AMERICA'S NATIONAL GAME

A. G. Spalding.

WHERE BASE BALL HAS ITS BEGINNING

America's National Game

HISTORIC FACTS CONCERNING
THE BEGINNING, EVOLUTION,
DEVELOPMENT AND POPULARITY
OF BASE BALL

*with personal reminiscences of its vicissitudes,
its victories and its votaries*

BY ALBERT G. SPALDING

*Introduction to the Bison Book Edition by
Benjamin G. Rader*

Cartoons by Homer C. Davenport

University of Nebraska Press
Lincoln and London

First Bison Book printing: 1992
Most recent printing indicated by the last digit below:
10   9   8   7   6   5   4   3   2   1

Library of Congress Cataloging-in-Publication Data
Spalding, A. G. (Albert Goodwill)
America's national game: historic facts concerning the beginning, evo-
lution, development, and popularity of base ball, with personal reminis-
cences of its vicissitudes, its victories, and its votaries / by Albert G.
Spalding; introduction to the Bison book edition by Benjamin G.
Rader; cartoons by Homer C. Davenport.
p.   cm.
Originally published: New York: American Sports Pub. Co., 1911. With
new introd. and index.
"Bison."
Includes index.
ISBN 0-8032-4220-4.—ISBN 0-8032-9207-4 (pbk.)
1. Baseball—United States—History—19th century.   2. Baseball—
United States—History—20th century.   I. Title.
GV863.A1S74   1992
796.35′0973—dc20
91-43078   CIP

Reprinted from the original edition published in 1911 by the American
Sports Publishing Company, New York. An index, as well as an introduction, has been added to this Bison Book edition.

To the memory of Henry Chadwick
"The Father of Base Ball"

To the memory of William A. Hulbert
The Savior of a Nation's Pastime

And to the National League
Of Professional Base Ball Clubs
That has borne the brunt of battle
During thirty-five years of development
Of America's National Game

This work is sincerely dedicated by

THE AUTHOR

INTRODUCTION

By Benjamin G. Rader

The first two decades of the twentieth century marked baseball's "coming of age." By then the game was no longer considered an oddity, an occasional diversion, or a trivial form of entertainment. Indeed, baseball had achieved a permanency and prominence in American life that was enjoyed by few other institutions. "Every city, town, and village in America has its ball team," observed the *St. Louis Globe and Commercial Advertiser* in 1905.[1] Boys everywhere grew up reading baseball fiction, learning the rudiments of the game, and dreaming of one day becoming diamond heroes themselves. Even the president of the United States unofficially extended his endorsement. In 1910 William Howard Taft, whose posterior was so broad that a row of seats had to be removed and replaced with a sofa in order for him to watch comfortably, established the precedent of the president opening each season by throwing out the first ball. *Take Me out to the Ball Game*, written by vaudevillian Jack Norworth in 1908, almost at once became the game's unofficial anthem. No other sport quite captured the essence of the nation's character as much as baseball. Such a contention was beyond debate, declared sporting goods magnate Albert Spalding in 1911. It was like saying that "two plus two equal four" (see p. 4).

In those days legendary players and managers populated the diamonds. There was the amiable John (Honus) Wagner, Pittsburgh's Flying Dutchman from the Pennsylvania coal mines, who, while playing shortstop, not only scooped up hard-hit ground balls but pebbles and dirt along with them. And then there was the demonic Ty Cobb, Detroit's outfielder from the Deep South, who was so driven by internal furies that he literally terrorized everyone in the American League, including even his own teammates. There was pitcher Christy Matthewson, the college boy and muscular Christian, who made it possible for young ladies to ask their escorts to take them to New York's Polo Grounds without sacrificing their respectability, and there was Matthewson's Napoleon-like manager, the pugnacious Irish-American, John J. McGraw, who made life miserable for umpires and opponents alike. There was "Shoeless Joe" Jackson, the country boy, a marvelous natural hitter who would leave the game in shame after revelations that the 1919 World Series had been fixed. And finally there was Andrew (Rube) Foster, a towering pitcher from Chicago, and later a field manager, club owner, league organizer, and league president, who could not play in the big leagues because of his skin color.

Baseball's coming of age included the construction of massive ball parks of concrete and steel, the "invention" of the game's immaculate conception, and the creation of an annual World Series. After several years of bitter warfare, the senior National League reached an agreement in 1903 with the upstart American League that permitted the playing of a championship series between the pennant winners of each league. The series soon became a national fall rite that equaled or surpassed the excitement and popularity of Independence Day, Washington's Birthday, or even tippling on New Year's Eve. In 1907 a specially appointed commission of men "of high repute and undoubted knowledge of Base Ball" concluded on the basis of strong feelings of patriotism but without systematic research that baseball had been conceived by Abner Doubleday in the bucolic village of Cooperstown, New York, in 1839. Thus was born the myth of baseball's uniquely American origins and a strengthening of its claim to being "America's national game." In the meantime, in order to seize upon the popularity of professional baseball, the sport's entrepreneurs replaced their hastily-built, wooden grandstands—structures that regularly succumbed to fire, the weight of fans, or boring termites—with sturdy new stands made of concrete and steel. Fifteen grand parks, all built between 1909 and 1923, joined with pillared public buildings, newly built skyscrapers, and mammoth railway terminals as edifices that local residents proudly pointed to as evidence of their city's permanence, size, and achievements. As depositories of collective memories, few if any other structures were as significant as the ball parks in linking the past and the present.

Only one thing was missing. That was an official chronicle, one that properly recounted the game's glorious past. The task befell Albert Goodwill Spalding (1850–1915), a former player, manager, and club owner who had become the world's biggest manufacturer of sporting goods. As a teenager in the 1860s, Spalding had been something of a sensation as a pitcher for the Forest City Club of Rockford, Illinois; in 1871 he joined the professional Boston team and in the following season pitched the team to the first of four consecutive National Association championships. "On receiving the ball," read a contemporary account of Spalding's pitching style, "he gazes at it two or three minutes in a contemplative way, and then turns it around once or twice to be sure that it is not an orange or a coconut. Assured that he has the genuine article . . . and after a scowl at the short stop and a glance at homeplate, [he] finally delivers the ball with the precision of a cannon shot."[2]

Although he was the game's first 200-game winner and acclaimed as "the champion pitcher of the world," Spalding soon turned his enormous energies elsewhere. In 1876 he joined the Chicago White Stockings as player-manager and helped businessman William Hulbert form the National League. From 1882 to 1891 he served as president of the Chicago club and was the single most important person in league councils. Along with Hulbert, he set out to alter the image of professional baseball by launching campaigns against drinking among the players and gambling and rowdiness at the ball parks. When faced with a player uprising in 1890, the National League owners naturally turned to Spalding to lead them in suppressing the rebellion.

Fourteen years earlier, while still a player, Spalding had charted yet another career. In February 1876, the *Chicago Tribune* announced that Spalding was opening a "large emporium in Chicago, where he will sell all kinds of baseball goods and turn his place into the headquarters for the Western Ball Clubs."[3] He obtained the exclusive right to furnish the league's official ball and to publish *Spalding's Official Baseball Guide,* an annual that included league rules, records, articles, and Spalding's views on the main issues confronting the game. He soon expanded his business into both the manufacturing and retailing of sporting goods.

As a baseball promoter, no one exceeded the bravado, energy, or imagination of Spalding. Spalding was to baseball what Phineas T. Barnum was to the circus. In 1888–89 he arranged and paid for a highly publicized world-wide tour that matched his Chicago team against a team of National League all-stars. Although the foreigners were singularly unimpressed with the exhibitions of America's National Game and Spalding lost money on the venture, the exotic nature of playing baseball games in far-off Australia, in the shadows of Egyptian pyramids, and on the leading cricket grounds of England intrigued Americans at home. In 1905, at the age of fifty-five and after having withdrawn from active participation in both business and league affairs, Spalding initiated an effort to obtain a book on "the Origins and History of Baseball."

To write the book, he called upon Henry Chadwick (1824–1908). No person was better suited for the job than the octogenarian sportswriter. Born in England as the son of a journalist, Chadwick emigrated with his parents at the age of twelve to Brooklyn, where he resided until his death. Beginning in the 1850s, in the infancy of baseball's development as an organized sport, Chadwick became the game's most distinguished journalist. He wrote voluminously for the *Brooklyn Eagle* (1856–94) and the *New York Clipper* (1857–88). From the English game of cricket, Chadwick adapted to baseball the box score and batting averages, both marvelous quantitative devices. He also invented the annual baseball guide, the first of which was published in 1860 as *Beadle's Dime Base Ball Player*. From 1869 to 1880 he edited *DeWitt's Guide* and then from 1881 to 1908 *Spalding's Base Ball Guide*. So important were his contributions to the game that he was soon hailed as "Father" Chadwick.

Upon obtaining an expression of interest by Chadwick in writing a history of the game, the imperious Spalding spelled out in detail what he wanted in the book. First of all, he ordered Chadwick to "*get busy, get action* and give me the manuscript of a first class history on Baseball, both professional and amateur, in this country and the rest of the world." Spalding needlessly reminded Chadwick, "You are not going to live forever." Spalding wanted the book to give special attention to the suppression of the "Baseball Revolutions" that had challenged the professional game. "Keep the book free of statistics as much as possible," continued Spalding. "In other words, make it a history of the game with principal reference to its government and development." Finally, he demanded that Chadwick send him carbon copies of what he had written "to show me how you are handling the work" and to offer an opportunity "now and then . . . [for me] to make a suggestion as we go along."[4]

How much, if any, of the manuscript Chadwick completed before his death in 1908 is uncertain. What is manifest is that much of the first half of *America's National Game* relies heavily upon Chadwick's assorted writings and his scrapbooks. Upon Chadwick's death, his widow turned over these materials to Spalding, who later gave them to the New York Public Library. Spalding also acknowledged that William D. Page, his longtime personal secretary, had a hand in writing the book; Page may in fact have written an initial draft. Nevertheless, nearly every page of the final edition bears the unmistakable imprint of Spalding. In 1911, six years after he had first conceived of the project, Spalding's own firm published his finished product as *America's National Game*.

Spalding launched an immense publicity campaign in behalf of the book. He had seventy-five autographed copies sent to prominent individuals and asked that they return their appraisals. Although President William Howard Taft and Pope Pius X, among others, had their aides prepare perfunctory replies, many persons sent back detailed, positive letters. The sporting editor of the *Boston Globe*, for example, declared it "a classic in American history," and Francis Richter, editor of *Sporting Life,* more accurately asserted: "Frankly, you have chosen the very best way to immortalize yourself in connection with the National Game."[5] Spalding had testimonials sent out to some two hundred newspapers; similar mailings went out to public libraries and in the advertisements of the A. G. Spalding Company. No official sales figures exist, but six months after publication the *Los Angeles Times* reported that 90,000 copies had been sold.

Spalding intended that *America's National Game* achieve two main goals. Although he specifically denied "any desire to exploit my name, my views, or my achievements," nearly every page of the book bears testimony to the contrary. "Indeed," as Peter Levine has observed, "the book is as much [Spalding's] autobiography as a history of baseball—a pastiche of personal reminiscences, narrative history, and pointed opinion."[6] Never suffering from the malady of undue modesty, Spalding made certain that everyone understood fully his immense contributions to baseball. Second, he sought to reassure skeptics that baseball, and more specifically professional baseball, was a respectable enterprise. He repeatedly asserted the sentiment that baseball had "all the attributes of American origin [and] American character," and that the game had been played by a "brilliant array" of "men of eminence in all professions and in every avenue of commercial and industrial activity." Baseball, "whether played on the village common or the splendidly appointed grounds of the modern professional club . . . satisfies and typifies the American idea of a manly, honest, entertaining recreation." According to Spalding, no other sport was so effective in cultivating the work ethic and self-restraint. Playing the game, he reassured anxious parents, instilled in youth "the psychology of success" (pp. 248, 542).

Spalding presented the game's history in terms of a morality play in which the forces of good repeatedly triumphed over the forces of evil. No force for righteousness exceeded that of the National League. Before the founding of the league in 1876, according to Spalding, the drinking, gambling, and dishonesty of the players had brought the game to the brink of utter ruin. The league's imposition and enforcement of stringent rules upon the players reversed the damage; it elevated and perpetuated baseball "into the most glorious and honorable sport on the green earth." Led by Spalding, the National League saved professional baseball again in 1890 when it suppressed the anarchy of the players' Brotherhood, and finally a third time when it put down Andrew Freedman's attempt in 1901 to transform the professional game into a trust. Indeed, Spalding's account of the National League not only made for a dramatic story, but it remained the standard work on early baseball history until the 1960s and continues to this day to shape our understanding of baseball's early history.[7] Furthermore, along with the inauguration of the World Series, the careers of the legendary players and managers, the myth of the game's origins, and the construction of magnificent ball parks, *America's National Game* made a large contribution to baseball's coming of age.

Notes

1. Quoted in Harold Seymour, *Baseball: The Golden Age* (New York: Oxford University Press, 1971), p. 4.

2. Quoted in Peter Levine, *A. G. Spalding and the Rise of Baseball* (New York: Oxford University Press, 1985), p. 11.

3. Arthur Bartlett, *Baseball and Mr. Spalding* (New York: Farrar, Straus & Young, 1951), pp. 98–99.

4. Quoted in Levine, *A. G. Spalding*, pp. 115–16.

5. Quoted in Levine, *A. G. Spalding*, pp. 120, 121.

6. Levine, *A. G. Spalding*, p. 116.

7. The most important recent works for the early era include the previously cited: Peter Levine, *A. G. Spalding* and Bartlett, *Baseball and Mr. Spalding*, as well as Harold Seymour, *Baseball*, 3 vols. (Oxford University Press, 1960, 1970); David Q. Voigt, *American Baseball*, 3 vols. (University Park: Pennsylvania State University Press, 1966–83); Ted Vincent, *Mudville's Revenge* (1981); Steven A. Riess, *Touching Base: Professional Baseball and American Culture in the Progressive Era* (Westport, Conn.: Greenwood Press, 1980); Riess, *City Games: The Evolution of American Urban Society and the Rise of Sports* (Urbana: University of Illinois Press, 1990); Melvin Adelman, *A Sporting Time: New York City and the Rise of Modern Sport, 1820–1870* (Urbana: University of Illinois Press, 1986); George B. Kirsch, *The Creation of American Team Sports: Baseball and Cricket, 1838–72* (Urbana: University of Illinois Press, 1989); Warren Goldstein, *Playing for Keeps* (Ithaca, N.Y.: Cornell University Press, (1989); and Benjamin G. Rader, *America's Game* (Urbana: University of Illinois Press, 1992).

Foreword

For several years I have been the recipient of frequent letters from admirers of our National Game in all parts of the country, urging me to write a history of Base Ball. For many adequate reasons I have felt impelled to decline these courteous invitations to enter the realms of literary endeavor, where I do not claim to belong.

First of all, the task was gigantic. It involved, under that title, not the writing of *a* book, but of *books*; not even the making of a few volumes, but of a library. I had neither time nor inclination for such an undertaking. It meant not only days, and weeks, and months, but *years* of patient application to a very exacting and not at all exciting line of research among musty records of long-forgotten facts.

I had been looking forward to the time when I might have a change and a rest from some of the active duties of life, and an enterprise involving so much of close personal application, although presenting a very wide divergence from my customary lines of labor, did not promise much in the way of absolute repose.

Recently, however, these requests have come with redoubled frequency and force. It is known that I have acquired possession of the Base Ball archives of Henry Chadwick, Harry Wright and other old-time friends and factors of the game; it is urged that I am duty bound to make public some of the contents of my storehouse of information pertinent to our national pastime, and I have been importuned to relate some of the reminiscences of the days when I was connected with it, either as player, manager or club official.

To all these requests and importunities I might have turned a deaf ear but for one incident which I will here relate. Some months before his demise I received a letter from Mr. Henry Chadwick, advising me that he had in his keeping the accumulations of years, embracing much valuable statistical and historical data bearing upon the national game. This he desired me to possess, but he wanted it to go into the hands of one who would make use of some part of it, at least. He then declared that he had written his will and bequeathed to me his Base Ball library, in the hope that I would write a book on the subject that had held so much of interest for him during his manhood's life.

Therefore, when, after his death I received word from Mrs. Chadwick that shipment had been made to me of her husband's Base Ball literature, I found myself facing the plea of an old and valued friend, now "on the other shore," adding to that of many others his request that I should write a book on Base Ball.

Hence, putting aside all personal inclinations, I find myself engaged in the undertaking of writing, not a *history* of Base Ball, but the simple story of America's National Game as I have come to know it. I wish again emphatically to disavow any pretense on the part of this work as a "history of Base Ball." I have simply sought in these pages to deal with the *beginnings* of things, leading the reader to the opening of paths the traversing of which will enable him to view certain historic scenes that in my opinion constitute the chief landmarks of Base Ball history.

I have undertaken briefly to touch upon the several epochs that impress me as of greatest importance; to consider abuses that crept into the game at the beginning; to note the inability of early Associations to control these evils; to dwell upon the nature of the struggle to eradicate wrongs and establish a form of government that would make for the integrity of Base Ball, and which *has* wrought the salvation of the game and made it the cleanest, most scientific and popular pastime known to the world of sport.

I have interspersed in this narrative some reminiscences in which the personal equation is conspicuously present. In the very nature of things that had to be the case. But I here and now disclaim any desire to exploit my name, my views or my achievements. This book is simply my contribution to the story of the game. In it I have reviewed facts as they have been presented to me. That others have seen them from other viewpoints and received impressions altogether different I know; and I accord to such the same sincerity that I maintain for myself.

In this work I have aimed to present only the truth. If in so doing I have on occasion seemed to speak harshly of the actions of some men who have sought to embarrass the noble sport, I plead in extenuation of what I have here written that it is the truth itself—not the one who utters it—that offends the doer of wrong.

A. G. Spalding

Point Loma, California, October, 1911.

ACKNOWLEDGMENTS

While the author of this work has dealt with his subject from viewpoints entirely his own, and has given many of the facts herein contained from personal observations and experiences during many years of active service in Base Ball, yet, in the nature of things, he has been obliged to call upon others to confirm data and amplify details.

To the following named gentlemen he desires here to make special acknowledgment:

To Hon. Morgan G. Bulkeley, of Connecticut; N. E. Young, of Washington, D. C.; A. G. Mills, James E. Sullivan and John B. Foster, of New York City; George Wright, John F. Morrill and F. W. Thayer, of Boston; A. J. Reach, of Philadelphia; Bruce Cartright, of Honolulu; Samuel E. Winslow and Ernest Thayer, of Worcester, Massachusetts, for valuable data supplied by each.

For illustrations he wishes to thank Mr. Homer C. Davenport, America's great cartoonist, to whose genius much of the interest of this volume is due. The cartoons were executed while Mr. Davenport was a guest at the author's home at Point Loma, California. After hearing some of the manuscript read, the artist felt inspired to illustrate certain leading features of the story of the game.

To Mr. William D. Page, a boyhood friend at Rockford, Illinois; later a well-known Indianian, resident at Fort Wayne (now a permanent resident of Point Loma, California), the author is particularly indebted. Mr. Page has given valuable assistance in the compilation and editing of this work.

To all these friends the author is glad to express his thanks and appreciation for favors always cheerfully extended.

POINT LOMA, CALIFORNIA, October, 1911.

TABLE OF CONTENTS

PAGE

LIST OF ILLUSTRATIONS

AMERICA'S NATIONAL GAME

CHAPTER I.

EAST AND WEST, NORTH AND SOUTH
"PLAY BALL"

CHAPTER I.

HAVE we, of America, a National Game? Is there
in our country a form of athletic pastime which
is distinctively American? Do our people recognize,
among their diversified field sports, one standing apart
from every other, outclassing all in its hold upon the
interest and affection of the masses? If a negative reply
may truthfully be given to all or any of these queries, then
this book should never have been published—or written.

But, if we have a National Game; if we know a form
of athletics which is peculiarly American, and have
adopted it as our own; if it is American in its spirit, its
character and its achievements; if it conforms in every
way to the American temperament; if we have a field sport
outranking all others in popularity, then it is indeed time
that the writing, in personal reminiscence, of its story
in book form should begin, "lest we forget" the salient
points in the inception, evolution and development of so
important a factor in the widespread entertainment of the
American people and the physical upbuilding of our
youth.

To enter upon a deliberate argument to prove that
Base Ball is our National Game; that it has all the
attributes of American origin, American character and

3

unbounded public favor in America, seems a work of supererogation. It is to undertake the elucidation of a patent fact; the sober demonstration of an axiom; it is like a solemn declaration that two plus two equal four.

Every citizen of this country who is blessed with organs of vision knows that whenever the elements are favorable and wherever grounds are available, the great American game is in progress, whether in city, village or hamlet, east, west, north or south, and that countless thousands of interested spectators gather daily throughout the season to witness contests which are to determine the comparative excellence of competing local organizations or professional league teams.

The statement will not be successfully challenged that the American game of Base Ball attracts more numerous and larger gatherings of spectators than any other form of field sport in any land. It must also be admitted that it is the only game known for which the general public is willing day after day to pay the price of admission. In exciting political campaigns, Presidential candidates and brilliant orators will attract thousands; but let there be a charge of half a dollar imposed, and only Base Ball can stand the test.

I claim that Base Ball owes its prestige as our National Game to the fact that as no other form of sport it is the exponent of American Courage, Confidence, Combativeness; American Dash, Discipline, Determination; American Energy, Eagerness, Enthusiasm; American Pluck, Persistency, Performance; American Spirit, Sagacity, Success; American Vim, Vigor, Virility.

Base Ball is the American Game *par excellence*, because its playing demands Brain and Brawn, and American manhood supplies these ingredients in quantity sufficient to spread over the entire continent.

No man or boy can win distinction on the ball field who is not, as man or boy, an athlete, possessing all the qualifications which an intelligent, effective playing of the game demands. Having these, he has within him the elements of pronounced success in other walks of life. In demonstration of this broad statement of fact, one needs only to note the brilliant array of statesmen, judges, lawyers, preachers, teachers, engineers, physicians, surgeons, merchants, manufacturers, men of eminence in all the professions and in every avenue of commercial and industrial activity, who have graduated from the ball field to enter upon honorable careers as American citizens of the highest type, each with a sane mind in a sound body.

It seems impossible to write on this branch of the subject—to treat of Base Ball as our National Game—without referring to Cricket, the national field sport of Great Britain and most of her colonies. Every writer on this theme does so. But, in instituting a comparison between these games of the two foremost nations of earth, I must not be misunderstood. Cricket is a splendid game, for Britons. It is a genteel game, a conventional game—and our cousins across the Atlantic are nothing if not conventional. They play Cricket because it accords with the traditions of their country so to do; because it is easy and does not overtax their energy or their thought. They play it because they like it and it is the proper thing to do. Their sires, and grandsires, and great-grandsires played Cricket—why not they? They play Cricket because it is their National Game, and every Briton is a Patriot. They play it persistently—and they play it well. I have played Cricket and like it. There are some features about that game which I admire more than I do some things about Base Ball.

But Cricket would never do for Americans; it is too slow. It takes two and sometimes three days to complete a first-class Cricket match; but two hours of Base Ball is quite sufficient to exhaust both players and spectators. An Englishman is so constituted by nature that he can wait three days for the result of a Cricket match; while two hours is about as long as an American can wait for the close of a Base Ball game—or anything else, for that matter. The best Cricket team ever organized in America had its home in Philadelphia—and remained there. Cricket does not satisfy the red-hot blood of Young or Old America.

The genius of our institutions is democratic; Base Ball is a democratic game. The spirit of our national life is combative; Base Ball is a combative game. We are a cosmopolitan people, knowing no arbitrary class distinctions, acknowledging none. The son of a President of the United States would as soon play ball with Patsy Flannigan as with Lawrence Lionel Livingstone, provided only that Patsy could put up the right article. Whether Patsy's dad was a banker or boiler-maker would never enter the mind of the White House lad. It would be quite enough for him to know that Patsy was up in the game.

I have declared that Cricket is a genteel game. It is. Our British Cricketer, having finished his day's labor at noon, may don his negligee shirt, his white trousers, his gorgeous hosiery and his canvas shoes, and sally forth to the field of sport, with his sweetheart on one arm and his Cricket bat under the other, knowing that he may engage in his national pastime without soiling his linen or neglecting his lady. He may play Cricket, drink afternoon tea, flirt, gossip, smoke, take a whiskey-and-soda at the customary hour, and have a jolly, conventional good time, don't you know?

Not so the American Ball Player. He may be a veritable Beau Brummel in social life. He may be the Swellest Swell of the Smart Set in Swelldom; but when he dons his Base Ball suit, he says good-bye to society, doffs his gentility, and becomes—just a Ball Player! He knows that his business now is to play ball, and that first of all he is expected to attend to business. It may happen to be his business to slide; hence, forgetting his beautiful new flannel uniform, he cares not if the mud is four inches deep at the base he intends to reach. His sweetheart may be in the grandstand—she probably is—but she is not for him while the game lasts.

Cricket is a gentle pastime. Base Ball is War! Cricket is an Athletic Sociable, played and applauded in a conventional, decorous and English manner. Base Ball is an Athletic Turmoil, played and applauded in an unconventional, enthusiastic and American manner.

The founder of our National Game became a Major General in the United States Army! The sport had its

CRICKET VS. BASE BALL

baptism when our country was in the preliminary agonies of a fratricidal conflict. Its early evolution was among the men, both North and South, who, during the war of the sixties, played the game to relieve the monotony of camp life in those years of melancholy struggle. It was the medium by which, in the days following the "late unpleasantness," a million warriors and their sons, from both belligerent sections, passed naturally, easily, gracefully, from a state of bitter battling to one of perfect peace.

Base Ball, I repeat, is War! and the playing of the game is a battle in which every contestant is a commanding General, who, having a field of occupation, must defend it; who, having gained an advantage, must hold it by the employment of every faculty of his brain and body, by every resource of his mind and muscle.

But it is a bloodless battle; and when the struggle ends, the foes of the minute past are friends of the minute present, victims congratulating victors, conquerors pointing out the brilliant individual plays of the conquered.

It would be as impossible for a Briton, who had not breathed the air of this free land as a naturalized American citizen; for one who had no part or heritage in the hopes and achievements of our country, to play Base Ball, as it would for an American, free from the trammels of English traditions, customs, conventionalities, to play the national game of Great Britain.

Let such an Englishman stand at the batter's slab on an American ball field, facing the son of an American President in the pitcher's box, and while he was ruminating upon the propriety of hitting, in his "best form," a ball delivered by the hands of so august a personage, the President's boy would probably shoot three hot ones over the plate, and the Umpire's "Three strikes; you're out," would arouse our British cousin to a realization that we have a game too lively for any but Americans to play.

On the other hand, if one of our cosmopolitan ball artists should visit England, and attempt a game of Cricket, whether it were Cobb, Lajoie, Wagner, or any American batsman of Scandinavian, Irish, French or German antecedents; simply because he was an American, and even though the Cricket ball were to be bowled at his feet by King George himself, he would probably hit the sphere in regular Base Ball style, and smash all conventionalities at the same time, in his eager effort to clear the bases with a three-bagger.

The game of Base Ball is American as to another peculiar feature. It is the only form of field sport known where spectators have an important part and actually participate in the game. Time was, and not long ago, when comparatively few understood the playing rules; but the day has come when nearly every man and boy in the land is versed in all the intricacies of the pastime; thousands of young women have learned it well enough to keep score, and the number of matrons who know the difference between the short-stop and the back-stop is daily increasing.

But neither our wives, our sisters, our daughters, nor our sweethearts, may play Base Ball on the field. They

may play Cricket, but seldom do; they may play Lawn
Tennis, and win championships; they may play Basket
Ball, and achieve laurels; they may play Golf, and receive
trophies; but Base Ball is too strenuous for womankind,
except as she may take part in grandstand, with applause
for the brilliant play, with waving kerchief to the hero
of the three-bagger, and, since she is ever a loyal partisan
of the home team, with smiles of derision for the Umpire
when he gives us the worst of it, and, for the same reason,
with occasional perfectly decorous demonstrations when
it becomes necessary to rattle the opposing pitcher.

But spectators of the sterner sex may play the game
on field, in grandstand or on bleachers, and the influence
they exert upon the contest is hardly less than that of
the competitors themselves.

In every town, village and city is the local wag. He
is a Base Ball fan from infancy. He knows every player
in the League by sight and by name. He is a veritable
encyclopædia of information on the origin, evolution and
history of the game. He can tell you when the Knickerbockers were organized, and knows who led the batting
list in every team of the National and American Leagues
last year. He never misses a game. His witticisms, ever
seasoned with spice, hurled at the visitors and now and
then at the Umpire, are as thoroughly enjoyed by all
who hear them as is any other feature of the sport. His
words of encouragement to the home team, his shouts of
derision to the opposing players, find sympathetic
responses in the hearts of all present.

But it is neither the applause of the women nor the

BASE BALL FOLLOWS THE FLAG

jokes of the wag which make for victory or defeat in comparison with the work of the "Rooter." He is ever present in large numbers. He is there to see the "boys" win. Nothing else will satisfy him. He is bound by no rules of the game, and too often, perhaps, by no laws of decorum. His sole object in life for two mortal hours is to gain victory for the home team, and that he is not overscrupulous as to the amount of racket emanating from his immediate vicinity need not be emphasized here.

And so it comes to pass that at every important game there is an exhibition in progress, in grandstand and on bleachers, that is quite as interesting in its features of excitement and entertainment as is the contest on the field of sport, and which, in its bearing upon the final result, is sometimes a factor nearly as potent as are the efforts of the contesting players.

It must be admitted that as the game of Base Ball has become more generally known; that is, as patrons of the sport are coming to be more familiar with its rules and its requirements, their enjoyment has immeasurably increased; because, just in so far as those in attendance understand the features presented in every play, so far are they able to become participators in the game itself. And beyond doubt it is to this growing knowledge on the part of the general public with the pastime that its remarkable popularity is due. For, despite the old adage, familiarity does *not* breed contempt, but fondness, and all America has come to regard Base Ball as its very own, to be known throughout the civilized world as the great American National Game.

Finally, in one other particular Base Ball has won its right to be denominated the American National Game. Ever since its establishment in the hearts of the people as the foremost of field sports, Base Ball has "followed the flag." It followed the flag to the front in the sixties, and received then an impetus which has carried it to half a century of wondrous growth and prosperity. It has followed the flag to Alaska, where, under the midnight sun, it is played on Arctic ice. It has followed the flag to the Hawaiian Islands, and at once supplanted every other form of athletics in popularity. It has followed the flag to the Philippines, to Porto Rico and to Cuba, and wherever a ship floating the Stars and Stripes finds anchorage to-day, somewhere on nearby shore the American National Game is in progress.

CHAPTER II.

BALL PLAYING IN ALL AGES AND ALL CLIMES

CHAPTER II.

ANTIQUITY OF THE GAME OF BALL——ARCHÆOLOGY, MYTH-
OLOGY, TRADITION AND HISTORY NOTE GAMES OF BALL
FROM THE BEGINNING OF RECORDED TIME——THE MAN
WHO DEVISED BASE BALL.

ARCHÆOLOGY contributes its testimony to the
antiquity of ball-playing by opening its storehouses
of ancient treasures; for, graven on tablets, and temples
and monuments, have been found pictures of human
figures in the act of playing with balls.

Four thousand years ago, in the 12th Egyptian
dynasty, a Coptic artist sculptured on the temple Beni
Hassan, human figures throwing and catching balls. A
leather-covered ball used in games played on the Nile
over forty centuries ago, has a place among the many
archæological specimens in the British Museum, at
London. It has a sewed cover and is still in a remarkable
state of preservation.

The game of ball was prized by the Greeks as giving
grace and elasticity to the human figure, and they erected
a statue to one Aristonicus for his proficiency in it. We
are told by Horace that Mæcenas amused himself during
his journeys by playing ball. In the Greek gymnasia
and in the Roman baths there were special compartments
for ball-playing, called Sphæristerii, where certain rules
and gradations of exercise were observed, according to
the health of the player. The balls used were of various

materials, the most common being of leather, filled with hair, while others were stuffed with feathers. Ancient medical practitioners were wont to prescribe a course of ball-playing, where the modern doctor would order a diet of pills.

It is supposed that ball-tossing had a deep symbolical meaning when played in the spring of the year; and that the tossing of the ball was intended to first typify the upspringing of the life of nature after the gloom of winter. And, whether this was the case among the people of antiquity or not, it is a remarkable fact that the ecclesiastics of the early Church adopted this symbol and gave it a very special significance by meeting in the churches on Easter Day, and throwing up a ball from hand to hand, to typify The Resurrection.

In the 16th century the game of ball was very popular in the courts of the Princes of Europe, especially in Italy and France. It was considered one of the best forms of exercise known for cultivating grace in motion, agility and strength, as well as for promoting general health of body and cheerfulness of disposition.

The Chinese have played ball in various ways from times of remote antiquity. For centuries games of ball have been known and played in Japan. Ethiopian and East Indian traditions refer to games with balls played many centuries ago. Britons, Celts, Scots, Scandinavians, Teutons and the early Latin races have played games of ball time out of mind.

But while it is true that ball playing in many forms has been engaged in by most nations from time immemorial, it is a proven fact that the game now designated "Base Ball," is of modern and purely American origin.

I have no intention, in this work, of reopening the discussion which waxed so warm a short time ago, as to the origin of the game. It would be an act of disloyalty to the Commission that was appointed at my suggestion in 1907, with instructions to consider all available evidence and decide the case upon its merits, were I ever again to enter upon the details of that vexed controversy—except in order to prove the righteousness of the verdict then rendered. It is quite enough here to say that the Commission referred to, after a long, thorough, painstaking investigation of all obtainable facts, unanimously declared:

"*First*—That Base Ball had its origin in the United States;

"*Second*—That the first scheme for playing it, according to the best evidence obtainable to date, was devised by Abner Doubleday, at Cooperstown, New York, in 1839."

The Commission rendering this important decision was composed of such able men and well-known friends of the game as

Mr. A. G. Mills of New York, an enthusiastic ball player before and during the Civil War, and the third President of the National League.

Hon. Arthur P. Gorman (since deceased), ex-United States Senator from Maryland.

Hon. Morgan G. Bulkeley, ex-Governor, and later United States Senator from Connecticut, and the first President of the National League.

Mr. N. E. Young of Washington, D. C., a veteran ball
    player, and the first Secretary and afterward the
    fourth President of the National League.

Mr. Alfred J. Reach of Philadelphia, and

Mr. George Wright of Boston, both well-known busi-
    ness men and two of the most famous ball players in
    their day.

Mr. James E. Sullivan of New York, President of the
    Amateur Athletic Union, accepted the position of
    Secretary of this Special Commission.

The report of the Commission, written by Mr. A. G.
Mills, and bearing date December 30th, 1907, is signed
by all the members named above, except Hon. A. P. Gorman, whose death occurred while his colleagues were
engaged in the work of research. The report closes with
these words:

"As I have stated, my belief had been that our 'National Game
of Base Ball' originated with the Knickerbocker club, organized in
New York in 1845, and which club published certain elementary rules
in that year ; but, in the interesting and pertinent testimony for
which we are indebted to Mr. A. G. Spalding, appears a circum-
stantial statement by a reputable gentleman, according to which
the first known diagram of the diamond, indicating positions for
the players, was drawn by Abner Doubleday in Cooperstown, N. Y.,
in 1839. Abner Doubleday subsequently graduated from West Point
and entered the regular army, where, as Captain of Artillery, he
sighted the first gun fired on the Union side (at Fort Sumter) in
the Civil War. Later still, as Major General, he was in command
of the Union army at the close of the first day's fight in the battle
of Gettysburg, and he died full of honors at Mendham, N. J., in
1893. It happened that he and I were members of the same veteran
military organization—the crack Grand Army Post (Lafayette), and
the duty devolved upon me, as Commander of that organization, to
have charge of his obsequies, and to command the veteran military
escort which served as guard of honor when his body lay in state,
January 30, 1893, in the New York City Hall, prior to his interment
in Arlington.

"In the days when Abner Doubleday attended school in Cooperstown, it was a common thing for two dozen or more of school boys

to join in a game of ball. Doubtless, as in my later experience, collisions between players in attempting to catch the batted ball were frequent, and injury due to this cause, or to the practice of putting out the runner by hitting him with the ball, often occurred.

"I can well understand how the orderly mind of the embryo West Pointer would devise a scheme for limiting the contestants on each side and allotting them to field positions, each with a certain amount of territory; also substituting the existing method of putting out the base runner for the old one of 'plugging' him with the ball.

"True, it appears from the statement that Doubleday provided for eleven men on a side instead of nine, stationing the two extra men between first and second, and second and third bases, but this is a minor detail, and, indeed, I have played, and doubtless other old players have, repeatedly with eleven on a side, placed almost identically in the manner indicated by Doubleday's diagram, although it is true that we so played, after the number on each side had been fixed at nine, simply to admit to the game an additional number of those who wished to take part in it.

"I am also much interested in the statement made by Mr. Curry, of the pioneer Knickerbocker club, and confirmed by Mr. Tassie, of the famous old Atlantic club of Brooklyn, that a diagram, showing the ball field laid out substantially as it is to-day, was brought to the field one afternoon by a Mr. Wadsworth. Mr. Curry says 'the plan caused a great deal of talk, but, finally, we agreed to try it.' While he is not quoted as adding that they did both try and adopt it, it is apparent that such was the fact; as, from that day to this, the scheme of the game described by Mr. Curry has been continued with only slight variations in detail. It should be borne in mind that Mr. Curry was the first president of the old Knickerbocker club, and participated in drafting the first published rules of the game.

"It is possible that a connection more or less direct can be traced between the diagram drawn by Doubleday in 1839 and that presented to the Knickerbocker club by Wadsworth in 1845, or thereabouts, and I wrote several days ago for certain data bearing on this point, but as it has not yet come to hand I have decided to delay no longer sending in the kind of paper your letter calls for, promising to furnish you the indicated data when I obtain it, whatever it may be.

"Yours very truly,

A. G. Mills

A Sketch from Life
Feb 15th 1910

Davenport

THE BISMARCK OF BASE BALL

" We, the undersigned members of the Special Base Ball Commission, unanimously agree with the decision as expressed and outlined in Mr. A. G. Mills' letter of December 30, 1907.

Morgan G. Bulkeley

Nicholas E. Young

A. J. Reach

Geo Wright

Senator Bulkeley, after affixing his signature, appended the following statement:

" I personally remember as a boy in East Haddam, Conn., before 1846, playing the game of One and Two Old Cat, and remember with great distinctness the early struggles in Brooklyn, N. Y., between the two rival clubs, the Atlantics and Excelsiors, and later the Stars, with Creighton as pitcher. This was some ten to fifteen years before the National organization. I was present, representing the Hartford club, at the formation of what is now the National League at the Grand Central Hotel, Broadway, New York City, about 1875 or 1876, and was its first President, with Nick Young, Secretary.

" M. G. BULKELEY."

Accepting the decision of the Commission appointed to consider the subject of the origin of Base Ball as final, I have nothing to add to their report. However, it is quite in keeping with the purpose of the story of our national game to present here a brief biography of the man who first perfected the system out of which the

MAJOR-GENERAL ABNER DOUBLEDAY

greatest of all out-of-doors pastimes has had its evolution. The following sketch is from Appleton's "Encyclopædia of American Biography":

"Major General Abner Doubleday was born in Ballston Spa, New York, June 26, 1819. He was a civil engineer in 1836-1838, when he was appointed to the U. S. Military Academy, and on his graduation in 1842, was assigned to the Third Artillery. He served in the First Cavalry during the Mexican War, being engaged at Monterey and at Rinconada Pass during the Battle of Buena Vista. He was promoted to First Lieutenant March 3, 1847, to Captain March 3, 1855, and served against the Seminoles (Indians) in 1856-1858. He was in Fort Moultrie from 1860 till the garrison withdrew to Fort Sumter on December 26th of that year, and *aimed the first gun* fired in defence of the latter fort on April 12th, 1861. He was promoted to Major in the Seventeenth Infantry on May 14th, 1861 ; from June till August was with General Patterson in the Shenandoah Valley, and then served in the defence of Washington, commanding forts and batteries on the Potomac. He was made Brigadier General of Volunteers on February 3, 1862, and was assigned to the command of all the defences of Washington on the same date, and commanded a Brigade on the Rappahannock and in the Northern Virginia campaign from May to September, 1862, including the second Battle of Bull Run, where he succeeded, on August 30, to the command of Hatch's Division. In the Battle of Antietam, his Division held the extreme right and opened the battle, losing heavily, but taking six battle-flags. On November 29, 1862, he was promoted to Major-General of Volunteers. He was at Fredericksburg and Chancellorsville, and succeeded General John F. Reynolds as Chief of the First Corps when that officer was appointed to that command of a wing of the army. On July 1, 1863, he was sent to Gettysburg to support Buford's Cavalry, and on the fall of General Reynolds, took command of the field till the arrival of General Howard, some hours later. His division fought gallantly in the battle that followed, and on the third day aided in the repulse of Pickett's charge.

"General Doubleday served on courts-martial and commissions in 1863, and on July 12, 1864, temporarily commanded the southeastern defences of Washington, when the city was threatened by Early's raiders. He was brevetted Colonel in the Regular Army on March 11, 1865, and Brigadier and Major-General on March 13, for his services during the war. In December, 1866, he was in command at Galveston, Texas; served as Assistant Commissioner of the Freedman's Bureau there until August 1, 1867, and, after being mustered out of the volunteer service, was made Colonel of the

Thirty-fifth Infantry, September 15, 1867. He was a member of the Retiring Board in New York City in 1868, and in 1869-1871 superintended the general recruiting service in San Francisco, where, in 1870, he suggested and obtained a charter for the first cable street railway in the United States. After commanding in Texas, he was retired from active service on December 11, 1873. He has published 'Reminiscences of Forts Sumter and Moultrie in 1860-1861,' New York, 1876; 'Chancellorsville and Gettysburg,' 1882; and articles in periodicals on army matters, the water supply of cities, and other subjects."

CHAPTER III.

AN EMBRYO BASE BALL STAR

CHAPTER III.

HOWEVER views of individuals may differ as to the origin of the American national game, all must agree that the sport had as its foundation—a Ball. Without that as its basis, the superstructure of the grandest pastime ever devised by man could never have been erected.

Josh Billings, in writing upon the general subject of Dogs, once said that, in order to realize on the different kinds of dogs, one must have environments calculated to develop the inherent traits of the varied breeds. Thus, in order to " realize " on a coach dog, one must be the owner of a carriage and team, that the canine might run along beneath the vehicle; in order to " realize " on a Newfoundland dog, he said its owner must have a pond of water and children, playing around, carelessly, that they might fall in and be rescued by " Faithful Nero," and so on.

Just so in this case, in order to " realize " on the Ball it is necessary to have someone to put it in motion. Happily, that one is not difficult to find. Placing the Ball in the hands of the first lad who happens along, we may be assured that he will do the rest. And he does. In

29

less time than it takes in the telling, he is bounding the sphere upon the ground. Down it goes; up it flies. Leaving the boy's hand, it strikes the ground, and, returning, is caught. In this completed act we have the first crude and elementary step in our National Game—with just a Boy and a Ball.

But the Boy, like other members of the human family, is a social creature. It is quite conceivable that the average boy, upon being presented with a Ball, would find immediate and pleasurable entertainment throwing it to the ground and catching it upon the rebound; but such pastime would be of temporary duration. The lad would soon tire of the monotony of the sport. Unselfish, he would want someone to share his fun—moreover, everybody recognizes that thing in human nature, in youth as well as maturity, which delights in the exploitation of ownership, possession. Given the boy's mother or sister in possession of a new gown, and it is immediately donned for exhibition before her less favored neighbor. The arrival of his new "Red Devil" sets the boy's dad rushing around town before he knows the first principles of the machine's construction, to the imminent danger of all resident mankind and incidentally that of any animal that may happen to come in his way. He simply *must* show Jones the new flyer, even though it decimates the population.

"Like father, like son." Tom wants his schoolmate, Dick, to see the new ball. In a very few minutes they are together, playing throw and catch, in an interesting elementary game of ball. Tom throws; Dick catches. Dick throws; Tom catches. Back and forth flies the ball till the school bell rings, and in this simple little form of exercise we have " Throw and Catch " as the second stage in the evolution of our game—with Two Boys and a Ball.

Now, human nature is not only social in its demands; it is also enterprising—and fickle. Bounding a ball on the ground is well enough if a lad is alone and can't get company. Throw and Catch beats no game at all; but it becomes tiresome after a while. And so, when school is over, or on Saturdays, when there is no school, we find Tom and Dick out behind the barn, inventing a new and different phase of the game of ball.

" I'll tell you what we'll do," says Tom. " I'll throw the ball against the barn. You get that old axe-handle over there and strike at it as it comes back. If you miss the ball and I catch it, you're out; or, if you hit the ball and can run and touch the barn and return before I can get the ball and hit you with it, you count one. If I hit you with the ball before you get back to your place, you're out. See?"

They try it; find it works well, and the third stage of the game is developed in " Barn-Ball "—with Two Boys, a Bat and a Ball.

Again, it happens sometimes that it is not altogether convenient to play barn-ball. The game requires a barn. Now, while most boys may usually be depended upon to have a large and varied assortment of things in pocket, it sometimes occurs that a barn is not one of them; so barn-ball is out of the question. Tom and Dick are coming from school with Harry. They tell the new boy about

BARN BALL

BOY AND BALL

the ball and the large amount of fun there is wrapped up in it. They dilate upon the proficiency they have already attained in throwing, catching and batting, and patronize Harry a trifle perhaps, because of his inexperience.

"Why can't we have a game of barn-ball, now?" asks the unsophisticated Harry.

"Oh, don't you know nuthin'? There isn't any barn," answers Dick.

"I'll tell you what we can do," says the inventive Tom. "Come on, Dick; you and I will throw and catch, just as we did the other day, and Harry can stand between us with the club. Now, Dick, when I throw to you, Harry can face me and try to hit the ball, and when you throw to me he can turn your way and strike at it. If Harry misses the ball, and either of us catches it before it hits the ground or on the first bound, he's out and the fellow who catches him out takes the club. If he hits the ball far enough to get to that rock over there and back before one of us gets the ball and hits him with it, he counts one tally; but if one of us hits him with the ball, he's out. See?" And thus the game of "One Old Cat" was born, and the fourth step has been evolved, with Three Boys, a Bat, a Ball and a Base.

The evolution of the next step in the game of Base Ball was natural and easy. It was a very simple sequence of One Old Cat. It grew out of the fact that Jim came along and wanted to play with the others.

"That's dead easy," says the resourceful Tom. "We'll just add another base, get another club, and there you are. All the difference there will be is that when

ONE OLD CAT

TWO OLD CAT

either one hits the ball you must both run and exchange places. If the ball is thrown and hits either one of you, that one must give way to the fellow who threw it." The game of Two Old Cat was thus developed in order to include Four Boys, Two Bats, Two Bases and a Ball.

By this time the game of Base Ball is becoming popular. Next Saturday, when Tom, Dick, Harry and Jim go out on the commons to have a game of Two Old Cat, Frank and Ned join them with hopes of getting into the game.

"No use," says the pessimistic Dick; "only four can play at this game. You see, we've got two catchers and two hitters now, and that's all we can have."

"Oh, I don't know," says Tom. "What's the matter with having a three-cornered game? then we all can play."

The game is tried three-cornered. It works all right, and Three Old Cat, with Six Boys, Three Bats, Three Bases and a Ball has added another step in the evolution of our American game.

The interest increases. Eight Boys want a chance to play at the same time. An equilateral ground is chosen, about forty feet each way. The sport is tried out in that form and is found to meet the purpose. But now the game is becoming cumbersome. It is slow and unsatisfactory in some respects. The multiplication of players introduces elements of discord. Dissensions arise. No two agree as to the proper way of playing the game. There are no printed rules available for the village commons. Interest, meanwhile, is growing, and more and

THREE OLD CAT

FOUR OLD CAT

still more players are clamoring for admission. The game of Four Old Cat has been developed all right, but, unlike the feline from which its name has been derived, the game is never a howling success; but it does afford pastime for Eight Boys, Four Bats, Four Bases and a Ball.

In Two, Three and Four Old Cat games, each individual player had his own score, and the players did not engage collectively as teams. Each tally was credited to the striker only. Every base gained by the striker was counted as a tally for himself alone. At the close of the game, if any record was kept, the player who was found to have the greatest number of tallies was declared the victor. Thus, in the days when a game which would accommodate no more than eight players would suffice, the "Old Cat," or "Individual Score," system of ball-playing answered the purpose; but as the pastime became more popular, and more boys wanted to play, it became necessary to devise a new form of the game which would admit a greater number of participants and at the same time introduce the competitive spirit that prevails in teamwork.

We are indebted to Four Old Cat for the square-shaped ball field, with a base at each corner. A natural step was then made by eliminating the four throwers and four batters of the Four Old Cat game, and substituting in place of them one thrower, or pitcher, and one batter. The pitcher was stationed in the center of the square and the striker, or batter, had his position at the middle of one of the sides of the square. In this form of the game,

TOWN BALL

BASE BALL

two sides, or teams, were chosen, one known as the Fielding Side, and the other as the Batting Side. The game was known as "Town Ball," and later, that is, in the decade beginning with 1850, it came to be known as the "Massachusetts Game of Base Ball," in contradistinction to the "New York Game of Base Ball," as played by the Knickerbocker Club of New York City in the decade of the '40s. Thus Town Ball came in vogue and made another step in the evolution of the American game of Base Ball.

In this game were present many of the elements of the game of Base Ball as we know it to-day—and then some. It accommodated thirty or more players and was played on town-meeting days, when everybody in the township took a hand. Sometimes there were so many playing that the grounds were full of fielders, and but for the large number and their indiscriminate selection, the sport might have developed more skill. The square field of Four Old Cat, but with the side lines lengthened to sixty instead of forty feet, obtained in Town Ball. Batsmen were out on balls caught on fly or first bound, and base runners were out by being "soaked" while running by a thrown ball. Town Ball was played quite generally throughout New England. It had, as before stated, fifteen or more players on a side, Catcher, Thrower, Four Bases, a Bat and a Ball.

The final step in the evolution of the game was the adoption of the diamond-shaped field and other points of play incorporated in the system devised by Abner Doubleday, of Cooperstown, New York, in 1839, and subse-

BASE BALL AS IT WAS

Second Championship Game between the Atlantics of Brooklyn and the Athletics of Philadelphia, 1866.   Score 33 to 33 quently formulated into a code of playing rules adopted by the Knickerbocker Base Ball Club, of New York, upon its organization in 1845. The number of players participating in a game was limited to eighteen—nine on a side; a Pitcher, a Catcher, a Short Stop, First, Second and Third Basemen, Right, Center, and Left Fielders, Four Bases, Bat and Ball, and was the game of Base Ball substantially as played to-day.

The following, from the Memphis *Appeal*, of date unknown to the writer, is a fair and interesting description of the game as played in the days of long ago:

" Time will not turn backward in his flight, but the mind can travel back to the days before Base Ball, or at least to the days before Base Ball was so well known and before it had become so scientific. There were ball games in those days, in town and country, and the country ball game was an event. There were no clubs. The country boy of those days was not gregarious. He preferred flocking by himself and remaining independent. On Saturday afternoons the neighborhood boys met on some well cropped pasture, and whether ten or forty, every one was to take part in the game. Self-appointed leaders divided the boys into two companies by alternately picking one until the supply was exhausted. The bat, which was no round stick, such as is now used, but a stout paddle, with a blade two inches thick and four inches wide, with a convenient handle dressed onto it, was the chosen arbiter. One of the leaders spat on one side of the bat, which was honestly called 'the paddle,' and asked the leader of the opposition forces, ' Wet, or dry? ' The paddle was then sent whirling up into the air, and when it came down, whichever side won went to the bat, while the others scattered over the field. The ball was not what would be called a National League ball, nowadays, but it served every purpose. It was usually made on the spot by some boy offering up his woolen socks as an oblation, and these were raveled and wound round a bullet, a handful of strips cut from a rubber overshoe, a piece of cork or almost anything, or nothing, when anything was not available. The winding of this ball was an art, and whoever could excel in this art was looked upon as a superior being. The ball must be a perfect sphere and the threads as regularly laid as the wire on a helix of a magnetic armature. When the winding was complete the surface of the ball was thoroughly sewed with a large needle and thread to prevent it from unwinding when a thread was cut. The diamond was not arbitrarily marked off as now. Sometimes there were four bases, and sometimes six or seven. They were not equidistant, but were marked by any fortuitous rock, or shrub, or depression in the ground where the steers were wont to bellow and paw up the earth. One of these tellural cavities was almost sure to be selected as 'the den,' now called the home-plate. There were no masks, or mitts, or protectors. There was no science or chicanery, now called 'head-work.' The strapping young oafs—embryonic preachers, presidents and premiers —were too honest for this. The pitcher was the one who could throw the ball over the 'den,' and few could do this. His object was to throw a ball that could be hit. The paddleman's object was to hit the ball, and if he struck at it—which he need not do unless he chose —and missed it, the catcher, standing well back, tried to catch it after it had lost its momentum by striking the earth once and bounding in the air—'on the first bounce' it was called—and if he succeeded the paddleman was dead and another took his place. If he struck it and it was not caught in the field or elsewhere, in the air or on the first bounce, he could strike twice more, but the third time he was compelled to run. There was no umpire, and very little wrangling. There was no effort to pounce upon a base runner and touch him with the ball. Anyone having the ball could throw it at him, and if it hit him he was 'dead'—almost literally sometimes. If he dodged the ball, he kept on running till the den was reached. Some of the players became proficient in ducking, dodging and side-stepping, and others learned to throw the ball with the accuracy of a rifle bullet. No matter how many players were on a side, each and every one had to be put out. And if the last one made three successive home runs, he 'brought in his side,' and the outfielders, pitcher and catcher had to do their work all over again. The boy who could bring in his side was a hero. No victorious general was ever prouder or more lauded. Horatius at the bridge was small potatoes in comparison. He was the uncrowned king. There were no foul hits. If the ball touched the bat ever so lightly it was a 'tick,' and three ticks meant a compulsory run. The score was kept by some one cutting notches in a stick, and the runs in an afternoon ran up into the hundreds. If a ball was lost in the grass or rolled under a Scotch thistle, the cry 'lost ball' was raised and the game stopped until it was found.

"Only the older country ball players can remember those days and games. They did not last long. When the change came, it came suddenly. Technicalities and rules began to creep in. Tricks between the pitcher and catcher, designed to fool the batter, began. The argot or slang of the game intruded. The country boys who went to college found more than their new homespun suits, of which they were so proud on leaving home, out of date. The ball game was all changed. They had to use a round club instead of a paddle to hit the ball. They had to change their tactics all through the game. They found the pitcher not intent upon throwing a ball that could be hit, but so that it would be hit at and missed. The bases were laid off with mathematical accuracy. They could be put out in many unknown and surprising ways. They could not throw a ball at a base runner. They could not wander at will over the field, but must occupy a certain position. All was changed. All has been changed since. The expert of even twenty years ago would be lost to-day. The game of ball has been growing more scientific every year. It will continue to grow more scientific for years to come. The home-spun-clad boys who returned home on vacation expecting to 'show off,' and teach their former companions the game of ball up to date, discovered the innovation had preceded them, and that those who had not left the old haunts knew all about the game excepting the very newest wrinkles. And they knew something which the college boys had not learned."

BASE BALL OR CRICKET—WHICH?

CHAPTER IV.

ALEXANDER J. CARTWRIGHT

CHAPTER IV.

1845–55

ALTHOUGH accepting the finding of the Commission of 1907 as definitely establishing the American origin of our national game, and that it was first put on record by the scheme devised by young Doubleday, in 1839, it is known that the game of Base Ball, in crude form, had been played for many years previous to that date, and it was doubtless from the fact of his familiarity with it in earlier years that the embryo Major General was inspired to formulate his system looking toward its perfection.

In his admirable little work, entitled "Base Ball," Mr. John Montgomery Ward, the famous old time player, and at present a member of the New York bar, declares that:

"Col. James Lee, elected an honorary member of the Knickerbocker Club in 1846, said that he had often played the game when a boy, and at that time he was a man of sixty or more years.

"Dr. Oliver Wendell Holmes said to the reporter of a Boston paper that Base Ball was one of the sports of his college days at Harvard, and Dr. Holmes graduated in 1829.

"Mr. Charles DeBost, the catcher and captain of the old Knickerbockers, played Base Ball on Long Island fifty years ago, and it was the same game which the Knickerbockers afterward played."

No longer ago than last year, the following appeared in the columns of the Erie (Pa.) *Tribune:*

47

To the Editor of *The Tribune.*

Sir: I find this morning in *The Tribune* an article on the "Origin of Base Ball" quoted from another periodical. In this article it is said that Base Ball probably grew out of the English game of "rounders."

I am in my eighty-third year, and I know that seventy years ago, as a boy at school in a country school district in Erie County, Pa., I played Base Ball with my schoolmates; and I know it was a common game long before my time. It had just the same form as the Base Ball of to-day, and the rules of the game were nearly the same as they are now.

One bad feature of the old game, I am glad to say, is not now permitted. The catchers, both the one behind the batter and those on the field, could throw the ball and hit the runner between the bases with all the swiftness he could put into it—"burn him," it was called. That cruel part of the game has been abolished; the ball is now thrown to the base before the runner reaches it, if possible, and this puts him out.

I never heard of the game called "rounders." "One old cat" or "two old cat" was played then as now; but it was in nothing like the Base Ball of my boyhood days. Real Base Ball, with some slight variation of the rules, as it has come down to the present day must be at least a hundred years old; it may be a thousand. Perhaps it has come down to us from the old times of the Greeks and Romans, as many games and other good things have done.

Erie, Pa., April 8, 1910.   ANDREW H. CAUGHEY.

At a Puritan banquet, held at Detroit, Mich., December 17, 1908, among the speakers were Ray Stannard Baker, the Michigan author; R. F. Sutherland, of Windsor, Speaker of the Canadian Parliament, and Samuel J. Elder, the prominent Boston lawyer. Mr. Elder replied to the toast, "The Puritans," and treated the subject in a rather anecdotal way. He told a number of instances of the humor of the early Puritans, among other things mentioning Gov. Bradford's account of a ball game at Plymouth. It seemed that some of the newcomers refused to work on Christmas Day because it was "against their conscience" to work on that day, and were duly excused on account of their scruples. Returning from work, however, the Governor found them playing ball in the streets, and told them it was "against his conscience" that they should play and others work. He therefore took away their ball and bats, and thus broke up what may have been the first ball game in America.

However, for lack of any organized clubs whose records were preserved, there is a dearth of information on the subject of Base Ball in its earlier years, save that which comes to us from the recollections of men such as gave utterance to the foregoing excerpts. But these were men of the past, not the present, century, and it is so far a cry, from 1911 to 1830, that memories of those now living who were old enough to play ball in the remote days referred to cannot be depended upon as a safe guide for the historian of to-day.

Nevertheless, it is of record that as early as the year 1842 a number of New York gentlemen—and I use the term "gentlemen" in its highest social significance—were accustomed to meet regularly for Base Ball practice games. It does not appear that any of these were world-beaters in the realm of athletic sports. Their records are not among those of famous athletes of their day. Indeed, there is reason to believe that these fine old fellows shone more resplendently in the banquet hall than on the diamond field. The records of the club, faithfully kept and most beautifully transcribed, indicate far less attention to achievements in the game of ball than to exploits in the realms of gastronomy.

The Knickerbockers! Dear old fellows! How the

THE KNICKERBOCKERS AT PRACTICE

very name of their organization suggests respectability! There is no photo of the players of that team on the field, but one almost unconsciously uniforms them in white silk stockings, shoes with silver buckles, silk knee breeches, blue swallow-tail coats and powdered wigs, under hats with the white cockade! They did not put up much of a game of Base Ball as we understand it now, those nice old boys; the curved ball was not in evidence, the spit-ball had not put in an appearance; the base on balls was an unknown factor, and if any player of that club ever slid to base, it was on skates or a hand-sled in the games regularly played by them every winter on frozen ponds.

But, while they left us no records of 1–0 twenty-four innings games, let us ever hold in memory the stamp of respectability imparted to Base Ball by its earliest champions. Let us never forget that the men who first gave impetus to our national sport in the way of organization for that purpose were gentlemen "to the manor born," men of fine tastes, of high ability, of upright character. It was not until long after the days of the Knickerbockers that Base Ball was nearly ruined by the ascendancy of rowdies and gamblers. But of this more anon.

It was in the year 1845—although the Knickerbockers had been playing practice games since 1842—that the desirability of effecting a formal organization was first conceived. Previous to that time its members had been held together by ties of congeniality; now, the element of business system was to be injected.

To Alexander J. Cartwright, beyond doubt, belongs the honor of having been the first to move in the direc-

tion of securing an organization of Base Ball players. It
is of record that in the spring of 1845 Mr. Cartwright,
being present and participating in a practice game of
ball, proposed to others the formal association of themselves together as a Base Ball club. His suggestion met
approval, and a self-constituted committee, consisting of
Alexander J. Cartwright, D. F. Curry, E. R. Dupignac,
Jr., W. H. Tucker and W. R. Wheaton, at once set about
securing signatures of those who were desirous of belong-
ing to such an organization. The result of the efforts of
this committee was the gaining of a nucleus for what
soon became the famous Knickerbocker Base Ball Club,
of New York, the first recorded association of Base Ball
players in the world. The organization was perfected
September 23, 1845.

Alexander J. Cartwright, whose portrait is presented
in connection with this chapter, was born in New York
City in the first decade of the Nineteenth Century. He
left his native city in 1849 and crossed the plains to California, attracted by the gold craze of that sensational
era. He remained in the Golden State for only one year,
sailing for the Hawaiian (then Sandwich) Islands, in
1850. There he spent the remainder of his active life,
dying at Honolulu in 1892.

From early boyhood, Mr. Cartwright was an enthusiastic devotee of Base Ball. Beginning as the originator
of the first Base Ball association in the world, and continuing his connection with that club as player and office-
bearer until the time of his departure in 1849, to seek his
fortunes in the Far West, he never lost interest in the

game. His son, Mr. Bruce Cartwright, a prominent citizen of Honolulu, in a personal letter to me, under date March 22, 1909, says:

" Although far removed from the field of his former activities, he never forgot Base Ball, and never missed an opportunity of being present whenever the game was played here."

Alexander J. Cartwright, among many other thousands, was one of the devotees of Base Ball disappointed by reason of the failure of the steamer "Alameda" to make schedule time, on the occasion of the visit of the " All America " and Chicago teams to Honolulu, on their world-tour in 1888–9.

This worthy man, whose loss was deeply mourned at the Hawaiian capital, where he was universally respected and beloved, had a life history contemporaneous with that of the birth and development of the game he so greatly admired. He had been present when the game was born. He had a part in its first organization. He had witnessed its progress throughout the years of its evolution and had seen it adopted not only as the national pastime of the land of his nativity, but had seen it become the favorite sport of the capital city of that far-off island of the Pacific which he had adopted as his home.

The first officers chosen by the Knickerbocker Club were Duncan F. Curry, President; William R. Wheaton, Vice-President; William H. Tucker, Secretary and Treasurer. The original playing grounds were on Manhattan Island and later on the Elysian Fields, Hoboken, New Jersey, at that time the city's most popular summer resort.

DUNCAN F. CURRY

The organization of the Knickerbocker Base Ball Club was the beginning of a most important era in the history of the game, for it was the first recorded movement of that kind. The right and title to the distinction of being the first organized Base Ball club in the world belongs to the old Knickerbocker Club. That honor has never been called in question. For more than thirty years the Knickerbocker Club maintained an amateur organization, and as such was regarded as a model in every respect.

But the claim to be the " only " club of ball players, was not long to remain unchallenged. The organization of the Knickerbockers soon bore fruit. In 1846 a party of players, styling themselves " The New York Nine," issued a challenge to the Knickerbockers to play a match— for a dinner, of course. The event came off at Hoboken, N. J., on the 19th of June, and it was the first contest of the kind ever played on those grounds.

The Knickerbocker team included Messrs. Turney, Adams, Tucker, Birney, Avery, H. and D. Anthony, Tryon and Paulding. The New York Nine comprised Messrs. Davis, Winslow, Ransom, Murphy, Case, Johnson, Thompson, Trenchard and Lalor.

The contest was a very one-sided affair. The challengers won by a score of 23 to 1, only four innings being necessary to secure the required 21 runs, and to teach the Knickerbockers that Base Ball is a game not simply for the cultivation of the social amenities. It was five years before the Knickerbockers engaged in another Base Ball match, but the annual banquets and occasional practice games continued as before.

In 1850 another team, under the title "The Washington Club," put in an appearance at the Old Red House grounds at Yorkville. Subsequently, in June, 1851, the Washingtons challenged the Knickerbockers. The game took place June 3d of that year. The Knickerbockers, having profited by their defeat at the hands of the New York Nine, had been giving more attention to practice than to pastry, and had greatly improved their game. They appeared upon the grounds in new uniforms, composed of blue trousers, white shirts and straw hats, creating a profound sensation. The score of this game was 21 to 11 in favor of the Knickerbockers, in eight innings.

It may be well to explain that, at this stage of the development of our national game, the final result was contingent, not upon the score as it stood at the end of nine innings, as now, but upon the winning of 21 runs in any requisite number of innings.

The return game of this series was played on June 17th, 1851, on the Hoboken grounds of the Knickerbockers. It was also won by the latter by a score of 22 to 20, in a hotly contested game of ten innings, which was followed by the usual banquet.

The Washington Club met defeat well. Undaunted by their double drubbing at the hands of the Knickerbockers, the team continued its practice games regularly, and greatly strengthened its play by the reception of a large number of new members from whom players were selected.

In 1852, the Washington Club (of New York), recognizing the apparent inappropriateness of title, changed its name to "The Gotham Club," and at once became a strong rival of the Knickerbockers. For two years the Gothams sought in vain to defeat their metropolitan adversaries. On June 24th, 1852, however, they at last succeeded, but only at the end of a contest unprecedented up to that time. The game lasted sixteen innings, the score finally standing 21 to 16 in favor of the Gothams.

The game of Base Ball played at this time was known as "The New York Game." It was played according to the printed rules of the Knickerbocker Club, which were recognized throughout the Empire State as authority. In New England, however, another code for the playing of the game was in operation. It was a modification of the old "Town Ball," which had been played in different sec· tions of the country for some years, and to which New England players had given the title of "Base Ball," which was clearly a misnomer, for it retained several of the features that had been eliminated by Doubleday's system, upon which the Knickerbocker rules were founded—notably the "soaking" of base runners with thrown balls.

About the time the Knickerbocker Club had been ten years in existence, the New York game had become quite generally established and widely accepted in New York and vicinity. Now, new clubs rapidly increased in numbers, and interest in the game became widespread.

Following the reorganization of the Gothams from the ranks of the Washingtons, in 1852, the Eagles, of New York, in 1854, began to soar. Next in order was the Empire Base Ball Club, in the fall of the same year, with Thomas G. Voorhis as President.

ECKFORD BASE BALL CLUB, OF BROOKLYN, 1858

C. Welling H. Manolt E. Brown P. Tostivan F. Pidgeon J. Vanderbilt W. Webster J. Grumm A. Mills
Dr. Bell, Umpire   William Butts, Scorer

The City of New York had now a quartet of fully organized clubs, every one of which became famous in the decade in which all were born. The splendid work done by these pioneers of the nation's game was productive of far-reaching results. It attracted the attention of sport-loving people all over the eastern part of the land to the fact that the game as played in New York was a sport worthy of adoption throughout the entire country.

It was impossible that so fine a game should long be monopolized by any city, so it came about in the natural order of things that as early as December, 1854, the Excelsiors, of Brooklyn, were organized, with J. Nelson Tappan as President. The Excelsiors, while retaining their organization intact, and playing frequent practice games, did not do much in the way of contests until 1860, when they won fame and favor as we shall see later on.

In the following May, 1855, the Putnams, of Williamsburgh, a suburb of Brooklyn, were organized, and a little later, in June, of the same year, the Eckfords, of Greenpoint, also an outlying community of Brooklyn, adopted articles of association. One year later, in July, 1856, the Atlantics, of Jamaica, were organized. And now the Knickerbockers, Gothams, Eagles and Empires, of New York, were offset by a Brooklyn quartet, composed of the Excelsiors, Putnams, Eckfords and Atlantics.

It must not be understood that these eight clubs constituted all the Base Ball organizations of the time. There were others, many others, and numerous clubs in many smaller cities were engaged during the decade of the fifties in active competition.

A very interesting story of one of these matches is preserved in the files of *Wilkes' Spirit of the Times*. Writing for that old time popular sporting periodical, Captain Frank Pigeon, pitcher of the Eckfords, of Brooklyn, thus chronicles the first match game in which that organization participated, and which was played at the Old Red House grounds, September 27th, 1856, with the Unions, of Morrisania. It will be noted that up-to-date journalism had not " caught on " sixty years ago as it has to-day. The report of a game of Base Ball nearly a year and a half old would hardly be regarded as news in this century of the world's progress. Captain Pigeon wrote:

" A year ago last August a small number of young men of that part of the city known as ' The Island.' were accustomed to meet for the purpose of enjoying the game. Being shipwrights and mechanics, we could not make it convenient to practice more than once a week; and we labored under the impression that want of practice and our having so few players from whom to select a nine would make it almost impossible for us to win a match even if we engaged in one. However, we were willing to do the best we could if some club would give us an invitation to play. But, alas, no such invitation came, and we began to doubt seriously if we were worth taking notice of.

" Still, we had some merry times among ourselves; we would forget business and everything else on Tuesday afternoons, go out on the green fields, don our ball suits, and go at it with a rush. At such times we were boys again. Such sport as this brightens a man up, and improves him, both in mind and body. After longing for a match, yet so dreading (not a defeat—we were sure of that) a regular Waterloo, we finally, through sheer desperation, expressed a wish to play the winners in a match between the Baltic and Union Clubs of Morrisania.

" The Unions won, and signified their willingness to play us. Well, we had got what we wanted—a match; and then, what? Why, we would have to do the best we could. The day came at last, on which we were to meet the conquerors of the Baltic; and nine determined, but badly scared men, whistling to keep up their spirits, might have been seen wending their way to the Red House. It would be difficult to describe the sensations we felt that day—such an intense desire to win, and such a dread of defeat. We knew that, if badly beaten, we could never succeed in building up a club. Many of our friends would not go to see the match because they did not wish to witness our defeat. * * *

"But the game. 'We pulled off our coats, and rolled up our sleeves;' we stood up to the rack, but were very nervous—first appearance on any stage. Our first man took the bat; tipped out; great dependence placed on him. Good Heaven, how unfortunate. Next man got scared; caught out. No use trying to win. Do the best we can, however. Steady, boys, steady. Third man gave the ball a regular crusher. One desperate yell burst from eight throats and I am not sure that the striker did not yell with the rest. First base, go it. Second base, come up. Go again, stay there. Another fortunate strike; man on third base got home. Glory. One run. Oh, how proud the Eckford club were at that run. Some ran to the umpire's book to see how it looked on paper.

"The innings ended with three runs for the Eckford. The Union took the bat, and made two runs. Could it be possible? We could scarcely believe it. We did the best we could to keep our end up, and by that means we overdid the matter, and the result was: Eckford, 22; Union, 8. About seven o'clock that evening, nine peacocks might have been seen on their way home, with tail-feathers spread. Our friends were astonished, as well as ourselves, and all felt rejoiced at the result."

This victory had a remarkable effect on the welfare of the Eckford Club, for henceforth members came flocking in by scores, and its game was greatly strengthened thereby.

The late Henry Chadwick, writing of this club, says:

"I remember seeing the Eckfords play a game in the fifties at the Old Manor House grounds in Williamsburgh. Their opponents that day were the Atlantics. It was then I first saw Frank Pigeon pitch. The visitors had no warrant to defeat the Eckfords; but the Atlantics had the prestige of success to help them, and the home team lacked confidence. Their captain saw what was the matter with them, and Frank said to them, 'Boys, just forget that you are playing the Atlantics, and go in as if you were facing a common nine.' There was philosophy in this advice, but the Eckfords could not get rid of the idea that they were playing against the champions, and, failing to play with confidence, they lost."

In an old copy of the *Baltimore Sun*, it is stated that

CHAMPION UNIONS, OF MORRISANIA

Smith, l.f.   Ketchum, 3b.   Shelly 3b.   Pabor, p.   Austin, c.f.   Goldie, 1b.
Beals, r.f.   Birdsall, c.   Akin, s.s.   Martin, 2b.

the first game of Base Ball played in Baltimore took place on a field located on ground that was later excavated for the bottom of a park lake. As to the inception of the game in Baltimore, the writer says: "Mr. George Beam, of Orendorf, Beam & Co., wholesale grocers, was invited in 1858 by Joseph Leggett to see a game in New York, in which the old Excelsiors of that city contested. Mr. Beam at once became an enthusiast, and returned to this city and organized the Excelsiors of Baltimore, in the wholesale trade on the wharf. Nearly all the players were business men. The Excelsiors lasted until 1861, and its members twice a week went to the diamond in an omnibus, which started from Exchange Place and Commerce Street. Large numbers of young men living on Madison Avenue would follow the bus to see the new game. The club soon moved to a lot at the southwest corner of Madison and North Avenues."

In 1860, the great Excelsiors, of New York, were invited over to give instructions in the game, and the Waverley Club, organized in 1860, offered its grounds, afterwards known as "Pastime Grounds," and there the games were played.

Among the New York players were Leggett, Creighton, Pearsall, Whiting, Flannery, Brainard, Polhemus. The Baltimore nine were Beam, Woods, Schriver, A. Woods, Mitchell, Pitman, Williams, Hank and Hazlett. The Excelsiors, of Baltimore, that night tendered to the Excelsiors, of New York, a regal banquet.

In addition to the New York and Brooklyn clubs composing the double quartet of which mention has been made, the names of the Mutuals, Harlems and Baltics, of New York, the Unions, of Morrisania, and the Continentals, of Brooklyn, might be quoted, but, with the exception of the Mutuals and Unions, none of these clubs ever attained that mark of excellence in play gained by the more famous organizations first referred to.

Before the decade of the fifties had ended, the game of Base Ball had reached a stage of popularity which called into being so many clubs—all of which, with the exception of the Libertys, of New Brunswick, N. J., were located within the present city limits of Greater New York—that a new epoch in the history of the game followed as a natural sequence in the order of development.

Following is a list of clubs organized up to and including 1857:

CLUBS	ORGANIZED	LOCATION OF GROUNDS
Knickerbocker	September 23, 1845...	Hoboken
Gotham..............	Spring of 1852........	Harlem
Eagle................	April, 1854...........	Hoboken
Empire..............	October 23, 1854.....	Hoboken
Excelsior............	December 8, 1854.....	South Brooklyn
Putnam..............	May, 1855	Williamsburgh
Newark..............	May 1, 1855..........	Newark
Baltic	June 4, 1855	New York
Eckford.............	June 27, 1855........	Greenpoint
Union	July 17, 1855.........	Morrisania
Atlantic	August 14, 1855......	Williamsburgh
Atlantic	August, 1855.........	Jamaica, L. I.
Continental	October, 1855.........	Williamsburgh
Harlem	March, 1856..........	New York
Enterprise	June 26, 1856........	Williamsburgh
Active..............	October, 1856	Hoboken
Star......	October, 1856........	South Brooklyn
Independent	January, 1857........	New York
Liberty.............	March 1, 1857........	New Brunswick, N. J.
Metropolitan........	March 4, 1857........	New York
Champion...........	March 14, 1857.......	New York
Hamilton	March 23, 1857.......	Brooklyn
St. Nicholas.........	April 28, 1857........	Hoboken
Mutual	June 24, 1857........	Williamsburgh

CHAPTER V.

(——)   Davis   De Bost   (——)   Stevens   H

KNICKERBOCKER AND EXCELSIOR TEAMS, 1858

(——) Kissam (——) Dr. Jones Polhemus Pearsall Leggett Holden Russell Dupont H. Brainard (——) (——)

CHAPTER V.

1855-60

IF it is true that the organization of the first Base Ball club, in the old Knickerbockers, marked the initial epoch in the history of the game, it must also be admitted that the coalition of numerous clubs, that they might work together for the advancement of common interests, inaugurated a second era of equal import.

For several years new clubs had been coming rapidly into existence. Thoughtful players of every team had views for the improvement of the game. It had long been apparent that some of the rules were inconsistent and prejudicial to the best development of the sport. All were agreed that certain modifications of the old Knickerbocker system ought to be introduced at as early a date as practicable. The need was pressing. Field contests were constantly increasing in numbers and interest, while misunderstandings, misinterpretations and dissensions on ball fields were multiplying in consequence.

Meanwhile, the Knickerbocker Base Ball Club, having served its important purpose of taking the initiative in organization, seemed to have outgrown its usefulness, and became an actual stumbling block in the path of progress.

This silk-stocking aggregation, never able to play a very brilliant game, had been reluctant to accept challenges from shipwrights, boilermakers and other grades of "greasy mechanics." Not wishing to be drawn into too close fellowship with the rabble, and perhaps dreading the humiliation of defeat at the hands of plebian upstarts, the Knickerbockers held aloof, practicing occasionally—between banquets—usually among their own exclusive membership, satisfied with the mouldy laurels won before live competition had appeared, and resting upon the glory of their unquestioned title as the first, if not "greatest ever."

The attitude of the Knickerbockers was for some time quite embarrassing to the interests of Base Ball. It was important that this organization, whose playing rules had been very generally adopted, but which needed so many changes, should co-operate with other clubs to that end. But no. The "Knicks" were satisfied with the rules, which were good enough for them—for anybody, they thought. And thus the matter rested, the original club declining overtures for matches, for conferences or for association. They were *it*, and *it* they proposed to remain.

Perhaps we ought not too harshly to criticize the Knickerbockers for their attitude at this period in the history of the game. They had been present at the accouchement and had witnessed the birth of Base Ball. Ever, since that glad day, the Knickerbockers had rocked the cradle of the infant prodigy, until they had come to regard themselves as in every way its special guardian and caretaker. They could not be induced to look with any favor upon the efforts of the Excelsiors, the Atlantics, the Gothams, the Putnams and other remote, aspiring relatives, to butt in under claims of ties of consanguinity. Especially were the Knickerbockers jealous of any attempts on the part of these rank outsiders to assume the functions of formulating rules for the disciplinary government of *their* child. The Base Ball infant had come into the world under the most auspicious conditions. From the very beginning, its surroundings had been pre-eminently respectable, and all its leadings had been along lines most proper and decorous. If the Knickerbockers had, in their fondness for the youngster, over-fed it at times and withheld a due amount of exercise, their intentions at least had been sincere and solicitous.

And now, it was proposed by these interlopers to introduce the kidlet into society—and such society! How were the Knickerbockers to meet the influences for evil which they thought would surely assail their darling if it came in touch with coarse and vulgar people who lived over on Long Island?

But that was not all. The Knickerbockers had been organized after the pattern of the ancient Marylebone Cricket Club, of England, which for centuries, more or less, had made every rule for the government of Cricket in Great Britain and her colonies—and which does so still. To question the right of the Marylebone Club to dictate in all matters of the British national game, on the other side of the Atantic, was rank heresy. And who were these pretenders, anyhow, who were disputing the Knickerbockers' right, which had never been questioned until now,

WILLIAM H. VAN COTT

to supervise and control Base Ball in America? And so the situation continued, full of embarrassments, full of disappointments, full of delays.

Finally a compromise was effected. It was agreed that the Great and Only Knickerbocker Base Ball Club, the First Base Ball Organization in all the Wide, Wide World, should, by reason of its seniority and lofty standing, call a convention in the interests of the game. This first convention was held in May, 1857, but, beyond adopting certain rules regulating matches for the ensuing year, no business affecting the game was transacted.

The second convention was also called by the Knickerbockers, on March 10th, 1858, but before this call was issued, the Knickerbockers, always refined and courteous, permitted the presidents of the Gotham, Eagle and Empire Clubs to add their signatures to the call.

Twenty-five clubs were represented at this convention by three delegates each, and the business transacted was of great importance to the future of Base Ball.

Hitherto the game had been controlled as to its playing rules largely by local prejudices. It was played under one set of rules in New York and another in New England, and other still widely different regulations were applied to the game elsewhere. In New York, batsmen were out on balls caught on the first bound; in New England, base runners were out by being "soaked" by thrown balls, and everywhere a batsman might wait all the afternoon for a strike ball, he alone being the judge of what he would strike at.

The organization of the National Association of Base

Ball Players, in 1858, therefore marked a new era in the history of the game, for it was then that there was put in operation for the first time a code of rules, framed by a special committee of the new association for that express purpose.

The officers elected in 1858, when the National Association of Base Ball Players was formed, were: President, William H. Van Cott, of the Gothams; First Vice-President, L. B. Jones, of the Excelsiors; Second Vice-President, Thomas S. Dakin, of the Putnams; Recording Secretary, J. Ross Postley, of the Metropolitans; Corresponding Secretary, Theodore F. Jackson, of the Putnams; Treasurer, E. H. Brown, of the Metropolitans.

It will be observed that the Knickerbockers, despite their former greatness, had already begun to fade away. Representatives from that club were conspicuous by their absence in the official roster of the new association. Practical politics had entered the game.

The first season after the organization of the National Association of Base Ball Players saw several series of remarkable games between picked nines representing the foremost clubs of New York and Brooklyn. Prior to these contests, the regular matches of each recurring season had attracted assemblages numbering only a few hundreds; but these games, inviting local partisanship, proved to be great drawing cards, bringing out the largest crowds ever seen at ball games up to that year.

The contests were held on the Fashion Race Course, on Long Island, during July, August and September of 1858. The first of the series of three games was played

on July 20th.   On account of the expense incurred in putting the grounds in order—and it was very poor order at
that—an admission fee of 50 cents was charged.

This was the first game of Base Ball on record where
gate money was demanded and received from spectators.
The difficulty of reaching the grounds was considerable.
Most of those in attendance came by small steamer from
the Fulton Ferry to Hunter's Point, and thence by the
Flushing Railroad to the Fashion Course.   This, of course,
materially lessened the numbers of the crowd.   Nevertheless, nearly 1,500 people saw the game, a great throng
for those days.

In this contest, the Brooklyn nine opened with a lead
of 3 to 0 at the end of the first innings, and at the end of
the second the score stood 5 to 1.   Then the New Yorks
struck a streak of luck and in the next three innings added
thirteen to their score, to six added by the Brooklyns,
showing a score at the end of the sixth of 16 to 13 in New
York's favor.   In the last three innings the Brooklyns
made five runs to six for the New Yorks, the final score
showing New York 22, Brooklyn 18.

Something of the nature of the game played at this
time may be known from the fact that of the 27 Brooklyn-
ites put out 13 were out on balls caught on a first bound,
while the New Yorks lost 14 on similar catches.   Eleven
bases were made on passed balls, charged to Brooklyn's
catcher, while New York's catcher lost only two.

The second match of the New York-Brooklyn series
took place on August 19th.   On this occasion the Brooklyns had considerably strengthened their nine.   As in the

OLD-TIME BASE BALL UNIFORMS

1. Pabor   2. Matt Yorston   3. "Deacon" Rogers

former game, Brooklyn took the lead in the start; but, unlike the previous game, the New Yorks failed to rally successfully. At the close of the sixth innings the Brooklyns led, 22 to 6, and at the end of the game were easy victors, having made 29 runs to 8 by their adversaries.

Another month elapsed before the final contest to decide the winner of two out of three matches came off. The date was September 10. By this time a widespread interest in the result had sprung up in both cities, and something of the spirit of local partisanship which characterizes league games at the present time was apparent. The crowd in attendance upon this event was the largest that had ever been seen on a ball field, numbering several thousands. In previous matches players from all the different clubs from each city were in the game; but in the final struggle, six players from the Atlantics and three from the Eckfords were on the Brooklyn team, while representatives from all of New York's quartet of clubs participated. The fight for supremacy in this game was very bitter. Both teams were on their mettle, every player feeling that the future welfare of the city represented by him depended upon the result. But it was apparent early in the game that the New Yorks were that day the better nine, and at the end of the ninth innings the score was 29 to 18 in favor of the boys from the big city.

In this game, a total of 27 men were out on balls caught on the first bound. In the entire contest no batsman was retired on strikes. During the three games only one home run was made, and on this run "hangs a tale" told by the late Henry Chadwick, in these words:

"Two Brooklyn cranks had a wager of $100 a side on John Holden's making a home run. One was an Atlantic rooter, the other an Excelsior fan. In this game I noticed that when Holden went to bat he was very particular in selecting his bat. It appears that the man who had bet on him went to him and told him that he would give him $25 of his bet if he made the hit; so Jack was very anxious. Matty O'Brien was pitching, and Jack, after waiting for a good ball, got one to suit him, and sent it flying over Harry Wright's head at right center, and made the round of the bases before the ball was returned, thus winning the $25."

Aside from the story itself, this tale is interesting as showing that already, almost at the inception of the playing of match games between organized teams in rival cities, betting on the result, which was to make so much for mischief in the future, was beginning to be in evidence.

CHAPTER VI.

EXCELSIORS, OF BROOKLYN

J. C. Whiting   H. B. Polhemus   E. Russell   A. Brainard
T. Reynolds   J. Creighton   A. T. Pearsall   J. R. Leggett   G. Flanley

CHAPTER VI.

1860

THE first recorded tour made by any Base Ball organization grew out of the series played between picked nines from the New York and Brooklyn quartets. Following the Fashion Course games of 1858, Base Ball clubs began to increase with great rapidity throughout the Atlantic States. Every city of considerable size soon had its team or teams of ball players. Interest in their prowess was manifested by larger attendance at matches between clubs of the same city, and by the multiplication of clubs everywhere. Now interest to know how the playing of nines of one city compared with that of teams of others began to develop.

Up to this time not much attention had been given to field sports in this country. Horse-racing was in vogue at all large places and in smaller cities in certain sections; but golf, lawn tennis, cricket, lacrosse and other games of the kind were without favor, save as here and there English and Scotch residents indulged in the national sports of Great Britain.

It was apparent now, however, that a new era had dawned in America, and while Base Ball had not yet earned the right to be denominated our national game, it

77

JAMES P. CREIGHTON

was forging ahead with rapid strides toward the goal of that distinction. It was quite natural that especial interest in the game should center in Brooklyn, the home of that splendid quartet comprising the Excelsiors, the Atlantics, the Putnams and Eckfords. But these were not all the Brooklyn clubs, by any means. Junior organizations had been formed in that city during the years in which their seniors were winning laurels, and before 1860 the older clubs were glad enough to find recruits for their ranks from strong players who were being developed in the minor organizations. In 1859, the Stars and Enterprise Clubs, both juniors, had been drawn upon by the Excelsiors, who profited greatly in securing several players, among them, from the Stars, James Creighton, afterwards famous as a pitcher.

The year 1860 saw the first tour of an organized Base Ball club, in the visit of the Excelsiors, of Brooklyn, to several cities in Central and Western New York. The trip is memorable, not alone as the first Base Ball tour, but because of its very remarkable record of victories.

The tour was made under the management of Captain J. B. Leggett. The team consisted of a trained nine from the Excelsiors, of Brooklyn. The first city visited was Albany, for which place they left on June 30th, 1860. On July 2d they met the champion nine of the capital city, defeating them in a nine innings game, the score of which was 24 to 6. The following day, July 3d, they encountered the Victory Club, of Troy, and again won, this time by a score of 13 to 7 in a full game. Taking train from Troy, after their victory there, the Excelsiors went to Buffalo, and on July 5th engaged the strong team of the Niagara Club. The score was 50 to 19, with victory on the banners of the visitors. This was the highest score that had ever been recorded in a Base Ball match up to that date, and, as games were measured in those days, it was regarded as a very fine exhibition of ball playing on both sides.

This record of consecutive victories, the tidings of which were flashed over the State, created a profound sensation, and bred a strong desire on the part of lovers of the game in every city having a team to see the invincible Excelsiors. Per consequence, invitations, which could not be accepted, came pouring in upon the victors from all points of the compass. Another effect of this first missionary tour in the interests of the game was to cause the formation of clubs in many places where none had theretofore existed.

From this time on the tour was one of triumphal ovations. The Niagaras, of Buffalo, took their guests over to the Falls, and entertained them at a fine banquet at the Clifton House, on the Canadian side. Returning from Buffalo, they played the Flour City nine at Rochester, July 7th, winning by a score of 21 to 1. Next day they met the Rochester Live Oaks, whom they defeated, 27 to 9. Stopping at Newburgh-on-the-Hudson, July 11th, they added another victory to their chain by a score of 59 to 14, in this game surpassing their large total in the Buffalo match.

Always and everywhere on this great journey of conquest the Excelsiors were the recipients of most gracious hospitality, a true sportsmanlike spirit possessing the hosts in every city visited. Moreover, at all points the game received fresh impetus, new clubs were organized, and word came from all over the State that Base Ball matches were being scheduled as never before.

Encouraged by the success of their trip through Western New York, the Excelsiors turned toward the South, and later, in July, 1860, took a trip in that direction, crossing the States of Pennsylvania, Delaware and Maryland. The first contest was with a picked nine from all the clubs of Baltimore. It came off July 22d, and was a repetition of the story of former experiences, the score being 51 to 6 in favor of the Excelsiors. True Southern hospitality marked the treatment of the Excelsiors at Baltimore. The day closed with a fine banquet at Guy's Hotel.

Returning, the Excelsiors stopped at Philadelphia, where, on July 24th, they played a nine composed of all the best players of the Quaker City, including the Olympics, the Athletics, the Winonas, the Equities, the United Base Ball Club and the Benedicts. The game was played on the old Camaco Woods Cricket Grounds and attracted a large attendance. The Excelsiors won by 15 to 4. Like the New York tour, this trip had a tremendous influence in promoting interest in the game in a new quarter. Upon their return, the Excelsiors found awaiting them an invitation from Boston, which they were compelled, reluctantly, to decline until a later date.

On July 20th, 1860, while resting on laurels won on their trip through New York—and before their South-

J. B. LEGGETT

ern tour—the Excelsiors met the Brooklyn Atlantics. This fine team had been their old time conquerors; but, flushed with their recently acquired string of victories, the Excelsiors felt that they might take their former rivals into camp. They had been greatly strengthened by the accession to their ranks of James Creighton, the star pitcher of the time, and other recruits from minor clubs. And so it came about that, in this first match game with their old adversary, the Excelsiors found no trouble in winning, the score standing 23 to 4. The crowd in attendance at this game numbered fully 2,000 spectators. The game was played on the new grounds of the Excelsiors. It was the prestige of this victory over the Atlantics, rather than their achievements in contests with less prominent clubs on the trip to Buffalo and return, that gave to the Excelsiors so much of notoriety on their visit to the South.

On the home-coming of the Excelsiors from Baltimore and Philadelphia, arrangements were made for the return match with the Atlantics, on the Atlantic Club Grounds. The game was played on August 10th, 1860. It was believed by most people interested in the contest that the Excelsiors had a "walk-away," and this opinion was strengthened when, at the end of the third innings, the score stood 8 to 0 in favor of that club; but the Atlantics were not yet beaten. In spite of the positive belief of the great throng that the Excelsiors were invincible, the Atlantics played that game with sublime courage and faith. At the end of the sixth innings, while the Excelsiors were still leading, the Atlantics had changed the score from 8 to 0 to 12 to 6. Then came one of those surprises peculiar to the game, and which gives always the assurance that the contest is not ended until the last man is out. The Atlantics in the seventh innings found the redoubtable Creighton for five clean hits, yielding nine runs and giving them a lead which the Excelsiors were unable to change. The final score was 15 to 14 in favor of the Atlantics. Thus ended a hitherto unbroken succession of victories, dating from the beginning of the Excelsiors' remarkable tour through New York.

The great rivals were now even in the race for championship honors of Brooklyn. Each had one game of the series. The next contest must decide the question of club supremacy. Interest in the result became intense. It was not confined to Brooklyn, but extended to all neighboring cities and villages. Under the agreement regulating the series of games, it was provided that the third game should be played upon neutral grounds. The new grounds of the Putnams, having just received their finishing touches, furnished just the requisite conditions. After a lapse of two weeks, namely, on August 23d, 1860, the final meeting took place.

The intense feeling of partisanship that had been engendered by the preceding contests increased as the time for the last game drew near, until it had become very bitter. It permeated all grades of society. Schoolboys, clerks, merchants, manufacturers, workingmen, and members of all the learned professions were profoundly interested. This would have been well enough, but, unfortunately, in those days all Eastern cities were noted for their utterly uncontrollable elements of thugs, gamblers, thieves, plug-uglies and rioters. Of these both New York and Brooklyn had more than their full quotas. It happened that public sympathy, as expressed in the views of the disorderly members of society, was strongly in favor of the Atlantics. They proposed that the Atlantics should win the deciding game of the series, and were on the grounds in large numbers for the purpose of securing a result to their liking, either by fair means or otherwise.

The Atlantics repudiated, but could not control, their belligerent partisans. Early in the game the actions of the disorderly among the spectators threatened trouble. Betting had been widely indulged in, and the class to which bettors belonged, and that never was particularly scrupulous in its acts, in this game, when the Excelsiors took the lead at the start, winning five runs to one for the Atlantics, began to show bad temper. At the close of the fourth the Excelsiors were still in the lead, by 8 to 4. From this time on the toughs began a crusade of blackguardism that became so unbearable as the game progressed that at the end of the sixth innings, with the score standing 8 to 6 in favor of his team, Captain Leggett, of the Excelsiors, took his players from the field, saying, as they entered the six-horse stage:

" Here, O'Brien, is the ball. You can keep it."

O'Brien replied, "Will you call it a draw?"

"As you please," responded the gentlemanly captain.

And thus ended the contest, for from that day to the date of disbandment of both clubs, in 1871, they never played together again.

CREIGHTON'S MONUMENT

This game saw the first recorded row at a Base Ball match.

The *Brooklyn Eagle*, of February 5th, 1898, contained the following article relative to James Creighton, one of the greatest ball players of ante-bellum days:

" On the crest of Tulip Hill, in one of the most picturesque portions of Greenwood Cemetery, a striking monument of granite marks the spot where one of Brooklyn's pioneer ball players lies buried. It is over the grave of James Creighton, a man whose ability in the national game, as it was known in its infancy, is well recollected by those whose memory extends back to the years before the Civil War.

" The stone in commemoration of Creighton faces the famous Firemen's Monument, and it would never be mistaken for anything else than the grave of a ball player. Across the face of the column, surrounded by a circle of oak leaves cut in the granite, is a design embodying a pair of bats crossed, a cap, a base and a score book, surmounted across the top by a scroll with the word " Excelsior " carved upon it. The old Excelsior Club of Brooklyn was the one with which Creighton made his reputation as a pitcher. On a level slab, just below the wreath, are carved the words: ' James Creighton, son of James and Jane Creighton, April 15, 1841; October 18, 1862.' A Base Ball, fashioned in stone, rests lightly upon the topmost pinnacle of the monument.

" Creighton's death occurred when he was twenty-one years of age, while he was still an active member of the Excelsiors. He was not only well known, but thoroughly popular among the followers of the early game, and his death came as a personal loss to every man who had been associated with him, either in the Base Ball field or in everyday life. Though he has been dead thirty-six years, Creighton's memory is still cherished by surviving members of the Excelsior Club.

" Creighton was in his day generally conceded to be the pitcher *par excellence* of the period. He was the first to introduce the wrist throw, or low underhand delivery, which was so puzzling to batsmen of that day. His forte was great speed and thorough command of the ball. His first appearance was as a member of the Niagara Club of this city in 1858. He was then playing second base, and J. A. Shields, U. S. Commissioner, was pitcher. He remained with the Niagaras throughout that season and the greater part of the following one, playing second base most of the time. In July, 1859, he began to loom up as a bright particular star in the Base Ball firmament. He first attracted attention as a pitcher in a game against the Star Club. Shields, the regular pitcher, was absent, and Creighton pitched so effectively that the Star Club tempted him to leave the Niagaras and join its nine, which he did, along with George H. Flanly, who had also been playing with the Niagaras.

"On September 3, 1859, the Stars met the Excelsiors on the latter's grounds in South Brooklyn, and the former won by a score of 17 to 12. On October 19, the Stars met the then famous old Atlantic nine on the Excelsior's grounds, and, after an interesting game, the Atlantics won by a score of 15 to 12. The contest was so evenly played that at the end of the seventh innings the score was a tie—11 to 11. Loose fielding, however, on the part of the Star players enabled the Atlantics to win. That season Creighton participated in six match games.

"During the following winter Creighton and Flanly joined the Excelsiors, and it was while with the latter that Creighton gained his greatest renown. In 1860 he participated in twenty match games, some of which are memorable ones. Probably the most noteworthy of these was the famous series between the Excelsiors and the Atlantics. The latter were pretty generally looked upon as being unconquerable. On May 17, 1860, the Charter Oaks defeated the Excelsiors by 12 to 11. Commissioner Shields pitched for the former and Creighton for the latter. On June 21 these clubs met again, and this time the Excelsiors won by 36 to 9. Creighton pitched for the Excelsiors and Shields for the losers. In July Creighton accompanied the Excelsiors on their great tour of victory through the State."

Under the caption, "Obsequies of a Celebrated Ball Player," the *Brooklyn Eagle* of October 20th, 1862, contained the following obituary:

"The remains of the late James P. Creighton, familiar in Base Ball and cricket circles as one of the best players in the Union, were yesterday conveyed to their last resting place, followed by a large number of friends and relatives.

"The circumstances of his death are very touching. In the late match with the Unions (Tuesday last) the deceased sustained an internal injury occasioned by strain while batting. After suffering for a few days, he expired on Saturday afternoon last at the residence of his father, 307 Henry Street. The remains were incased in a handsome rosewood coffin, with silver mountings, and upon a silver plate was inscribed the name, age, etc., of the deceased—'James P. Creighton, 21 years, 7 months and 2 days.'"

CHAPTER VII.

THE CALL FOR VOLUNTEERS—1861

CHAPTER VII.

AS HAS been already stated, the years 1857-8-9 saw rapid progress in the multiplication and quality of Base Ball organizations. The decade of the fifties had developed the game from one of crude beginnings to a sport that was attracting widespread attention because of its easily discernible possibilities. The year 1860, however, was the banner year in early Base Ball history. The triumphal tour of the Excelsiors had wrought wonders in the way of creating public sentiment favorable to the game. The contests at Albany, Troy, Buffalo, Philadelphia and Baltimore had inspired the young men of those cities to emulate the example of the youth of New York and Brooklyn, and had begotten within them the hope that they might win for their cities a glory akin to that which had been achieved for the city on Long Island. As a result, clubs were organized by the hundreds, the fever spreading to all parts of the country, East, West, North and South, and matches, which developed strong new players, were scheduled everywhere.

But in 1861 a serious check was given to the progress of Base Ball. The news that Fort Sumter had been fired upon turned the thoughts of men of the North to a subject more grave than ball playing, while Southerners, believing that the President's call to arms meant the invasion of the "Sunny South," prepared to give their Northern visitors a less hospitable reception than that which had been accorded to the Excelsiors a few months previous at Baltimore. Thoughts of contests on fields of sport were banished from the minds of men in every section, while all looked forward to a greater, fiercer struggle that should be decided by the arbitrament of arms on fields of battle.

And yet, while the game of ball, during those four years of fratricidal strife, was held in abeyance—the attention of its votaries being more deeply engaged in the game of war—it was nevertheless undergoing an evolution of greatest import to its future. For, during those years of unhappy conflict, on both sides of the line "Yanks" and "Johnnies" were playing ball and laying the foundation for a game which, when war's alarms should cease, would be national in its spirit and national in its perpetuity.

No human mind may measure the blessings conferred by the game of Base Ball on the soldiers of our Civil War. A National Game? Why, no country on the face of the earth ever had a form of sport with so clear a title to that distinction. Base Ball had been born in the brain of an American soldier. It received its baptism in bloody days of our Nation's direst danger. It had its early evolution when soldiers, North and South, were striving to forget their foes by cultivating, through this grand game, fraternal friendships with comrades in arms. It had its

best development at the time when Southern soldiers, dis-
heartened by distressing defeat, were seeking the solace of
something safe and sane; at a time when Northern soldiers, flushed with victory, were yet willing to turn from
fighting with bombs and bullets to playing with bat and
ball. It was a panacea for the pangs of humiliation to
the vanquished on the one side, and a sedative against the
natural exuberance of victors on the other. It healed the
wounds of war, and was balm to stinging memories of
sword thrust and saber stroke. It served to fill the enforced leisure hours of countless thousands of men suddenly thrown out of employment. It calmed the restless
spirits of men who, after four years of bitter strife, found
themselves all at once in the midst of a monotonous era,
with nothing at all to do.

And then, when true patriots of all sections were
striving to forget that there had been a time of black and
dismal war, it was a beacon, lighting their paths to a future of perpetual peace.   And, later still, it was a medium
through which the men who had worn the blue, found
welcome to the cities of those who had worn the gray,
and before the decade of the sixties had died the game
of Base Ball helped all of us to "know no North, no
South," only remembering a reunited Nation, whose game
it was henceforth to be forever.

It is very unfortunate that the records of games
played by soldiers during the Civil War are inscribed only
upon the memories of those who participated in them.
Interesting, indeed, would it be to read the details of
struggles which served so well to break the monotony of

ON TENTED FIELDS—IN PRISON PENS

camp life in the early sixties. Especially would it be of interest to note that while Americans of the North were fighting Americans of the South, between battles both were playing a game that had been devised nearly a quarter of a century before by a youth who, in the pending struggle, had sighted the first gun in defense of Fort Sumter, and who, later on, was to wear the epaulets of a Major General.

It was during the Civil War, then, that the game of Base Ball became our national game; for against it there was no prejudice—North or South; and from that day to this it has been played with equal fervor and with equal prowess in every section of our beloved country.

It is said that in Virginia, in the long campaign before Richmond, at periods when active hostilities were in abeyance, a series of games was played between picked nines from Federal and Confederate forces. I have heard rumors of this series repeatedly, but have not been able to trace them to any authoritative source. I refer to them here, not as history, but simply as of sufficient interest to be worthy of mention. I have not found any soldier of either army to corroborate these rumors or to deny them. Several have told me that they took part in many games, on one side or the other, and that they believed the rumors might be founded on fact, because they had themselves known of cases where good-natured badinage had been exchanged between Union and Confederate soldiers on the outposts of opposing armies in the field.

However, it is of record that many games of Base Ball were played by soldiers during the war. On Christmas

Day, December 25th, 1862, a team from the 165th New York Volunteer Infantry, Duryea's Zouaves, engaged a picked nine from other Union regiments in that army. The game was witnessed by about 40,000 soldiers. It was played at Hilton Head, South Carolina, and was discussed for many a week thereafter. Among those participating in this game was Mr. A. G. Mills, of New York City, afterwards President of the National League, and to him I am indebted for the interesting incident.

Writing under date March 8th, 1909, Mr. N. E. Young, former President of the National League, says:

"In my native town in New York State the modern game of Base Ball had not been introduced prior to the breaking out of the Civil War. In my regiment we had a full cricket team, all of whom had played together at home, and our first match was arranged and played near White Oak Church, Va., in the early spring of 1863, against the Ninety-fifth Pennsylvania Regiment's team, hailing from Philadelphia. About this time (1863) a Base Ball club was organized in the Twenty-seventh New York Regiment, so we turned our attention to Base Ball, and kept it up as we had the chance until the close of the war. It was here that I played my first regular game of Base Ball."

In *Collier's Weekly* of May 8th, 1909, Will Irwin writes as follows:

"Then came the Civil War, and the place of the Boston boys was the ranks. The number of clubs in and about New York City dwindled from sixty-two in 1860 to twenty-eight in 1865. But the enlisted players took their game with them into the camps of Virginia and Tennessee. Whenever, in summer or fall, the Federal armies rested for a week, some one was sure to take a Base Ball out of his haversack and start a game. They played it on the Peninsula while the Army of the Potomac waited for the latest incompetent general to replace the last incompetent general. They played it before Fort Fisher, dropping one game mid-innings to fall in and run to the firing line. They played it in Confederate prisons, where they taught it to their captors. The Ohio, Illinois, Wisconsin and Indiana regiments turned out to watch and remained to learn. A young cricketer from Amsterdam, New York, who had enlisted in the ranks, saw the Eighth New York, recruited from Manhattan, playing a new game. It looked like cricket, for which his soul thirsted; he begged into the game. It was Nicholas E. Young, for a quarter of a century President of the National League. A volunteer private returned invalided to Rockford, Illinois, in 1863. He saw the boys batting up flies, and he told them that he knew a better game. He had learned it in the army. One tall, wiry boy took a special interest. It was Al. Spalding, great pitcher, great manager, great organizer— prime figure in Base Ball from that day to this. On Roanoke Island Hawkins' Zouaves formed two scrub teams. A young volunteer pitcher won for his side by a weak, puzzling delivery which baffled the batsmen. It was Alphonse Martin, first in the line of great American pitchers.

"The same leaven was working in the Confederate ranks. The New Orleans boys also carried base balls in their knapsacks. A few of them found themselves in a Federal prison stockade on the Mississippi. They formed a club. Confederate prisoners from Georgia and South Carolina watched them, got the hang of it and organized for rivalry. In the East and West Series that followed the West won triumphantly by unrecorded scores."

James L. Steele, writing in *Outing* Magazine, has the following relative to newspaper treatment of the sport in days before the war:

"The first newspaper report of a Base Ball game that I remember reading was an account of a game played at Hoboken, N. J., in 1859. It appeared in an illustrated weekly, and was such a novel and interesting event that the weekly gave a double-page illustration.

"There were no Base Ball schedules in those days, and nobody lay awake nights hatching up reasons why Harvard should not play Princeton and why Yale should play Pennsylvania. All that was needed was an occasion such as a Fourth of July celebration, a county fair, a house-raising, or some other event of that nature. The occasion for this particular game was the entertainment given to a team of English cricketers then touring this country and defeating 'United States Twenty-Twos' with commendable regularity. We had evolved a game called Base Ball, and we wanted to show our cousins what a high old game it was.

"It may have been the 'humors of the day' editor who wrote the report, which was as follows:

"'Base Ball differs from cricket, especially in there being no wickets. The bat is held high in the air. When the ball has been struck, the "outs" try to catch it, in which case the striker is out;

or, if they cannot do this, to strike the striker with it when he is running, which likewise puts him out.

"'Instead of wickets, there are, at this game, four or five marks called bases, one of which, being the one at which the striker stands, is called "home."

"'As at cricket, the point of the game is to make the most runs between bases; the party which makes the most runs wins the day.'

"The fact that the reporter thought it necessary to explain how the game was played, indicates the extent of the public's knowledge of Base Ball at that time, and even he wasn't quite sure whether there were four bases or five. When he says a base runner may be put out by hitting him with the ball, he makes no mistake, for that was an actual fact, and it was considered a good play on the part of the base runner to draw a throw from the pitcher, for usually the runner would dodge the throw and gambol around the bases while the fielders were hurrying after the ball. This rule was abolished as soon as the game became popular, for a baseman, instead of touching a runner with the ball, would often 'soak' him at short range, which generally brought forth unprintable remarks from the soakee.

"The artist, in illustrating this game, was not far behind the reporter. The picture shows us several hundred spectators, and, with the exception of a few ladies and gentlemen, seated in carriages, the only person sitting down in the entire assemblage is the umpire; and, as if to show the perfect tranquility of his mind and his contempt for foul tips, he leans back in his chair with his legs crossed. The basemen, instead of playing 'off,' are standing, each with one foot on his base, and a base runner is 'glued to third,' although the pitcher is ready to deliver the ball. In short, the general aspect of the field is enough to give a modern Base Ball captain nervous prostration."

CHAPTER VIII.

HON. ARTHUR PUE GORMAN

CHAPTER VIII.

1865

A S SHOWING the rapid growth in popularity of Base Ball from the time of the formation of the National Association of Base Ball Players, in 1857, to the breaking out of the Civil War, in 1861, the following figures, though often published heretofore, will be found of interest:

The number of clubs represented by delegates in the first convention, held in 1857, was 16; in 1858, 25; in 1859, 49; in 1860, 54, and in 1861, only 34. The great falling off in '61 was due, of course, to the beginning of hostilities in that year, and from that time until the close of the war the attendance of club representatives at national annual meetings was very small.

But in 1865, at the close of the Civil War, so great was the furore for Base Ball that 91 clubs had representation in the convention—over 48 being from the State of New York alone, while 14 clubs had representation from Pennsylvania and 13 from New Jersey. The presence of scattering delegates from Portland, Me.; Leavenworth, Kansas; St. Louis, Mo., and Louisville, Ky., showed how the fever was spreading.

The tenth annual convention of the National Association of Base Ball Players, held in 1866, had a most sensational attendance, in the largest assemblage of representatives ever gathered in a similar convention up to that time. Delegates were present from clubs in New York, Pennsylvania, New Jersey, Connecticut, the District of Columbia, Maryland, Ohio, Massachusetts, Iowa, Tennessee, Missouri, Kansas, Delaware, Virginia, West Virginia, Kentucky, Oregon, Maine.

It was at this convention that Arthur Pue Gorman, afterward United States Senator from Maryland, was elected President of the National Association.

The eleventh annual convention, held in 1867, was another surprise. It had representation from 237 clubs from the following States: Connecticut, 22; Illinois, 56; Indiana, 21; Maryland, 20; New York, 24; Ohio, 42; Pennsylvania, 27; Wisconsin, 25.

An analysis of these figures is of interest as showing that between the tenth and eleventh conventions of the National Association an epidemic of Base Ball fever had swept out into the West, and that, whereas in 1866 only a few Western States were represented by a mere handful of delegates, in 1867 the four States of Illinois, Indiana, Ohio and Wisconsin had 145 clubs represented, which was nearly double the representation of the entire country the year previous. There was also something to inspire conjecture in the fact that in this year, while the great State of New York, where Base Ball had its birth, was represented by only 24 clubs, Illinois alone had 56—more than double the number of the Empire State, and delegates from Indiana and Wisconsin were about equal in numbers to those from New York.

This great and rapidly increasing interest in the game throughout the West was productive of noteworthy results. Not only were many clubs being formed in the Mississippi Valley and beyond the Rockies, but really formidable teams were springing up on every hand. The great clubs of the Atlantic States, too, were beginning to sit up and take notice of the records of some of the players of the Middle West, while a very natural longing to "take the conceit out" of the "farmers" gained possession of the Eastern clubs.

Meanwhile the names of the foremost players of the Eastern clubs were becoming as familiar as "household words" to Western fans, so that desire to see the Wright Brothers (Harry and George), Leggett, Berthrong, Williams, McBride, Reach, Fox, Start, Chapman, Ferguson and other notables, was prevalent everywhere. Thus it came about naturally, through the wish of the Eastern players to vanquish the West, and the hope of the Western boys to test conclusions with the fellows who had made the game famous, that a tour was arranged having as its object the playing of a series of matches between an Eastern club and teams in cities of the West.

The National Base Ball Club, of Washington, D. C., though an amateur organization, with membership largely confined to government employes who had developed ability to put up a strong game, conceived the idea of taking upon itself the task of cleaning up the "Wild and Wooly West." Mr. Arthur Pue Gorman, of Maryland, himself a fine player and an enthusiastic supporter of the game, favored the scheme and at once gave to it his personal aid and encouragement.

On the 11th of July, 1867, therefore, the Nationals, accompanied by a party of friends, started upon a trip to the West that was to include in its itinerary the States of Ohio, Indiana, Kentucky, Missouri and Illinois. The club was under the personal management of its President, Col. Frank Jones, and with him were the following players:

George Wright, shortstop and captain; W. F. Williams, a young law student, pitcher; Frank P. Norton, clerk in the Treasury Department, catcher; G. H. E. Fletcher, clerk in the Third Auditor's Office, first base; E. A. Parker, clerk in Internal Revenue Office, second base; George H. Fox, student at Georgetown College, third base; S. L. Studley, clerk in Treasury Department, left field; Harry W. Berthrong, clerk in Comptroller's Office, center field; Harry C. McLease, of the Auditor's Office, right field; E. G. Smith, clerk in the Fourth Auditor's Office, substitute. Henry Chadwick was a member of the party and official scorer.

The President of the Nationals had arranged a schedule of games to be played on this trip, the list being as follows:

Capital Club, of Columbus, Ohio; Cincinnatis and Buckeyes, at Cincinnati, Ohio; Louisville Club, at Louisville, Ky.; the Westerns, at Indianapolis, Ind.; the Empires and Unions, at St. Louis, Mo.; the Excelsiors and Atlantics, at Chicago, Ill., and the Forest City Club, of

Rockford, Ill., which had been winning favor at the game, also at Chicago.

This schedule involved the playing of games in five States of the South and West and traveling a distance of over 3,000 miles by rail and boat, at an expense of more than $5,000. The sportsmanlike nature of the game in those days may be known from the fact that, from beginning to end, the visiting club bore all its own expenses, absolutely refusing to share any gate money at any game on the trip.

The tourists left Washington at four o'clock p. m. of the day of their departure, a large company of friends being present to see them started on their journey, and the following gentlemen having interest enough in players and game to accompany the Nationals on their tour: Messrs. Hodges, Cronin, Brown, Patterson, Munson, St. Clair, Ewer, Gramar, Dorsey, Stewart, Corvan and Price. They were met on their arrival at Annapolis, Md., by Mr. Gorman, who subsequently joined the party at Chicago.

At Columbus, the scene of the first game, the Nationals were received with demonstrations of marked favor and most profuse hospitality. On July 12th they met the Capital Club nine on a very poor field in the suburbs of the city. Two namesakes were pitted against each other as pitchers in this contest, J. Williams, afterwards Secretary of the American Association, appearing for the Capitals, while W. Williams filled the pitcher's box for the Nationals. The Western Williams did not make good in this game, a total of twenty-seven base hits being made from his delivery, while the Columbus team got only ten hits from the National Williams. The score at the end of seven innings—which were quite enough to satisfy spectators and players—was 90 to 10 in favor of the Washington club, an unprecedented score for the West up to that date.

After the customary banquet and other social functions common to the game in those days, the Nationals left for Cincinnati, where they arrived on the 14th, and on the 15th, after a full day's enjoyment of the hospitality of Cincinnati's players and people, they played the Cincinnatis, on the Union grounds, which had been opened on July 4th. As at Columbus, the Nationals were again victorious, this time by a score of 53 to 10 in a full game. For the Cincinnatis, the afterwards famous Harry Wright pitched, and the noted cricketer, Rogerson, caught.

I have already remarked that cricket is not Base Ball. It was not until Harry Wright put cricket in the background that he became noted as a Base Ball player and manager.

The following day the Nationals met the rivals of the Cincinnati Club, in the Buckeyes, also of the same city, and defeated them, 88 to 12, in a six innings game. On July 16th the Nationals left Cincinnati for Louisville, by the steamer "General Buell," and next day engaged the Louisville team at the Cedar Hill grounds. The result was a defeat for Louisville by a score of 82 to 21, in nine innings.

July 19th, the club from the Nation's capital city arrived at Indianapolis, en route to St. Louis. Here they played the Western Club, of the Hoosier capital, winning by the score of 106 to 21 in a full game. It was in this game that McVey, afterward to win enduring fame on the diamond, played at second base for the Westerns, and made his bow to the public as a future great one. The game was played on the old Camp Burnside Grounds.

On the 22d of July the Nationals played their first game at St. Louis with the Unions of that city, on one of the hottest days of a very hot season, the mercury registering 104 in the shade on the ball grounds. Notwithstanding the torrid heat, the game lasted four hours and a half, and the poor clerks from the government offices at Washington had to circle the bases for a grand total of 113 runs to 26 for the Unions in a nine innings game. Next day the Nationals had no trouble in defeating the Empire Club of St. Louis by 53 to 26, in six innings.

From St. Louis the Nationals went to Chicago, where occurred the most sensational incident of the entire trip. On July 25th this great team of splendid ball players, that had visited Columbus, Cincinnati, Indianapolis, Louisville and St. Louis, winning every game played, and by scores ranging from 113 to 26 to 53 to 26, in large cities, met a nine from the pretty little city of Rockford, Illinois, and suffered their first and only defeat; for, utterly crushed and humiliated by the unexpected drubbing by the schoolboys, after a game next day with the Chicago Excelsiors, which they won easily by a score of 49 to 4, the Nationals turned their faces homeward, and the players were soon again at their desks at Washington, D. C.

The late Henry Chadwick, in his Base Ball memoranda, which came into my possession at his death as the gift of his estimable wife, describes the National-Forest City game in these words:

"A Base Ball tourney had been held in Chicago on July 4, 1867, in which the Excelsiors of that city and the Forest City Club, of Rockford, had been the leading contestants. The former had defeated the Forest City nine in two games, by very close scores of 45-41 in one, and 28-25 in another, when the Forest Citys were invited to meet the Nationals at Chicago on July 25th, a day which proved the most notable of the tour. The contest took place at Dexter Park, before a vast crowd of spectators, the majority of whom looked to see the Nationals have almost a walk-over. In this game A. G. Spalding was pitcher, and Ross Barnes shortstop for the Forest City nine; these two afterwards becoming famous as star players of the Boston professional team of the early seventies. Williams was pitcher for the Nationals and Frank Norton catcher. The Nationals took the lead in the first innings by 3 to 2; but in the next two innings they added but five runs to their score, while the Forest Citys added thirteen to theirs, thereby taking the lead by a score of fifteen to eight, to the great surprise of the crowd and the delight of the Rockfords. The Nationals tried hard to recover the lost ground. The final result, however, was the success of the Forest Citys by a score of 29 to 23 in a nine innings game, twice interrupted by rain."

The Chicago papers taunted the Nationals on their defeat, and anticipated a signal victory for their "Champions of the West," the Chicago Excelsiors, next day. The crowds present on the 26th, when the Excelsiors met the Nationals, was the largest ever seen at a match out West up to that time, though the admission fee was half a dollar. From the very outset of the contest the Nationals played the finest game of their tour, not only in pitching and batting, but especially in fielding, while the Excelsiors, after the first innings, which ended seven to nothing against them, "went up in the air," as the saying is, and came out of the fight the most demoralized set of ball players ever seen in Chicago. To be beaten at all was bad enough, but to be whipped by a score of 49 to

4 by a nine their Rockford rivals had beaten the day before, was galling in the extreme.

Next day the Chicago *Tribune* charged the Nationals with throwing the game to Rockford "for betting purposes." Mr. A. P. Gorman and President Jones, of the Nationals, visited the *Tribune* office and compelled a retraction of the charges.

Thus ended the great Western tour of the Washington Nationals, the first tour of an Eastern Base Ball club to the West.

I recall an incident in connection with this game which may be of interest. I was the pitcher of the Forest City Club in this victory over the famous Nationals, and, as a lad of seventeen, experienced a severe case of stage fright when I found myself in the pitcher's box, facing such renowned players as George Wright, Norton, Berthrong, Fox, and others of the visiting team. It was the first big game before a large audience in which I had ever participated. The great reputations of the Eastern players and the extraordinary one-sided scores by which they had defeated clubs in Columbus, Cincinnati, Louisville, Indianapolis and St. Louis, caused me to shudder at the contemplation of punishment my pitching was about to receive. A great lump arose in my throat, and my heart beat so like a trip-hammer that I imagined it could be heard by everyone on the grounds.

I knew, also, that every player on the Rockford nine had an idea that their kid pitcher would surely become rattled and go to pieces as soon as the strong batters of the Nationals had opportunity to fall upon his delivery.

COLONEL FRANK JONES

They had good grounds for that fear.   Every member of the team cautioned me to take my time and keep cool; but I was not so rattled but that I recognized the fact that everyone of them was so scared that none could speak above a whisper.   The fact is, we were all frightened nearly to death, with possibly the exception of Bob Addy, who kept up his nerve and courage by "joshing" the National players as they came to bat with his witticisms, which made him famous among ball players for many years.

In the first innings, the Rockfords made two runs and the Nationals three, which in those days was called good ball playing.   In the second innings, five runs by the Nationals and eight by the Rockfords gave the latter a lead by ten to eight.   In the third, the Nationals drew a blank and Rockford made five runs, thus putting Rockford to the good by a score of fifteen to eight for the Nationals. The fourth and fifth yielded three runs to the Nationals and one to the Rockfords.   In the sixth innings the Nationals made seven runs and the Rockfords eight, which made the score at the end of the sixth innings, Nationals, 18; Rockford, 24.

While the Forest Citys had by this time gotten pretty well settled and their stage-fright had disappeared, yet none of us even then had the remotest idea that we were destined to win the game over such a famous antagonist. The thought or suggestion of such a thing at that stage would probably have thrown us into another mental spasm.

At this psychological moment, Col. Frank Jones, President of the National Club, rushed up to George Wright, who was about to take his position at the bat, and said, in a louder voice possibly than he intended:

"Do you know, George, that this is the seventh innings and we are six runs behind? You must discard your heavy bat and take a lighter one; for to lose this game would be to make our whole trip a failure." Col. Jones' excited manner plainly indicated his anxiety.

This incident inspired the Rockfords with confidence and determination, and for the first time we began to realize that victory was not only possible, but probable, and the playing of our whole team from that time forward was brilliant. I have always given Col. Jones credit for Rockford's victory.

None but a ball player can understand how much of a factor little incidents of this kind are in a closely contested match.

In the game of the following day, when the Nationals administered their crushing defeat to the Chicago Excelsiors, George Fox, of the Nationals, made the longest hit I ever saw in any game on any grounds. It was one of those terrific, swift drives just over the heads of the outfielders that is so difficult to judge. The ball was hit in such a way and with so much force that it flew on a straight line to such an amazing distance that it became a subject of comment to all who witnessed it for years thereafter.

CHAPTER IX.

FOREST CITYS, OF ROCKFORD, ILL.

T. J. Foley, 3b.   A. Barker, l.f.   Fred Cone, 1b.   A. G. Spalding, p.   Scott Hastings, 2 b.
R. C. Barnes, s.s.   D. Sawyer, c.f.   R. E. Addy, c.   Geo. E. King, r.f.

CHAPTER IX.

1865–70

AMONG other agencies which at this time wrought so marvelously in the making of popularity for our national game, and in the production of great ball players, none was more potent than the city just emerging from the chrysalis stage of villagedom. It required the quality of young manhood which had been developed in field and furrow, in combination with that which had come from cash desk and counter, from forge and furnace, to present the American game in all its requirements of strength, agility and capacity to deal with emergencies. For, be it known, comparatively few of those whose names have found a place on the Base Ball Scroll of Fame came originally from the big cities of our land. It was towns like Rockford, Illinois, from whence came Ross Barnes; Marshalltown, Iowa, with Anson to its credit; Fort Wayne, Indiana, with Matthews as its contribution; Rochester, N. Y., with Sutton among its products; Corning, N. Y., with Jim White, and a long list of other cities of the third and fourth classes, whose splendid players attracted attention of the country in the early seventies, giving hope even to the small town, village and hamlet, that, enclosed in the overalls of some of their vigorous sons

115

might be an embryo pitcher or catcher, or shortstop or baseman, or batsman, whose future achievements on the diamond would make famous the burg that had nurtured an artist of such phenomenal prowess.

In this chapter it is my purpose to write, briefly, the story of the Forest City Base Ball Club, of Rockford, Illinois, presenting it as a type of clubs in other small cities, which in the early development of the game did so much to add prestige to the pastime, and whose influence for the upbuilding and maintaining of the dignity of the sport, as well as skill and science in play, is felt unto this hour. I write of the Forest City Club, not because it was in all respects greater than any other—although I shall be able to disclose for it a record of which no friend need be ashamed—but because I was a part of it; because with it I began my active Base Ball career, and because I know its story better perhaps than I do that of any other Base Ball organization.

In writing of the Forest City Club, of Rockford, I am compelled by the very nature of the case to introduce local facts, probably of greater interest to me than to any-one else in the world; but I would be guilty of gross injustice, of base ingratitude, were I not in this, my only work on the game, to acknowledge appreciation of the sound and unselfish advice of some, the kind words of cheer and encouragement from others, and were I to withhold an expression of the high regard I have ever entertained for my first comrades in the game, to whom I bade a regretful farewell when I elected to make a business of what had been theretofore simply a pleasant pastime.

Hence, as an apology for and in explanation of that which seems purely personal in the few following pages, I beg the reader to have in mind that much of sentiment still clings to the memories of those days of my early Base Ball career, and I could not refer to the times without also recalling the men with whom I was then so closely and so agreeably associated.

My association with the game of Base Ball began at Rockford, in 1865. As a school boy, I belonged to a club called the Pioneers. Since nobody in the team was over sixteen years of age, the title may have appeared to some as a misnomer; but it sounded all right. Most of us had heard our fathers spoken of as "pioneers," and we knew it could not mean anything bad. The Pioneers put up a pretty fair article of ball, for boys—if I do say it— and it was not long before we became ambitious. There were at Rockford at that time two amateur rival nines— the Forest Citys, just organized, and the Mercantiles. These played occasional matches, the Forest Citys having rather the better of the argument.

Ross Barnes, afterwards to win fame on the diamond as one of the greatest second basemen of his time, and in my opinion one of the best all around players the game has produced, was a member of the Pioneers, and he and I conceived the idea that we could "do" the Mercantiles, whose players were for the most part salesmen in the several stores of the city. A challenge was therefore sent; but the tradesmen at first regarded it as a joke; they were not in the game to play with children. However, after much insistence on our part, and some chaffing, perhaps, by members of the Forest Citys, the Mercantiles finally accepted. The game took place one fine day in the fall of 1865, with the Forest City players present and rooting good and hard for "the kids." The game resulted in a score of 26 to 2, in favor of the Pioneers.

Call it science, skill, luck, or whatever you please, I had at that time, when only fifteen years old, acquired the knack of pitching winning ball, and in the game with the Mercantiles it was first recognized. The Forest Citys immediately made overtures to Barnes and me and in 1866 we both became members of that club.

The Forest City Club, at the time Barnes and I were admitted to membership, consisted of Dr. S. J. Sawyer, pitcher; A. Barker, catcher; H. S. Warner, shortstop; G. E. King, first base; T. T. Webster, second base; S. Lakin, third base; W. Stearns, left field; M. L. Wheeler, center field; J. Brown, right field, and J. H. Manny, scorer. The executive officers of the club were: H. H. Waldo, President; I. S. Hyatt, Vice-President; George E. King, Secretary; George P. Ross, Treasurer. The Directors were E. C. Dunn, H. N. Starr and C. G. Manlove.

In the games following the reorganization of the Forest City Club, the line-up was changed and the following players appeared: Spalding, pitcher; King, catcher; Cone, first base; Addy, second base; Stearns, Lighthart or Stires, third base; Barnes, shortstop; Wheeler or Warner, right field; Cheney or Osborne, center field; Barker or Waxham, left field.

With a team thus placed, the Forest City Base Ball Club entered upon its public career in 1866. Previous to this time it had devoted its energies almost entirely to practice games and matches with local and nearby nines. Now, however, it began to receive and issue challenges, with the result that in nearly every instance victory favored the Rockford players.

It was thus early in my Base Ball career that I came face to face for the first time with the business end of the game. It came about in this way: The Forest Citys, although a comparatively young organization, as we have seen, had already attracted considerable attention by reason of many victories; and commercial travelers from Chicago and other cities, who were fond of Base Ball, would so schedule their trips as to be at Rockford when we played. I was employed at the time at a very small salary in a Rockford grocery, whose proprietor affected to be quite proud of my efficiency as a pitcher—but who regularly "docked" me when absent from the store. Therefore, when I was approached one day by a Chicago man with an offer of $40 per week to take a position as bill clerk with a wholesale grocery house of that city, with the understanding that my store duties would be nominal, and a chance given to play ball frequently, without affecting my salary to reduce it, I found no difficulty so far as my Rockford job was concerned in making up my mind as to what I ought to do.

But there were other considerations that might not be so easily disposed of. I was a mere youth both in age and in experience. I dared not trust my own judgment as to what was best. My home was and had long been at Rockford, with my widowed mother. Ought I, just as I was becoming a man, to leave her whose tender care and fond affection had been so lavishly bestowed upon me through the years of my boyhood life? Would she approve of my going to a large city, with its dangers in the busy whirl, and its greater dangers in the temptations that so thickly abound?

Moreover, what did this offer mean? That it meant separation from the Forest City Club was quite apparent; but that problem did not count; I could not afford to rest my business interests on a mere sentiment. But there was a moral side to the question which I might not ignore. Were my services worth the proffered salary? What did I know of the wholesale grocery business that I should be offered $40 per week as bill clerk? Was I not being paid for my skill as a ball player rather than as an expert in the grocery trade? And, if so, would I not be violating at least the spirit of that rule of the National Association of Base Ball Players that forbade the payment of salaries to players?

Again, from a mere business standpoint, would it be wise for me at my age to sever the relations that had been established at the home of my youth? All my acquaintances were at Rockford. Did not they constitute an asset with which I might not lightly part? All these, and many other questions, presented themselves to my mind, and I did what I would now advise any other boy to do in like circumstances. I carried the whole subject to my mother. I knew that she approved of my connection with the game of Base Ball as a pastime; but how she would view it as a vocation I was not sure at all.

When I broached the subject, I saw at once that it distressed her. She, far better than I, realized what it meant. The commercial aspect of the case, in making use of whatever skill I possessed as a ball player to gain a competence, made her shrink at first. She had looked upon the game as a means of health-giving exercise, and had rejoiced in it. She had followed the early victories of our club, and, like a loyal mother, had gloried in them. But, to make a business of ball playing! That was altogether different; it required consideration; perhaps advice.

Finally, the problem reduced itself—as have so many problems in other Rockford households in the last half century and more—to an appeal to Rockford's Grand Old Man, Hiram H. Waldo, to whom I here pay the homage of man's sincere tribute to man. I held him in honor in the days of my youth. I esteemed him in my early manhood, and now, in my maturer years, I count him as one of the noblest, purest, most unselfish men I have ever known.

Mr. Waldo was at that time President of the Forest City Club, and yet we laid the severing of my connection with that organization before him, assured that his advice would be fair, honest, unbiased; as, indeed, it proved. I remember well how we received the announcement of the offer made to me to go to Chicago; how we placed before him the situation in all its bearings; how I rather earnestly pleaded the opportunity it presented for my advancement in life. He heard the case quite patiently and then said:

"You know, my boy, that, as a citizen of Rockford, I don't want you to go; and perhaps, as President of the

Forest City Club, I ought to urge you to stay; but, as a friend to whom you have come for advice, I must say to you, accept the offer and go; but," he added, smiling, "you needn't tell that I advised it."

And so, in the fall of 1867, I went to Chicago, ostensibly to accept a clerkship in a wholesale grocery, but really to become a member of the Chicago Excelsior Base Ball Club. It may interest some to know that I never played but one game with the Excelsior team. Before the next springtime had rolled around the great wholesale house with which I had become connected failed—not entirely on account of the size of my salary, I trust—and a few days later saw me back at Rockford, again a member of the Forest City Club, where I was warmly welcomed, having received employment in the insurance office of A. N. Nicholds, Secretary of the club, and on the *Rockford Register*, at moderate salary, under the management of E. H. Griggs, who had meantime been elected Secretary of the National Association of Base Ball Players.

As to the question of my agreeing to accept a semi-professional position on the Excelsior team of Chicago at a time when professionalism of every kind was "tabu," I have this to say: Although at this date there was no strictly professional club in existence—the Cincinnati Red Stockings not being organized as such until 1869—the rule prohibiting salaries was nevertheless a dead letter. Most clubs of prominence, all over the country, had players who were either directly or indirectly receiving financial advantage from the game. Some held positions like that proffered me; others were in the pay of individual lovers of the game. I believed that I foresaw the day soon coming when professional Base Ball playing would be recognized as legitimate everywhere. I was not able to understand how it could be right to pay an actor, or a singer, or an instrumentalist for entertaining the public, and wrong to pay a ball player for doing exactly the same thing in his way. I did not like the roundabout schemes that were being worked in all large cities to secure good players, by giving them nominal employment in stores, warehouses, etc. It seemed to me to be educating young men in a school of false pretense. I felt that the only right thing to do was to come out openly and honor the playing of the game as a legitimate avocation, and this position I have ever since consistently maintained.

From the time Barnes and I became connected with the Forest City Club, that organization had an almost uninterrupted succession of victories. No team in the Northwest was able to win from the Rockford nine until the tournament in July, 1867, when the Chicago Excelsiors took two games by close scores—and these games were subsequently offset by a series, best two out of three, played the following season for the championship of the Northwest, in which the Forest Citys were victorious by scores of 20 to 18 and 36 to 27, respectively.

It is not the scope or purpose of this work to publish records. Those interested in statistics will find voluminous tables in the annual Base Ball Guides. But in the case of the Forest City Club, whose story is unique among amateur organizations, I feel that I owe it to that club to make public its remarkable achievements:

1866

Forest City,	123 to	8	Mystic, Belvidere, Illinois.
" "	37 to	23	Shaffer, Freeport, Illinois.
" "	13 to	14	Cream City, Milwaukee, Wisconsin.
" "	39 to	16	Clipper, Rochelle, Illinois.
" "	50 to	11	Sinissippi, Rockford, Illinois.
" "	24 to	10	Cream City, Milwaukee, Wisconsin.
" "	42 to	3	Badger, Beloit, Wisconsin.

1867

Forest City,	56 to	0	Phoenix, Belvidere, Illinois.
" "	59 to	4	Byron, Byron, Illinois.
" "	41 to	45	Excelsior, Chicago, Illinois.
" "	24 to	16	Phoenix, Belvidere, Illinois.
" "	25 to	28	Excelsior, Chicago, Illinois.
" "	29 to	23	National, Washington, D. C.
" "	35 to	57	Bloomington, Bloomington, Illinois.
" "	63 to	8	Star, Marengo, Illinois.

1868

Forest City,	43 to	25	Byron, Byron, Illinois.
" "	73 to	7	Harvard, Harvard, Illinois.
" "	20 to	18	Excelsior, Chicago, Illinois.
" "	13 to	94	Athletic, Philadelphia, Pennsylvania.
" "	29 to	31	Atlantic, Brooklyn, New York.
" "	36 to	27	Excelsior, Chicago, Illinois.
" "	28 to	9	Capitol City, Madison, Wisconsin.
" "	43 to	12	Capitol City, Madison, Wisconsin.
" "	88 to	6	Mutual, Janesville, Wisconsin.

1869

Forest City,	110 to	11	Harvard, Harvard, Illinois.
" "	37 to	9	Beloit College, Beloit, Wisconsin.
" "	103 to	6	Stillman Valley, Illinois.
" "	49 to	6	Beloit College, Beloit, Wisconsin.
" "	76 to	1	Clipper, Monmouth, Illinois.
" "	32 to	4	Amateur, Chicago, Illinois.
" "	25 to	4	Aetna, Chicago, Illinois.
" "	13 to	32	Cincinnati, Cincinnati, Ohio.
" "	31 to	10	Garden City, Chicago, Illinois.
" "	43 to	9	Garden City, Chicago, Illinois.
" "	14 to	15	Cincinnati, Cincinnati, Ohio.
" "	40 to	1	Buckeye, Cincinnati, Ohio.
" "	83 to	14	Independent, Mansfield, Ohio.
" "	32 to	10	Detroit, Detroit, Michigan.

Forest City,	32 to 53	Cincinnati, Cincinnati, Ohio.
" "	7 to 28	Cincinnati, Cincinnati, Ohio.
" "	47 to 2	Clipper, Monmouth, Illinois.
" "	52 to 7	Occidental, Quincy, Illinois.
" "	44 to 11	Union, St. Louis, Missouri.
" "	70 to 6	Empire, St. Louis, Missouri.
" "	66 to 3	Relic, Jacksonville, Illinois.
" "	101 to 13	Liberty, Springfield, Illinois.
" "	34 to 22	Picked Nine, Chicago, Illinois.
" "	41 to 10	Illinois, Morris, Illinois.

Early in the spring of 1870, the business men of Rockford, proud of their ball team, and recognizing how much it had done in the way of advertising that enterprising young city, raised a purse of $7,000 that the Forest City Club might make the first tour ever made by a Western amateur Base Ball club to the Eastern States. and match their playing ability with that of the strong nines of that section.

The following table shows the result of the tour as to games won and lost, with the scores of each:

Forest City,	65 to 3	Maple Leaf, Hamilton, Canada.
" "	44 to 13	Niagaras, Buffalo, New York.
" "	57 to 16	Eckfords, Syracuse, New York.
" "	17 to 2	Ontarios, Oswego, New York.
" "	21 to 3	Haymakers, Troy, New York.
" "	36 to 4	Mutuals, Springfield, Massachusetts.
" "	4 to 4	Unions, Morrisania, New York.
" "	13 to 21	Mutuals, New York, New York.
" "	17 to 16	Atlantic, Brooklyn, New York.
" "	10 to 16	Athletics, Philadelphia, Pennsylvania.
" "	1 to 0	Marylands, Baltimore, Maryland.
" "	21 to 11	Pastimes, Baltimore, Maryland.
" "	8 to 7	Olympics, Washington, D. C.
" "	10 to 4	Nationals, Washington, D. C.
" "	15 to 6	Jeffersons, Washington, D. C.
" "	24 to 18	Forest Citys, Cleveland, Ohio.
" "	14 to 28	White Stockings, Chicago, Illinois.

An analysis of the record shows that out of a total of 65 games played the Forest City Club won 51. In these games the Rockford Club made 2,592 runs to 959 for all the other clubs combined—nearly three to one!

In October of this year the Forest City team defeated the great Cincinnati Red Stockings by a score of 12 to 5.

Such, then, was the career of the Forest City Base Ball Club. When it is remembered that this organization was composed entirely of young men living in and about Rockford; that the club was strictly an amateur organization, no player receiving salary; it must be conceded that the record here published is unparalleled in the history of the game for a similar club.

Before closing this chapter, which I fully realize has dealt too much with things of which I was myself a part, I desire once more to express my appreciation of the membership of that club, one and all—not only as players; their records speak plainly enough on that point; but as gentlemen and friends whom I shall ever remember with feelings of fraternal regard.

CHAPTER X.

CINCINNATI RED STOCKINGS

Hurley, sub.   G. Wright, s.s.   Allison, c.   McVey, r.f.   Leonard, l.f.
Sweasy, 2b.   Waterman, 3b.   H. Wright, c.f.   Brainard, p.   Gould, 1b.

CHAPTER X.

1869-70

BEFORE the close of the decade of the 60's there were mutterings of discontent, disparagement, if not of actual disgust with existing conditions. It has already been noted that from the very beginning of Base Ball history betting had been openly, widely, almost generally indulged in at all contests of importance.

It is unnecessary, perhaps impossible, to catalogue all the evils that followed in the train of this pernicious practice. It is essential to the story, however, to mention the fact that one of the earliest legitimate effects of this illegitimate custom was to beget another practice even more prejudicial to the interests of Base Ball; for betting on the result of games naturally begot collusion between those who bet their money and some of those who played the game. Per consequence, it was soon discovered that unprincipled players, under pretense of accident or inability to make points at critical stages, were "throwing" games.

Nor was this all. The determination of the founders of Base Ball to maintain it as an amateur pastime had been only partially successful from the start. The perfectly natural desire of every club to strengthen its playing corps found its earliest expression in the drafting, by senior clubs, from the ranks of local junior teams the best players among them. This absolutely legitimate practice was soon followed by that of inducing the best players in clubs of small cities and villages to join those of larger cities, the ostensible advantage being set forth as the increased opportunities of getting on in life.

It was, of course, but a very short step from this custom to that of offering to exceptionally good players positions in commercial or industrial enterprises, with the understanding that salaries would be forthcoming. These were usually paid in part by promoters of the ball clubs, and partly by the firms in whose employ the players were enrolled. It was always understood in such cases that, while the player was ostensibly engaged by the house he served, he was really expected to participate in all match games played by the club to which he was to become attached.

It will readily be seen that such a state of things could not long continue. The public lost confidence in a game the results of whose contests depended upon the interests of the gambling fraternity, or the presence of veiled professional players. Upright ball players knew that games were occasionally sold by their unscrupulous companions. Having lost faith in their fellows, they began to lose hope in the future of the pastime itself, and, one by one, conscientious players were dropping out. The system, too, of securing players by underhanded subterfuge also had a demoralizing effect on the sport, so that after a while players and public became outspoken in their criticisms of

conditions existing everywhere, and violent in their denun-
ciations of the management of the National Association
of Base Ball Players, under whose regime these outrageous abuses obtained.

It should be stated in this connection that the evils
complained of were not authorized by either the letter or
the spirit of the National Association rules. On the contrary, all practices prejudicial to the game were not only
not encouraged, but were vigorously forbidden by the
language of the rules and violently denounced by delegates at each recurring convention of that body. But that
the National Association of Base Ball Players was unable
to deal with the problem of needed discipline confronting
it was quite apparent. It either lacked the will or the
courage or the ability to control the situation, and so, as
always and everywhere, abuses unchecked became intolerable. Having lost respect for the governing body, players
paid little heed to its mandates, interest in the sport sub-
sided, attendance at games fell off, while the small number
of clubs represented at annual conventions showed widespread demoralization.

In addition to the factors already named, that were
rapidly leading up to the dissolution of the National
Association of Base Ball Players, was the political propa-
ganda. Under the original by-laws of the Association—
which had never been amended as to this point—representation by proxy was provided for. This resulted in
all kinds of trouble. Men of mediocrity from remote districts and obscure organizations were able to collect
proxies enough so that they could and did have themselves

HARRY WRIGHT

elected to places of influence and importance that they were not qualified to fill, and this in order that they might manipulate the game to selfish ends. Thus the legitimate purpose of the sport, which was to provide entertainment for the public and healthful exercise for its participants, was prostituted to ends of graft and greed. The question prompting these mischief-makers was not "How may we perpetuate the game of Base Ball in its integrity and perfection?" but, "How may we secure the largest personal advantage while in office?" I do not make this charge of officers of the Association as a rule, but that there were present in power at this time officials who wrought havoc with the game will not be disputed.

Mutterings, loud and deep, showing the dissatisfaction that was present in the minds of the press and public, were heard everywhere from those who had any interest whatever for the welfare of Base Ball in America. It was quite apparent to everybody that something must soon occur to change the existing order of things—and in this one case it was the "expected" that happened.

The leading Base Ball club of Cincinnati, seeing the inevitable, unwilling to be bound by rules which nobody respected or obeyed, holding in utter contempt an organization that had failed to uphold the dignity and integrity of a game of which it was the nominal executive head, threw down the gauntlet of defiance to the National Association of Base Ball Players—not by a flaming pronunciamento, but by manly declaration that henceforth it would be known as a professional organization.

It required a great deal of moral courage on the part

of Harry Wright and his confreres to take this step. There were at least three elements to be dealt with. First, that portion of the public—and it was at that time probably in the majority—who believed that Base Ball was simply an ordinary form of outdoor sport, a pastime, like cricket in England, to be played in times of leisure, and by gentlemen, for exercise, and only incidentally for the entertainment of the public, had to be reckoned with. This class felt that the game would suffer by professionalism; that it meant the introduction into the ranks of any man who could play the game skillfully, without regard to his "race, color or previous condition of servitude." It meant, they thought, the introduction of rowdies, drunkards and dead-beats. Somehow, it was felt that the game would lose in character if it departed from its original program, and they honestly deplored the proposed innovation.

Another class to be dealt with was the gambling element, and this opposition was not to be lightly considered. They had so long been a controlling influence, that anything threatening their ascendancy was sure to meet with stubborn resistance. Of course, their chief interest in Base Ball was what they could make out of it in the line of their nefarious profession. They feared that if the executive control of the game passed into the hands of men who also had cash at stake, it was a sure thing that just in so far as the management made money they must lose. They knew, of course, that the clubs must depend upon gate receipts for their income; that gate receipts depended upon the restoration of public confidence, and that public confidence could only be won back by the eradication of the gambling evil. So the gamblers would fight, and fight hard.

A third element, well worthy of sober thought, was that represented by players in other clubs still affiliating with the National Association, and obeying the letter, if not the spirit, of its non-professional requirements. What this class would do only the future could determine, though the fact that many of them were even then in an underhanded way practicing semi-professionalism gave force to the belief that they would not long hold out.

Finally one club, actuated by the spirit that has characterized every pioneer movement in history, decided to blaze the way. Consequently, in 1869, under the management of Harry Wright, who had then been playing Base Ball for about ten years, the Cincinnati Red Stockings, formed in 1866 as an amateur team, now determined to organize as an out-and-out professional club, with a view of measuring skill with the heretofore invincible clubs of the East.

This club consisted of trained players, the best men procurable, and every one to receive a substantial salary. The players were Brainard, pitcher; Allison, catcher; Gould, first base; Sweasy, second base; Waterman, third base; George Wright, shortstop; Leonard, left field; Harry Wright, center field; McVey, right field.

A. B. Champion, a prominent lawyer of Cincinnati, was President of the Club, and to him very largely was due the success of the new professional movement.

The Eastern tour of the Red Stockings, in 1869, was

GEORGE WRIGHT

preceded by a series of uninterrupted victories over Western clubs. The trip Eastward saw its first contest with the Buffalo Niagaras, after which the Cincinnati Club passed through Western New York to Massachusetts and then to New York City, where they played their first important game with the Mutuals. The result of this contest was a score, unprecedented up to that time, of 4 to 2, the Red Stockings winning. Next day they met and defeated the celebrated Atlantic Club by 32 to 10. The Eckfords were next to go down to defeat, and by a score of 24 to 5. From New York the Red Stockings went to Philadelphia, en route disposing of the Irvington, N. J., team by 20 to 4. At Philadelphia they encountered the Olympics, winning, 22 to 11, and following this by a defeat of the great Athletics of that city by 27 to 18, and the Keystones by 45 to 30. Later the Westerners visited Baltimore and Washington, easily defeating the best teams of both cities, the Marylands by 47 to 7, the Washington Nationals by a score of 24 to 8, and the Olympics of the capital city by 16 to 5.

Thus ended the first Eastern tour of a Western Base Ball club. It was also the first tour of a professional ball club in any direction. Every game played was won by the Red Stockings, presenting an important object lesson in professionalism, for it demonstrated at once and for all time the superiority of an organization of ball players, chosen and trained and paid for the work they were engaged to do, over any and all organizations brought together as amateurs for the simple purpose of playing ball for exercise and entertainment.

Returning to Cincinnati, the Red Stockings were visited by the Olympics, of Washington, which nine they defeated in three straight games, the score of one being 71 to 15. They then played visiting nines from the West for over a month, being victorious in every contest.

Next, they received the Haymakers, of Troy, New York, which club they had previously defeated, but which, on this occasion, played them to their first tie game, 17 to 17. About this time they won a close game from the Forest City Club, of Rockford. The score was 14 to 13 in their favor, the Red Stockings making three runs and winning the game in the ninth inning.

Having met every club in the East without a reverse, and having conquered every team in the Middle West, the Red Stockings now conceived the idea of visiting the Pacific Coast, stopping at St. Louis en route. At San Francisco they defeated the Eagles, Pacific and Atlantic nines of that city, every score but one being marked by fifty runs to single figures. Returning, they defeated clubs at Omaha and Nebraska City, and completed their triumphant record on their own home grounds by victories over the Philadelphia Athletics and the Mutuals.

This sensational record, without a parallel then, has never been equalled. Aside from its spectacular effect, in calling attention to the great players of a great club and their wonderful achievements, it exerted a tremendous influence, afterwards to be felt in the game itself, for it portended the birth of a new era in which professional ball should become thoroughly established, though not without its serious vicissitudes.

The Red Stockings had now played every prominent club from Massachusetts to California without losing a game, and this wonderful succession of victories was continued not only through 1869, but also from April to June in 1870, without a defeat.

From a record kept by Harry Wright, the great captain and manager of the Red Stockings, the following facts concerning that club, its players and its record are gleaned: Out of 57 games played the Red Stockings won 56 and tied 1. In these games they scored a total of 2,395 runs to 574 for their adversaries. The nature of the batting done is shown in a total of 169 home runs, or an average of nearly three to a game. The number of miles traveled by rail and boat was 11,877, without a serious accident of any kind. Over 200,000 people witnessed the games. The individual score of George Wright, the famous shortstop, was the highest of any player on the team. He played in 52 of the 57 games. His batting average was .518. He made 339 runs, of which 59 were home runs; one of them the longest hit up to that time.

Such is the story of the first professional Base Ball club, as taken from the records. Aside from the achievements of the Red Stockings during their brief but meteoric career, it will not be easy to estimate the influence of their performances upon the future of the game. The club, as organized by Harry Wright, passed out of existence in the fall of 1870, but it had paved the way for the introduction of new means, new measures, new methods, soon inaugurated, and which are an integral part of the system to-day.

SOME OF THE RED STOCKINGS

D. Allison, c.
A. J. Leonard, l.f.
Cal. A. McVey, r.f.
C. J. Sweasy, 2 b.
C. H. Gould

As pertinent to the question of professionalism, I recall very distinctly a bit of controversy with Harry Wright when, in 1871, he came to Rockford to secure the services of Roscoe Barnes, Fred Cone, and myself for the Boston Club. The professional Red Stockings, of Cincinnati, the pioneer professional club, had disbanded. That organization, under Mr. Wright's management, had demonstrated that professionalism not only stood for a marked improvement in playing, but that the dreaded opposition on the part of the public did not materialize, since the simple announcement that the Red Stockings were to appear had been sufficient always to attract crowds.

But the experiment had not yet been tried in an Eastern city. Hence, when Wright came with his overtures to Barnes, Cone, and myself, it was to join a club ostensibly amateur but really professional; for all were to receive good salaries. I knew, of course, that the manager of the Bostons felt exactly as I did with regard to the subject; but I could see that he was reluctant to break over the custom in vogue in New England and oppose the honest prejudice existing in that section and all over the East against professional Base Ball.

However, I was inclined to be obstinate in my views of the matter. I had determined to enter Base Ball as a profession. I was neither ashamed of the game nor of my attachment to it. Mr. Wright was there offering us adequate cash inducements to play on the Boston team. We were willing to accept his offer. Why, then, go before the public under the false pretense of being amateurs? The

FRED WATERMAN, HARRY WRIGHT, ASA BRAINARD

assumption of non-professionalism would not deceive any-body. It was not possible that any could be found so simple as to believe that George and Harry Wright, Cal McVey and the rest were in the game merely for healthful or philanthropic reasons. Then why engage in duplicity?

We went over the whole subject, threshed it out in all its bearings, and finally agreed to come out openly and above-board as a professional organization. The result was even more gratifying than we had hoped. Opposition in the East faded rapidly away. Soon after the organization, in 1871, of the National Association of Professional Ball Players, professionalism was firmly rooted and established.

SOUVENIRS OF ATLANTIC VICTORIES

CHAPTER XI.

ATLANTICS, OF BROOKLYN

Mills Zettlein Pearce Start Smith Ferguson Crane Pratt Chapman

CHAPTER XI.

1870-71

I T IS the plan of this work, while telling in a general
way the story of our national game, to deal rather
with beginnings than with details. It has required
libraries of volumes to chronicle facts of which here only
the briefest outline can be given. Already consideration
has been given to the first ball, the first bat, the first
bases, the first diamond, the first grounds, the first club,
the first association, the first contest, the first gate money
receipts, the first row, the first tour, the first visit of an
Eastern club to the West, the first trip of a Western
club to the East and the first tour of a professional club
in any direction. But it is manifestly impracticable to
trace in these pages the history of all the good clubs, of
all the skillful players, their many tours, their countless
victories and their occasional reverses. Hence, those who
might expect the minor details of the successful trips of
the Athletics, of Philadelphia, and the Atlantics, of
Brooklyn, to have a place just here, where they would
chronologically belong, are reminded that these tours were
simply less sensational repetitions of that of the pioneer
Excelsiors and Nationals, whose triumphant journeys
have been heretofore quite fully given.

Something is due, however, to Base Ball organizations which at this period demonstrated the possession of surprising and surpassing excellence, and that obligation is met by giving the story of the games in which the great Red Stockings, of Cincinnati, were first made to acknowledge defeat—a calamity that seemed not only to break the record of that club but the hearts of its players as well—for the Red Stockings, under that title, did not outlive another year.

It was on the 14th of June, 1870, that the World's Champions of 1869, the theretofore unconquered Red Stockings, of Cincinnati, had their victorious career checked by the Atlantics, of Brooklyn. The game was played at the City of Churches, on Long Island, and attracted an immense concourse of spectators for the time. The line-up of the Atlantics was as follows: Ferguson, catcher; Zettlein, pitcher; Start, first base; Pike, second base; Smith, third base; Pearce, shortstop; Chapman, right field; Hall, center field; McDonald, left field. The gate receipts, at 50 cents as the admission fee, disclosed an attendance of 9,000 lovers of the game. No grandstand, with upholstered cushions, contributed to the comfort of the onlookers, but the entire crowd stood throughout the long and exciting contest.

The Red Stockings had their regular championship team, composed of the following professional players: Allison, catcher; Brainard, pitcher; Gould, first base; Sweasy, second base; Waterman, third base; George Wright, shortstop; McVey, right field; Harry Wright, center field, and Leonard, left field. At the end of the first innings the score stood 3 to 0 in favor of the Red Stockings, who were playing with their usual confidence and in splendid form. In the next three innings, however, the Atlantics got in four runs and shut out the visitors, thereby securing a lead of one run. Friends of the Atlantics began to enthuse over the situation; but the Cincinnati players, with the sublime courage that ever characterized their game, rallied, and in the next two innings gained two runs to one for the Atlantics, tieing the score, which remained unchanged in the ninth.

At the end of the ninth innings the Atlantics gathered up their bats, and the crowd, assuming that the game had ended with a draw, were preparing to leave the grounds, when Harry Wright, captain and manager of the Reds, with the bulldog tenacity for which his race— the English—is famed the world over, protested to the umpire that the game was not ended. He knew that the rules required a tie game, under such circumstances, to be continued. A sharp controversy ensued, in which the captain of the Atlantics, quite satisfied to having played the world-beaters to a tie, contended that the game was over. Finally the umpire and captains of both teams agreed to refer the question to Mr. Henry Chadwick, Chairman of the Committee on Rules of the National Association of Base Ball Players, who was in attendance at the game, and to abide by his decision. Mr. Chadwick without hesitation declared that Mr. Wright's contention was in accordance with the rules and that the game must at once be resumed.

The tenth innings began under renewed excitement,

PETER O'BRIEN

though it was the general opinion that the Red Stockings would win. In this innings the Atlantics had two men on bases—McDonald on second and Pearce at first—when Smith, the next man up, hit a pop-fly to George Wright at short. Then was introduced the first recorded instance of a play that later was not infrequently witnessed. Holding up his hands as if to catch the easy ball, Wright signalled to Waterman to get to his base. McDonald and Pearce, certain that the batsman would be out on such an easy fly—and not reckoning upon the fielder's choice—stood quietly at their bases. Then Wright purposely trapped the ball by scooping it up on the first bound and threw it to Waterman at third, who passed it to Sweasy at second, and McDonald and Pearce being forced by Smith's hit, made fair by Wright's strategic play, were both declared out before they realized what had happened to them. Of course, Smith made first in safety, but the double play had cost the Atlantics two men, as Wright intended, and the side was out, with ten innings played and the score tied.

In the eleventh innings, the Red Stockings went to bat and added two to their score. At this point the Brooklyn crowd of spectators, losing all hope of victory for the home team, started to leave the grounds—when the unexpected happened.

The score now showed the Cincinnati team two runs to the good, with two to tie and three to win as the demand from the Atlantics in their half of the eleventh. Brainard, of the Reds, who up to that innings had been pitching a great game, suddenly had a streak of ill luck, or something. At any rate, he let down in the quality of his work. The Atlantics, taking advantage of the fact and playing the game for all there was in it, began to bat fiercely. Smith opened with a clean base hit, and on a wild pitch made third. Start then hit a long fly to the outfield which McVey could not get because of the intervening crowd. Smith tallied and Start reached third. Ferguson made a clean hit, on which Start scored and the game was a tie, with Ferguson on first and nobody out.

The excitement at this situation was intense. For a while, so wild was the crowd over this unexpected turn in the fortunes of the game, that it was impossible to proceed. The turmoil and confusion were so great that nothing could be done. Things certainly did look good to Brooklyn, and they seemed brighter still when, immediately after resuming the game, Zettlein hit a swift grounder to Gould, which the first baseman failed to get, thus advancing Ferguson to second. Gould, chagrined at his mishap in failing to get Zettlein's ball, attempted to stop Ferguson, threw wild, and Ferguson, seeing that the ball was not well handled, took a forlorn chance and succeeded in beating it home, scoring the winning run in this historic eleven-inning game, which ended 8 to 7, breaking the Red Stockings' theretofore uninterrupted series of victories, lasting for over an entire year.

After this signal check to their long and triumphant career, the Red Stockings did not encounter another defeat until July 7th, on which date they played their return game with the Philadelphia Athletics, at Cincinnati. On June 22d the Cincinnati team had beaten the

Athletics at Philadelphia in a very close game, 27 to 25. But on this occasion the Athletics had their revenge, beating the Red Stockings on their own grounds by a score of 11 to 7. In this year, in addition to their victory over the Red Stockings, in the game here referred to, the Athletics played seventy-seven games, winning sixty-six and tieing one. The official record, in its table of runs, credits the Athletics with a grand total of 2,222 to 710 for their opponents.

The death of the National Association of Base Ball Players, which occurred in 1871, was expected, natural and painless. Everybody who was interested in the welfare of our national game had been looking forward to this consummation, not only with resignation, but with some degree of impatience. The organization had outlived its usefulness; it had fallen into evil ways; it had been in very bad company; and so, when the hour of its dissolution came, no sorrowing friends were there to speak a tearful farewell. If the National Association of Base Ball Players, following its demise, had any obsequies, they do not appear of record. The "dear departed" seems to have gone to its long rest unmourned, unhonored and unsung.

The following, from the pen of the late Henry Chadwick, at that time editor of *Beadle's Base Ball Player*, the official organ of the game—from which publication this excerpt is made—will be of interest as telling the story of the last hours of the Association:

"The National Association of Base Ball Players, which was organized in 1857, existed until 1867 on the basis of individual club representation. In the latter year, however, the original constitution

ATLANTICS, OF BROOKLYN

Fred. Crane, 2 b.   R. J. Pearce, s.s.
J. Galvin, c.f.   J. C. Chapman, l.f.   J. Start, 1b.   S. Smith, r.f.
F. Norton. c.   C. J. Smith, 3b.   Peter O'Brien   T. J. Pratt. p.

was practically ignored, its laws set aside and a reorganization effected on the basis of a representation by delegates from State Base Ball associations, a system perfect in its theory, and one which would be thoroughly successful if carried out under a well written constitution. Each annual convention since 1867, however, has seen a diminished interest in the Association and its meetings at the hands of the amateur class of the fraternity; the crude and incomplete constitution under which the reorganized association has governed the fraternity having allowed the meetings to be controlled almost entirely by an unscrupulous clique of men hailing from the professional clubs, assisted by tools selected from some of the amateur organizations. Under such circumstances, it is not surprising that the close of the season of 1870, was marked by a so-called 'National Convention' which, in the character of its general proceedings and in the election of its chief official, afforded a practical illustration of the fact that the National Association, under its existing organization, had ceased both to elicit and merit any further respect or consideration at the hands of the reputable class of the fraternity.

"In the first place, the several State associations found it difficult to obtain a representative quorum at their preliminary conventions. New York, which by some peculiar tactics—well known in certain political circles—entered the convention with a representation based on the existence of eighty-five clubs, could scarcely raise a quorum of delegates at the State convention, not over a dozen clubs sending delegates; not over forty clubs existing in the State, nor has there been for two years past. The clique in question obtained the controlling power in the convention by presenting nine delegates, the majority of whom were merely their serviceable tools. Massachusettss could not raise even ten clubs, and had to come under the claim of fractional club representation. New Jersey had but eleven clubs represented at the State convention; Indiana but three; the District of Columbia but five; Connecticut but ten, and Missouri the same. Illinois claimed twenty odd, while other States, having State associations, ignored the Association altogether.

" From the initiatory proceedings to the very close of the convention, ample evidence was shown that the majority vote of the delegates had been manipulated in the interest of one man. Some few there were of the delegates present, hailing from amateur clubs, who manfully battled against the ruling clique for the interests of the amateur class of the fraternity, but they finally had to succumb, and all of these retired in disgust from the farce in which they had been involuntary participants. It was well for the general interests of the fraternity, however, that matters should have taken the course they did, or otherwise we should have had to suffer the infliction of another like convention. One result of the proceedings of this convention was to occasion a movement to be started in favor of the organization of a

National Amateur Association, in which no such characters as controlled the convention in question can ever obtain influence or position.

"Before this convention adjourned, it rescinded the penalty attached to Wansley since 1865, and that player, who instigated the plot to sell the game between the Eckford and Mutual Clubs in 1865, is now a player 'in good standing' in the professional fraternity. Unluckily, the professional delegates afterwards not only violated their written constitution, but stultified themselves, by adopting a resolution of expulsion against Craver, of the Haymakers. In the one case, however, the Mutual and Chicago delegates favored Wansley's admission, and in the other they were bitterly down on Craver. It was pointed out that no such action as that expelling Craver could constitutionally be taken by the convention, as all matters of that kind must be adjudicated by the judiciary committee. But the explanation had no weight and the constitutional law was ignored. So ended the last convention of the National Association of Base Ball Players."

In December, 1871, a meeting was called for the formation of an Amateur Association, and subsequently, in March, 1872, an adjourned meeting was held for the same purpose at New York. At this meeting seventeen clubs were represented, seven of which were from leading colleges. The election of officers resulted in the choice of F. B. Wood, of the Champion Club, of Jersey City, as President, who thus became the chief executive of the first National Association of Amateur Base Ball Players. This new amateur association continued for one year and then ceased to exist. Since that time the game has been under the direction and control of the professional element.

CHAPTER XII.

HAYMAKERS, TROY, N. Y.

"Mart" King, c.f. Michael McAtee, s.s. Thomas Abrams, p. William Craver, c. Steve King, l.f.
James Ward, 2 b. Peter McCune, r.f. S. Leavenworth, 1 b. Cal. Penfield, 3 b.

CHAPTER XII.

FIRST PROFESSIONAL BASE BALL ASSOCIATION——CONDITIONS LEADING UP TO ITS ORGANIZATION——PROFESSIONALISM THOROUGHLY ESTABLISHED——LIST OF THE FIRST PROFESSIONAL PLAYERS. 1870–75

THE decade which opened with the year 1871 saw several very important events in the history of Base Ball, the first being the formal organization into a national association of the professional ball players. Heretofore professionals not only had been without an organized status, but until recently they had been under the ban of disapproval by the only recognized national association. It may be well at this point, in order to avoid confusion, to note the difference between the titles of the new and the old bodies. The earlier and first organization of Base Ball clubs was known as "The National Association of Base Ball *Players*." The one now organized was "The National Association of *Professional* Base Ball Players," with the accent on the word "professional."

The meteoric career of the Cincinnati Red Stockings had wrought a very great change in public sentiment, and in the minds of players as well, regarding professionalism. Genuine lovers of the sport, who admired the game for its real worth as an entertaining pastime and invigorating form of exercise, saw in the triumphs of the Reds the dawn of a new era in Base Ball; for they were forced, *nolens volens*, to recognize that professionalism had come

159

to stay; that by it the game would be presented in its highest state of perfection; that amateurs, devoting the greater portion of their time to other pursuits, could not hope to compete with those whose business it was to play the game—and play it as a business. Hence public opposition to professional Base Ball melted quickly away. The best players needed no other incentive to make them accept the situation, even gleefully, than was found in their love for the sport, coupled with the prospect of gaining a livelihood in a manner so perfectly in accord with their tastes and inclinations.

Even before 1870, several full professional and semi-professional clubs were in existence. Aside from the Red Stockings, of Cincinnati, almost every large city had clubs whose players were directly or indirectly in receipt of forbidden emoluments from the game. In 1871 the following clubs were known as professional, and were playing in that class: Athletics, of Philadelphia; Atlantics, of Brooklyn; Bostons, of Boston; White Stockings, of Chicago; Forest Citys, of Cleveland; Forest Citys, of Rockford; Haymakers, of Troy; Kekiongas, of Fort Wayne; Marylands, of Baltimore; Mutuals, of New York; Nationals, of Washington; Olympics, of Washington; and Unions, of Morrisania.

However, at the meeting at which the National Association of Professional Base Ball Players was formed at New York, March 4th, 1871, only the following cities were represented: Boston, Brooklyn, New York, Philadelphia and Troy, in the East; Chicago, Cleveland, Fort Wayne and Rockford, in the West. At this, the first meeting of the new Association, Mr. J. W. Kerns, of Troy, President of the Haymakers, was elected President of the National Association of Professional Base Ball Players.

Of the ten professional clubs entering the National Championship contest of 1871 only eight finished the season. The champion Red Stockings, of Cincinnati, had disbanded. The Kekiongas, of Fort Wayne, played no official game after July. The Eckfords, of Brooklyn, which did not enter the race until August, lost representation in the pennant contest on account of tardiness. The race closed with the clubs in the following order: Athletics, of Philadelphia; Bostons, of Boston; White Stockings, of Chicago; Haymakers, of Troy; Mutuals, of New York; Forest Citys, of Cleveland; Nationals, of Washington, and Forest Citys, of Rockford.

As showing the players who were prominent in the game at that time, and who were the first recognized professional players of Base Ball, the following list of contestants should be of interest:

Athletics, of Philadelphia—Malone, catcher; McBride, pitcher; Fisler, first base; Reach, second base; Meyerle, third base; Radcliffe, shortstop; Cuthbert, left field; Sensenderfer, center field; Heubell, right field.

Bostons, of Boston—McVey, catcher; Spalding, pitcher; Gould, first base; Barnes, second base; Shaffer, third base; G. Wright, shortstop; Cone, left field; H. Wright, center field; Birdsall, right field; Jackson, substitute.

Eckfords, of Brooklyn—Hicks, catcher; Martin, pitcher; Allison, first base; Swandell, second base; Nelson, third base; Holdsworth, shortstop; Gedney, left field; Shelly, center field; Chapman, right field; Allison, substitute.

Forest Citys, of Cleveland—White, catcher; Pratt, pitcher; Carleton, first base; Kimball, second base; Sutton, third base; Bass, shortstop; Faber, left field; Allison, center field; White, right field.

Forest Citys, of Rockford—Hastings, catcher; Fisher, pitcher; Mack, first base; Addy, second base; Anson, third base; Fulmer, shortstop; Ham, left field; Bird, center field; Stires, right field.

Haymakers, of Troy—McGeary, catcher; McMullin, pitcher; Flynn, first base; Craver, second base; Bellan, third base; Flowers, shortstop; King, left field; Yorke, center field; Pike, right field.

Mutuals, of New York—C. Mills, catcher; Wolters, pitcher; Start, first base; Ferguson, second base; Smith, third base; Pearce, shortstop; Hatfield, left field; Eggler, center field; Patterson, right field.

Olympics, of Washington—Allison, catcher; Brainard, pitcher; Mills, first base; Sweasy, second base; Waterman, third base; Force, shortstop; Leonard, left field; Hall, center field; Berthrong, right field.

At the First Annual Convention of the National Association of Professional Ball Players, held at Cleveland, in March, 1872, Robert Ferguson, of the Brooklyn Atlantics, was elected President, and it was declared as the policy of the association not to permit any outsider—that is, anyone not a professional Base Ball player—to hold office.

Eleven clubs, from Boston, Brooklyn, Baltimore, Chi-

cago, Cleveland, Mansfield (Conn.), New York, Philadelphia, Troy and Washington, entered for the National
Championship series of 1872. Two clubs entered from
Washington — the Nationals and Olympics; but the
Nationals withdrew before the close of the season and had
no standing in the race, which closed with clubs in the following order: Bostons, Athletics, Marylands, Mutuals,
Haymakers, Forest Citys, of Cleveland; Atlantics, Olympics, Mansfields and Eckfords.

In 1873 Mr. Robert Ferguson was elected to succeed
himself as President of the National Association of Professional Ball Players.

As indicating the crudity of the game as played even
so late as that year (1873), it may be remarked that it
was thought necessary to adopt a rule forbidding the
catching of a fly ball in hat or cap, and giving the base
runner his base as penalty for any ball so caught.

It was further provided by this rule, that a ball so
caught became a dead ball, and could not be put in play
until returned to the pitcher, in his position. I recall an
amusing incident growing out of this "cap catch" rule.
In those early days of Base Ball, when the game was in
its formulative period, it was quite customary for bright
players to study out new schemes of play that would show
up defects in the playing rules, and, by applying these
technicalities in a regular match, attract the attention of
rule-makers and effect the desired change.

The players of our team—the Bostons—were sitting
in the hotel one evening, at Cleveland, when someone, commenting on the rule, asked what would happen in case the

MUTUALS, NEW YORK, N. Y.

Nelson, 3 b.   Martin, p. and r.f   Swandell, 2 b.   Eggler, c.f.

E Mills, 1 b.   Hatfield, s.s.   C. Mills, c.   Walters, p. and r.f.   Patterson, l.f.

bases were full and a ball should be caught in a cap by
one of the players fielding his position. The official
umpire of the pending series of games, Ellis by name, was
present, and the case was put up to him for a decision.
He was asked what he would rule in such an emergency.
He replied, "I don't know; but I hope I may never be
called upon to decide that point in a close game."

A few weeks later we were playing the Athletics at
Philadelphia. We always had a hard fight in the "City
of Brotherly Love," and the contest this day was particularly close and strenuous, with the local crowd very bitter
against the "Bean Eaters" because of the intense rivalry
between these two leading clubs.

It happened that the Athletics got three men on bases
in the last innings, when the opportunity to test the "cap
catch" rule presented itself to my mind. Prompted by a
spirit of mischief, no doubt, I suggested to George Wright,
who was near me, playing at short, that this would be a
good time to try out the "cap catch" rule if an opportunity presented. I had a slow ball at that time, the
delivery of which was frequently followed by a pop-fly,
and this I pitched to the batsman, with the result that,
sure enough, he sent a nice, easy one over to short field.
Wright, reaching for his cap, deftly captured the ball
therein. He then quickly passed it to me, standing in
the pitcher's box. Under the rule, the ball was now in
play. I threw it home, from whence it was passed to third,
second and first, and judgment demanded of the umpire
on the play.

As a coincidence, it happened that the umpire on duty

that day was Ellis, the same with whom the subject had been discussed one night at Cleveland. The effect of the play on the crowd was simply paralyzing. None present had ever seen anything like it, and nobody knew what was up. The umpire, passing me, hissed: "That was mean of you, Spalding." The spectators were wild with rage. Shouts of "dirty ball," "Yankee trick," etc., etc., came from all quarters. Interest was at once centered on poor Ellis, the umpire. It was clear that if he declared the base runners out he would be mobbed. If he decided otherwise, he would do so in direct violation of the strict letter of the rule. Meanwhile the crowd became more and more riotous, now threatening our team, and now the umpire. Through it all I kept a stiff upper lip, demanding "judgment." "It's up to you, Mr. Umpire," I shouted. "What's your decision?"

"I decide," said he after a short pause, during which he looked into the faces of the angry mob, "that nobody's out and that the batsman must resume his place at bat as though nothing had happened."

I do not recall which team won that game, but I do recall the fact that at the close of the contest four burly policemen came on the field to escort me from the grounds.

"What's the matter now? Am I under arrest?"

"Naw, you ain't under arrest; but the management thought we'd better be on hand to protect you."

After the game was over and we had returned to our hotel, I was plied with all kinds of questions about that trick: "What about the umpire?" "Was his decision right?" and I made this reply:

"Technically, if for no other reason, he was wrong; but as a matter of policy he was right; for if he had decided otherwise than as he did there would have been a riot, and somebody would have got a sore head."

Upon mature reflection, I am convinced that the decision of Umpire Ellis in this instance was right from every standpoint; for, as umpire, it was his duty to see that the spirit as well as the letter of the law was observed, and this was a clear case where the letter of the rule had been followed but the spirit violated. Umpire Ellis' decision in this case was absolutely correct under the circumstances, for there are times in Base Ball games when an umpire is justified in going outside the rules to preserve fair play and make secure the dignity of the sport.

This incident is narrated, not so much on account of the interest attaching to it, as to indicate how the evolution of the game of Base Ball, from its crude form in the earlier days to its present degree of perfection, has been largely wrought through observation and experience of incongruous rules by players themselves.

The season of 1873 saw nine clubs entered for the championship. Only eight, however, were accorded a place at the close. Boston again won the first honor, with other clubs following in this order: Philadelphias, Marylands, Athletics, Mutuals, Atlantics, Washingtons, and Resolutes, of New Jersey. In this year Adrian C. Anson, who had heretofore played with the Forest Citys, of Rockford, and Tim Murnane appeared in the Athletic nine.

In 1874 a new rule for the playing of Base Ball was

ATHLETICS, OF PHILADELPHIA—1874

Hall   Fisler   Anson   Bechtel   McBride   Force   Craver   Sutton   Clapp
       Eggler

adopted. It provided for ten men and a ten innings game. The argument that led to the adoption of this rule was that, as played, the game had a lopsided field; that between first and second bases was a hole that needed protection by a second shortstop. The experiment was tried, but was soon abandoned and the rule rescinded, as the innovation had added nothing to the interest or perfection of the game.

In this year, 1874, eight clubs again entered the championship contest, only one (the Chicago Club) being from the West. Eastern cities represented were Boston, Baltimore, Brooklyn, Hartford, New York and Philadelphia. The City of Brotherly Love had two clubs. Out of 232 games scheduled 96 were not played at all, clubs ignoring them, consulting only their own desires or convenience. The Bostons again led in the race, the standing at the close being as follows: Bostons, Mutuals, Athletics, Philadelphias, Chicagos, Atlantics, Hartfords and Marylands.

Thirteen clubs entered the lists in 1875 for the Association championship pennant. But the number thirteen proved to be unlucky, for the season's play was characterized by so many flagrant abuses that it sounded the death knell of the National Association of Professional Base Ball Players and opened up another important era in the game.

The pennant for the season of 1875 was again won by Boston, and for the fourth time in succession. Other clubs followed in this order: Athletics, Hartfords, St. Louis, Philadelphias, Chicagos Mutuals, St. Louis Reds,

A HOT PROPOSITION IN THE EARLY DAYS

Washingtons, New Havens, Centennials, Westerns and Atlantics.

It was during this season's play that a remarkable game occurred between the Chicago White Stockings and the Hartford Dark Blues. Billy McLean, the quondam prize fighter, of Philadelphia, acted as umpire. Ten innings had been played without a run being scored on either side, when the Chicagos got in one in their half of the eleventh innings, winning by 1 to 0.

In evidence of the tremendous strides that had been taken in the playing of the game in the few years since contests were characterized by two figures on each side, and occasionally by three figures for the winners, the following record of games won by the Bostons in the contest of 1875 will be in point: Boston vs. St. Louis, 2 to 1; Hartfords, 3 to 1; Mutuals, 4 to 1; Hartfords, 3 to 2; Hartfords, 4 to 0; Hartfords, 4 to 1; Philadelphias, 4 to 3; Centennials, 5 to 0; St. Louis, 5 to 0. On the other hand, Boston was defeated by Chicago in this season's contest 1 to 0; and by the same club a second time by 2 to 0, and by St. Louis by a score of 5 to 3. Here was a demonstration of what professional Base Ball had accomplished in the improvement of the game.

In 1876 eight clubs, representing Chicago, Hartford, St. Louis, Boston, Louisville, New York, Philadelphia and Cincinnati, contested for the championship, and closed the season in the order above printed.

Next year, 1877, only six clubs comprised the circuit, and of these one (Cincinnati) forfeited its membership by non-payments. Boston again took its place as winner, the teams closing the season as appears below: Boston, Louisville, Chicago, Hartford, St. Louis.

In the following year, 1878, the Louisville, New York and Hartford clubs withdrew, but as Cincinnati had made good its shortage and been reinstated, and as Providence, Indianapolis and Milwaukee had been admitted, the circuit was again composed of six clubs, the championship season closing with the clubs in the following order: Boston, Cincinnati, Providence, Chicago, Indianapolis, Milwaukee.

In 1879, Buffalo, Cleveland, Syracuse and Troy added clubs to the contest, but, as Indianapolis and Milwaukee had withdrawn, eight clubs were left to close the season as follows: Providence, Boston, Chicago, Buffalo, Cincinnati, Syracuse, Cleveland and Troy.

Thus ends the championship story of the decade of the seventies, a story which chronologically overlaps the period that saw the death of the National Association of Professional Base Ball Players, and the birth of the National League of Base Ball Clubs, which must form the subject for another chapter.

CHAPTER XIII.

BOSTON CHAMPIONS

Cal. McVey   A. Leonard   A. G. Spalding   H. Wright   J. White   Ross Barnes
J. O'Rourke   G. Wright   Harry Schaefer   G. Hall   Dave Birdsall

CHAPTER XIII.

THE decade of the seventies recorded an event of considerable import to Base Ball, which chronologically belongs here. During the life of the National Association of Professional Base Ball Players, and before, the leading cricketers of England had been making frequent pilgrimages to the United States, with a view of exploiting Great Britain's national game, and also to win additional cricket laurels from Americans, who had become somewhat interested in the sport. Finally, in 1874, promoters of Base Ball in this country conceived the idea of returning the compliment by sending exponents of the American game to England, that the new sport might be presented in the Old Country, and perhaps gain a footing there.

While playing with the Boston team, in 1874, I became possessed with an intense yearning to cross the Atlantic. I wanted to go to England, but I hadn't the price. How to " raise the wind," therefore, was the problem I had to face. It occurred to me that since Base Ball had caught on so greatly in popular favor at home it might be worked for a special trip for me, to be followed by a second one, in which a couple of teams could be

175

taken over to introduce the American game to European soil. I was sanguine enough to believe that, once our English cousins saw our game, it would forthwith be adopted there, as here. I didn't know our English cousins then as well as I have come to know them since.

The preliminaries were not difficult of arrangement. I had already entered into a sort of conspiracy, in collusion with Father Chadwick and other writers for the sporting press, and very soon the scheme was so urgently fostered and so successfully promoted that "the magnates" were quite convinced, and I found myself en route to England, as the *avant courier* of such an undertaking.

I had been provided with so many excellent letters of introduction, that upon my arrival in Britain I was able to secure an early audience at the celebrated Marylebone Cricket Club, with a membership composed very largely of members of the nobility. Upon a date appointed, I was received with utmost courtesy, and was asked to state, in open meeting, the purpose of my mission.

It should be remembered that I was at that time a mere stripling, with very little experience in business or observation of society. It goes without saying that I had not been hobnobbing with "Dooks" on this side the Atlantic, and when I found myself suddenly in the presence of so much nobility it nearly took away my breath. However, I did the best I could. I explained to them that America had just developed a new form of outdoor sport, and that, because all the world knew that the home of true sportsmanship in all its phases was England, we turned naturally to their country to exploit our game. They had been for years sending their splendid cricketers to America, and now we would like to bring over a couple of Base Ball teams, and give a few exhibitions. Of course I knew that there would be no use to come without the favor and patronage of the great Marylebone Cricket Club, but even that honor, in the interests of sport, I hoped might be forthcoming. I talked at some length and with great earnestness, because I began to feel the responsibility of my position. It was no longer a question of my personal picnic; but a sort of international problem, with the sportsmen of Great Britain possibly inviting sportsmen of America to visit them and exhibit to the old nation the new nation's adopted game. I think, in my ardor to win out, I made mention of the fact that we had some cricketers among our players, and might be able to do something in the national games of both countries.

At last I finished. I knew my face was red with the oratorical effort, and I could feel the perspiration trickling down my spinal column. Then, just as I supposed all was over except the fireworks, I saw approaching me an attenuated old fellow, of about eighty, bearing in his hand an ear trumpet as big as a megaphone. I could tell by the deference paid to the old gentleman that he was "classy," and I awaited his approach with some trepidation. He came, took a seat beside me and asked:

"Young man, will you kindly repeat to me what you have been saying to the others?"

Please remember that the Marylebone Cricket Club

ADRIAN C. ANSON

is composed of gentlemen. They didn't shout or scream
with laughter at my plight, as a company of my fellow
countrymen would have done, and as I felt perfectly
assured that they would do, but even they were unable to
entirely control their risibilities, for, as I began the trying
task of retelling my story to His Lordship, the Deaf, I
could detect here and there a smile struggling with the
facial muscles of my well-bred hosts.

Next day I was officially notified that the Marylebone
Cricket Club would be very pleased to welcome the American Base Ball clubs, would arrange grounds for their
exhibitions, and would be delighted to schedule games of
Cricket to be played between American and British
Cricketers. I saw that I had been too previous perhaps
in suggesting the cricket contests, and when I began to
"work" the newspapers, in my capacity as press agent,
I found that the cricket end was altogether most attractive from their viewpoint.

Mr. Charles W. Allcock, the recognized cricket
authority of England, upon whom I most depended for
help along publicity lines, was especially enthusiastic
about the cricket. The fact is, he didn't know an earthly
thing about Base Ball, and he knew that he would be out
of ammunition in a short time so far as our game was
concerned. Therefore, when we arrived, late in the season, with eighteen American ball players, we found the
British public thoroughly advised of the forthcoming
cricket matches and only slightly informed about the
exhibition ball games.

Now, it happened that, aside from Harry and George

Wright and Dick McBride, and possibly two or three others, there wasn't a man in the whole American bunch who had ever played a game of cricket in his life, and most of them had never seen one. Meanwhile, the London sporting papers were promising a series of fine cricket matches—and we were certainly up against it. However, as we had eighteen men—and I urged that no one wanted to be left out of the cricket games—it was agreed that we should, in all cricket matches, play at the odds of eighteen to eleven in our favor, which, considering the fielding ability of the Americans, was greatly to our advantage.

I recall very distinctly an incident that occurred one morning preceding our first cricket match. We had gone out to practice on the Liverpool Cricket Grounds, and Mr. Allcock was present. We had hardly begun when he came to me and said:

"For Heaven's sake, Spalding, what are your men trying to do?"

I explained that they were just engaging in a little preliminary practice.

"But, man alive," he expostulated, "that isn't cricket. Why, you led me to suppose that your fellows were cricketers as well as ball players, and here have I been filling the London papers with assurances of close matches. Why, Spalding, your men don't know the rudiments of the game."

I confess that I was quite as worried as he; but this was no time to show my anxiety, and so I told him not to be uneasy. "You'll see," said I, "when the game comes

off what we can do. Of course we don't pretend to play
cricket in the fine, graceful form you are familiar with;
but we get there, just the same. We are not much in
practice, but we are great in matches."

It happened that our first contest at cricket was with
the famous Marylebone " All-English " eleven, the finest
cricketers in England. The game opened with the Britishers at bat. We had so many men in the field that it
seemed impossible that any balls could get away, and yet,
at the close of the afternoon's play, the Englishmen had
scored 105 runs in their inning. Next day the game was
resumed, with two of our three cricketers—Harry Wright
and McBride—first at bat. Harry went out on the first
ball bowled, and, after making two runs, McBride followed suit. I followed Wright, and Anson took McBride's
place.

In cricket, as I knew, the duty of the batter is to
defend his wicket and prevent it being bowled over.
Incidentally, he is expected to hit the ball and make
some runs, and, whether in defending his wicket or making his runs, he is expected to play gracefully and in
"good form." I shall not undertake here to explain
what "good form" requires. I gave no thought whatever to the gracefulness of my posing or to anything
else than making points. The first ball that threatened
my wicket I knocked over the fence, outside the grounds,
and the umpire shouted: "Four runs; you needn't leave
your place on a hit like that."

I had been accustomed to bat with a small, round ash
club, and with the great board paddle now in my hands it

GREAT BRITAIN'S NATIONAL GAME

just seemed impossible to miss. The second ball bowled was also hit outside the grounds, and likewise the third, and I felt myself immortalized by making twelve runs on my first "over" without leaving my position. Before I was bowled out, I had started our score with twenty-three runs, and Anson had scored fifteen runs. My experience at bat was repeated in the performances of others. The boys, seeing how easy it was, gained confidence and batted the ball all over the South of England. Harry Wright and McBride, the only members of our crowd who were accounted first-class cricketers, and who played in strictly "good form," were easy picking for the English bowlers; but George Wright put up the real thing, both as to form and achievement, and helped our score amazingly.

Harry Wright was captain of the American team and an experienced cricketer of English birth. He naturally felt considerable chagrin at our lack of "form."

He was inclined to instruct our men to play carefully and guard their wickets by more "blocking" and less wild slugging. I expostulated with him on these instructions, insisting that for an American ball player to attempt to "block" as a trained cricketer would do was an utter impossibility, but that slugging, or rather lunging at every ball bowled, was our only hope of success. "Good form" in cricket requires the batsman to invariably block all balls bowled on the wicket and to strike at balls off the wicket; but in Base Ball the batsman should strike at good balls, over the plate (or wicket), and let the bad balls, or those off the wicket, go by.

This natural instinct of the ball player could not be readily changed to conform to the cricketer's custom of "blocking," so it was decided to violate all conventional cricket "form" and slug at every ball bowled. The better and more accurately the Englishmen bowled, the more hits we could make, for such balls in our eyes were what we would term "good balls."

The result was that we made 107 runs in our inning to 105 for the Britishers, and American cricket stock went soaring. The London newspapers, in commenting on the play of the American ball players, declared that while in cricket they were not up to much in "form," their batting and fielding were simply marvelous.

The history of that day's game was repeated in every subsequent contest played in Great Britain. Not once were we defeated. Following the first game, which was played at the Lords' Grounds, in London, with the above score of 107 to 105 in one inning to each side, at the Prince's Grounds we defeated the Cricket Club by 110 in one inning against 60 in their two innings. At the Richmond Grounds the game was drawn, the English cricketers being disposed of for 108 in their innings, while the Americans had 45 with only six wickets down when rain stopped the game. At Surrey Oval the ball players scored 100 in their first inning to 27 by the cricketers, the game not being played out. At Sheffield the Americans defeated a Sheffield team by 130 runs in one inning to 43 and 45, a total of 88 in their two innings. At Manchester they defeated the Manchester twelve by 221 to 95 in a two-innings game. In playing against an "All-

Irish" team, at Dublin, the ball players won by 168 to 78.

The American ball players who accompanied me to Great Britain upon the occasion of this first visit of such an organization to foreign shores constituted two teams that had demonstrated their superiority in many hard-fought contests. They were the players of the Boston Champions and the Philadelphia Athletics, with the following line-ups for each team:

BOSTONS.		ATHLETICS.
A. G. Spalding	*Pitcher*	J. D. McBride
C. McVey	*Catcher*	J. E. Clapp
J. O'Rourke and Kent.	*First Base*	W. D. Fisler
Ross C. Barnes	*Second Base*	J. Battin
H. Shaffer	*Third Base*	E. B. Sutton
George Wright	*Shortstop*	M. H. McGeary
A. J. Leonard	*Left Field*	A. W. Gedney
Harry Wright	*Center Field*	J. F. McMullen
G. W. Hall	*Right Field*	A. C. Anson

Thos. J. Beals, J. B. Sensenderfer, S. Wright, Jr., and Tim Murnane accompanied the teams as utility men. Mr. Chas. H. Porter, President of the Boston Club, and Mr. Ferguson, President of the Athletics, had general charge of the trip. About eighty American tourists accompanied the two clubs on this memorable tour.

The teams as above listed played in fourteen exhibitions of the American National Game of Base Ball in England and Ireland; two at Liverpool, two at Manchester, seven at London, one at Sheffield and two at Dublin. Of these the Bostons won eight and the Athletics six.

The result of this tour of American Base Ball clubs to the British Isles in its effect was even more than had been hoped for, since it elicited from the London *Field,* the leading sporting journal of that city, the following commendation, in addition to setting the minds of the British sporting public at work to conjecture how the Americans came to be successful in all their cricket matches:

"Base Ball is a scientific game, more difficult than many, who are in the habit of judging from the outward semblance, can possibly imagine. It is, in fact, the cricket of the American continent, considerably altered since its first origin, as has been cricket, by the yearly recourse to the improvements necessitated by the experiences of each season. In the cricket field there is sometimes a wearisome monotony that is utterly unknown in Base Ball. To watch it played is most interesting, as the attention is concentrated for but a short time, and not allowed to succumb to undue pressure of prolonged suspense. The broad principles of Base Ball are not by any means difficult of comprehension. The theory of the game is not unlike that of 'Rounders,' in that bases have to be run; *but the details are in every way dissimilar.* To play Base Ball requires judgment, courage, presence of mind and the possession of much the same qualities as cricket. To see it played by experts will astonish those who only know it by written descriptions, for it is a fast game, full of change and excitement, and not in the least degree wearisome. To see the best players field, even, is a sight that ought to do a cricketer's heart good, the agility, dash and accuracy of timing and catching by the Americans being wonderful."

CHAPTER XIV.

ROBERT FERGUSON
Only Player-President of Major League

CHAPTER XIV.

1875–80

IT IS the purpose in this chapter to consider events leading up to the organization of the National League of Professional Base Ball Clubs, an alliance which, through many trials and discouragements, has successfully weathered all the storms that have beaten about its head during thirty-five years of all kinds of weather, and which stands to-day the honored pioneer Major League in Base Ball history.

The seasons of 1873 and 1874 had been characterized by an increase of the abuses and evils which the National Association of Professional Base Ball Players had inherited from the National Association of Amateur Base Ball Players. It may be possible that had the professional management been in control of affairs at the beginning of organized Base Ball things might have been different. We have, however, to deal with things as they were, not as they might have been. And they were "rotten." Gambling, in all its features of pool selling, side betting, etc., was still openly engaged in. Not an important game was played on any grounds where pools on same were not sold. A few players, too, had become so corrupt that nobody could be certain as to whether the issue of any

189

game in which these players participated would be determined on its merits. The occasional throwing of games was practiced by some, and no punishment meted out to the offenders. Years before, one Wansley, convicted of selling a game between the Eckfords and Mutuals, had been reinstated "in good standing." Liquor selling, either on the grounds or in close proximity thereto, was so general as to make scenes of drunkenness and riot of every day occurrence, not only among spectators, but now and then in the ranks of the players themselves. Many games had fist fights, and almost every team had its "lushers." The effect of this condition was exactly what might have been expected. A game characterized by such scenes, whose spectators consisted for the most part of gamblers, rowdies, and their natural associates, could not possibly attract honest men or decent women to its exhibitions. Consequently, the attendance fell away to such a degree that the season of 1875 closed with bankruptcy facing every professional club in the country.

It was at this time in the fortunes of the American game that Mr. Henry Chadwick, with true prophetic vision, drew the following pen picture of existing conditions in the official publication of 1873, which he was then editing:

"When the system of professional ball playing as practiced in 1872 shall be among the things that were, on its tombstone—if it have any—will be found the inscription, 'Died of Pool-Selling.' When professional playing was first inaugurated, the first obstacle presented in its slow progress to a reputable popularity was 'revolving' (a term used to designate contract jumping). This evil, however, soon disappeared when the system was governed by official authority emanating from a regular organization of professional clubs. In its place, however, an evil of far greater magnitude has sprung up, and the past season's experience stands forth as affording unmistakable evidence of the fact that the greatest evil the system of professional ball playing ever encountered or is likely to encounter is that arising from the pool-selling business inaugurated in 1871. The cause of its introduction was a very loose system of arranging wagers on the games, there being constant disputes arising from the want of some reliable depository of the stakes of the betting class. To remedy this, the pool-selling system was introduced, with the sole view of putting an end to the quarreling and bickering incident to the 'betting exchange' business which had previously prevailed. Unfortunately for the professionals, this pool-selling innovation has proved more damaging in its results than any one dreamed of, the evils before existing in the betting-mart being trifling in comparison. Before pools were sold on games, it was only by a rough and unreliable estimate that any idea of the amount bet on a match could be ascertained, except in such cases of individual investments where a man would bet $1,000 or more in place of $25 or $50 on a match. But now the amount of money pending in a contest on which pools have been sold can be known to the interested few to a dollar, and hence the temptation to fraudulent arrangements for losing matches for betting purposes becomes so great as almost to be irresistible. Since the introduction of pool-selling at Base Ball matches, pools amounting to over $20,000 have been known to be sold on a single match, and it has been in the power of parties knowing the aggregate amount of money invested, and who also knew which club the larger amount was invested on, to so manipulate things as to make the contest terminate just as the special 'ring' of the day desired it should. What benefit therefore pool-selling yielded in supplying a regular responsibility in the payment of bets in the place of the previous loose way of staking money was more than offset by the great temptations to fraud the knowledge of the amounts invested on the favorite club afforded and which the pool business admitted of. But, aside from the special evil of the system referred to, the very existence of the betting mart on the ball field has been found to be demoralizing in the extreme. Where this system of open betting exists, it is characterized by a suspicion of foul play by the contesting nines whenever either glaring errors or one-sided scores mark the playing of the game. Besides, during the contest, the class of fellows who patronize the game simply to pick up dollars by it, indulge in the vilest abuse and profanity in their comments on those errors of the play which damage the chances of winning their bets or pools. In fact, in every way likely to affect the interests of professional ball playing, is the pool-selling business an evil, and one, too, that has done more to lower the status of professional ball playing and to bring into question the honesty of the professional class than half a dozen such exposures of fraud as the Wansley case of 1865."

As shown heretofore, there was no stability in the fabric of the organization. A club standing well at the front in one season's race for the pennant would be out of the game the following year. There was no tie to bind the clubs in a bond strong enough to hold them together. The game had loyal friends and true, many of them, who were willing to back it with time and money; but a single season was usually quite sufficient to satisfy any capitalist who was willing, temporarily, to act as "angel," that the emissaries from the lower regions had control of the sport and that Base Ball, under then existing conditions, was only a hole in the ground into which he might pour his wealth as water, without hope of possible recovery.

What, then, was the matter? It was quite evident that the National Association of Professional Base Ball Players was no better equipped to deal with the situation than had been its predecessor. The abuses that had played havoc with the old association were not only continued, but were rapidly increasing in numbers and strength under the new organization. It was not conceivable that the men who were depending upon the game as a means of obtaining a livelihood were desirous of deliberately wrecking it. Nor could it be imagined that those who year after year met in convention and roundly denounced the outrageous practices that had attached themselves to Base Ball were dishonest in their clamor against those wrongs. All were agreed that the game must be reformed. But how?

About this time it began to be apparent to some that

the system in vogue for the business management of the sport was defective; that means ought to be adopted to separate the control of the executive management from the players and the playing of the game. The idea was as old as the hills; but its application to Base Ball had not yet been made. It was, in fact, the irrepressible conflict between Labor and Capital asserting itself under a new guise.

The experiment of business control of Base Ball by the men who played the game had been tested under several administrations of the National Association of Base Ball Players and the National Association of Professional Base Ball Players. No further evidence of the inability of ball players, whether amateurs or professionals, to manage both ends of the Base Ball enterprise at the same time was needed than was presented in conditions apparent to everybody—and especially in the overdrawn bank accounts of those who had undertaken to finance the sport.

Now, this picture of the situation as it was carries with it no reflection whatever upon the business acumen or executive ability of ball players as individuals. Scores of those who have won fame on the diamond have also won fortunes in business. But no ball player, in my recollection, ever made a success of any other business while he was building up his reputation as an artist on the diamond. The two branches are entirely unlike in their demands. One calls for the exercise of functions differing altogether from those which are required in the other. No man can do his best at ball playing unless his whole soul is in the effort. The man whose whole soul is absorbed in the business of playing ball has no soul left for the other business—just as important in its way—of conducting the details of managing men, administering discipline, arranging schedules and finding the ways and means of financing a team.

And so there came a day in the fall of 1875 when certain men—to be spoken of more personally later on—desirous of the success of the national game, determined upon a reorganization on lines differing entirely from those that had previously obtained. They proposed an organization that should draw a sharp line of distinction between the terms "Club" and "Team." Heretofore Base Ball *Clubs* had won and lost games, matches, tournaments, trophies. Henceforth this would be changed. The function of Base Ball *Clubs* in the future would be to manage Base Ball *Teams*. Clubs would form leagues, secure grounds, erect grandstands, lease and own property, make schedules, fix dates, pay salaries, assess fines, discipline players, make contracts, control the sport in all its relations to the public, and thus, relieving the players of all care and responsibility for the legitimate functions of management, require of them the very best performance of which they were capable, in the entertainment of the public, for which service they were to receive commensurate pay.

This then was the germ, yet in its chrysalis state, that was incubating in the minds of devotees of the game—some of them players and some not—during the closing hours of the life of the National Association of Professional Base Ball Players, in 1875.

Just here a word should be spoken in justice to the memory of the man who for the greater part of its existence was President of the National Association of Base Ball Players. Robert Ferguson was not only one of the best ball players of his time, but he was a man of sterling integrity and splendid courage. He knew all about the iniquitous practices which had become attached to the game as barnacles to a ship, and he was sincerely desirous of eradicating them. But he lacked the essential qualifications of a reformer. It was written and widely published at the time, that, upon occasion of one of the notable contests in which the club that he headed as captain-manager was engaged, he went among the members of the gambling fraternity, who, as usual, were practicing their nefarious calling on the grounds, and, in the presence of a great throng attracted by the vehemence of his language and actions, berated the gamblers with fierce invective, charging them with having conspired to debauch the honor of his players, and threatening them with personal chastisement if they did not at once desist.

Had Ferguson at this time been surrounded by men such as later on took control of the game, much of humiliation might have been spared to players in coming years, and the game itself would never have suffered the disgrace that came to it from failure to act along sane lines at this important juncture.

The trouble with Ferguson—as with many other players in those days—was not lack of intelligence, courage or integrity; but, rather, a want of diplomacy. He was no master of the arts of finesse. He had no tact. He knew nothing of the subtle science of handling men by strategy rather than by force. Could it have been possible to eliminate gambling by physical demonstrations, Robert Ferguson would have cleared the Base Ball atmosphere of one of its most unsanitary conditions at that time; and this was true of many other well meaning but inefficient leaders in those days of the game's early evolution. It was this fact that later on made it very clear that there must be a separation between the playing and business ends of the sport; that no man could be a success in both offices at the same time; that the manager must be equipped to *manage*, while the player need only be qualified to *play* the game.

CHAPTER XV.

WILLIAM A. HULBERT

CHAPTER XV.

1875–76

AS IN the history of nations, so in that of all enterprises of magnitude, there arise from time to time men cast in heroic molds, the impress of whose acts upon the issues at hand is felt for many years. At the time of the organization of the National League of Professional Base Ball Clubs such a man was present in the person of William A. Hulbert.

He was not a professional ball player; had never been a player of the game. He was simply one among countless thousands of Americans who enjoyed the great national pastime, and was a frequent spectator at its exhibitions. His home was at Chicago. Being a loyal partisan of the city where he lived, he stood for the interests of the great Western metropolis, and incidentally for those of the whole Mississippi Valley. It was borne to him one day that the reason why Chicago—whose phenomenal achievements on other lines were attracting the wonder of all the world—could make no better showing on the diamond was because the East was in league against her; that certain Base Ball magnates in the Atlantic States were in control of the game; were manipulating things to the detriment of Chicago and all Western cities; that if

199

the Chicago Club signed an exceptionally strong player he was sure to be stolen from her; that contracts had no force, because the fellows down East would and did offer players increased salaries and date new contracts back to suit their own ends.

To a man of William A. Hulbert's fibre this sort of thing was a firebrand to kindle all the heat of an ardent and combative nature.

It was something to be resented, to be fought, to be overcome. And so when, in 1875, he was urged to accept the Presidency of the Chicago Base Ball Club, he did not turn the matter down, as he might have done under different circumstances, but took it under advisement, and asked for time.

It was at this stage that I first met Mr. Hulbert. I had been playing on the Boston team as a professional for several years. Our nine had won the pennant three years in succession and had it cinched for the fourth. It was becoming monotonous. The effect of such an uninterrupted succession of all-season victories was to destroy interest in the game. "There's no use going." "Boston's sure to win." "She's hasn't lost a game on the home grounds this year." Such expressions were heard every day, and gate receipts were small. For myself, I felt that the time was ripe for a change. Moreover, I was heartily disgusted with what I saw going on all about us. I knew that gambling was practiced everywhere; that such players as had not stamina to resist the overtures made to them were being caused to swerve from the legitimate ends of the game, and to serve the illegitimate purposes of the gamesters. I do not claim for myself any degree of puritanical perfection; but I was sick and sore of existing conditions; ready to get away from them—the sooner the better. I had made up my mind fully to one thing; that unless a change soon took place in the management of the game, I was done with it at once and forever.

I was greatly impressed by the personality of Mr. Hulbert at our first meeting, in Chicago, early in 1875. He seemed strong, forceful, self-reliant. I admired his business-like way of considering things. I was sure that he was a man of tremendous energy—and courage. He told me of the interest of Chicago in Base Ball; how that thousands of lovers of the game at Chicago were wild for a winning team, but couldn't get one; how she had been repeatedly robbed of her players, and, under Eastern control of the Professional Association, had no recourse. It seemed to me that he was more deeply chagrined at the insult to Chicago than over that city's failure to make a creditable representation in the game. I told him that I was quite familiar with the entire situation; that it was the same all over the West—no city had any show under the present regime; that the spirit of gambling and graft held possession of the sport everywhere; that the public was disgusted and wouldn't patronize the pastime, and, finally, that unless there was a new deal throughout, with a cleaning out of the gamblers, both in and outside the Base Ball profession, I, for one, proposed to quit.

We talked for quite a while upon the different phases of the situation, and then he said to me: "Spalding, you've no business playing in Boston; you're a Western

MORGAN G. BULKELEY

boy, and you belong right here. If you'll come to Chicago, I'll accept the Presidency of this Club, and we'll give those fellows a fight for their lives."

I gave him to understand that I was not averse to such a movement, and said that, if I did come, I would bring a team of pennant winners. Later in the season, in June, 1875, he called upon me at Boston, as President of the Chicago Club. He there and then signed Barnes, McVey, White and myself, and I accompanied him to Philadelphia, where Anson and Sutton had already been secured through my efforts. This left three places on the team which could be readily filled from strong players on the Chicago nine, consisting of Hines, Glenn and Peters.

Every effort was made to keep this matter a secret until the close of the season, chiefly because there was a rule in force at that time to the effect that a player signing a contract with any club during the playing season, except with the one with which he was then engaged, would subject him to expulsion from the Association, which meant expulsion from professional Base Ball.

This secret lasted about two weeks, when an announcement appeared in a Chicago paper that the four Boston and two Philadelphia players above named had been signed for the Chicago Club for 1876. This announcement occasioned a great sensation in Boston and Philadelphia, and, in fact, everywhere throughout the country.

As I write this story, many amusing incidents are recalled of our experiences at Boston during the balance of that season. The Monday morning when the announcement appeared in the Boston papers it so happened that

I, being out of the city, spending Sunday with some friends, did not read the papers, and I arrived at the grounds just in time to don my uniform and get onto the field in time to play in a game against the St. Louis team.

I was alone in the dressing room, when Ross Barnes came in and said:

"Well, you will get a chilly reception when you come on the field."

"What's the matter now?" I asked.

"Why, don't you know?" said Barnes. "Haven't you read the morning papers?"

I replied that I had not, whereupon he continued:

"The jig is up. The secret is out and H——'s to pay. McVey, White and I took to the woods early in the day and just arrived at the grounds a few minutes ago. Everybody seems to take it as a huge joke," added Barnes, "and we have treated it the same way, and have neither affirmed nor denied the rumor."

I knew that the Boston crowd would consider me the head devil in this secession movement, so I made a clean breast of the whole affair, and turned the joke into a reality by announcing that the statement was absolutely true. We had been dubbed the "Big Four," and for the balance of that season were caricatured, ridiculed, and even accused of treason. Boys would follow us on the streets, shouting "Oh, you seceders; your White Stockings will get soiled," and would hurl all kinds of facetious remarks at us.

The "Big Four" had certainly been popular in Boston up to the time of our so-called secession movement.

We knew that we had been magnificently treated by the Boston public and the Boston Club officials, and our associations with the two Wright brothers and other members of the original Boston team had been exceedingly pleasant. If at that time we had felt free to follow our inclinations, we would most gladly have given up the whole business and remained in Boston. But we had gone too far. We had signed contracts with President Hulbert to go to Chicago the following year. Because of this he had accepted the Presidency of the Chicago Club and assumed financial obligations based upon our assurance that we would be with him in 1876. Our inclinations drew us back towards Boston, but our duty surely called us to Chicago. We therefore unanimously decided to go, regardless of what inducements might be offered to remain.

To the credit of Mr. N. T. Appolonio, then President of the Boston Club, who was criticised severely for permitting the "Big Four" to leave, I have to say that, while regretting our action, he did not put a stone in our path, nor did he urge us to break our contracts with Chicago, although he did intimate that, if it was simply a matter of salary, Boston would pay us higher salaries than Chicago had offered or would give.

The professionals of that period never looked kindly upon the rule expelling a player for signing a contract with another club during the playing season. The club officials gave it out that the reason for the rule was that players might lose interest and not do their best to win for their club if permitted to sign contracts to play elsewhere next season.

N. E. YOUNG

Now, it is just as natural for a ball player to play his best to win as it is for a duck to swim. They don't know any other way to play the game. The "Big Four" and their associates on the Boston team of 1875 were determined to show the fallacy of the idea that good players ever lose interest in Base Ball. We rather overdid the thing, for the Boston nine never lost a game during 1875 on the home grounds, and closed the season with a record of 71 games won and 8 lost, or a percentage of .899, which record has never been equalled in professional Base Ball.

After the close of the season of 1875 there were mutterings in the press to the effect that at the next annual meeting of the National Association of Professional Base Ball Players, which was to be held in March, 1876, the Boston "Big Four" and Anson and Sutton, of the Philadelphia Athletics, would be expelled for violation of the rule prohibiting players from signing contracts with other clubs during a pending season. I discussed this phase of the question with Mr. Hulbert while visiting at his home in Chicago in the fall of 1875. I probably exhibited some uneasiness on that subject, but Mr. Hulbert answered by assuring me that whatever happened Chicago would pay the salaries of her players in full. Chicago, he said, had been working for years to get a winning ball team, and now that she had finally secured one, he proposed that Chicago should have what was coming to her.

William A. Hulbert was a typical Chicago man. He never spoke of what *he* would do, or what *his club* would do, but it was always what *Chicago* would do. "I would rather be a lamp-post in Chicago than a millionaire in any other city," was one of his frequent and characteristic expressions.

In again referring, that same evening, to our possible expulsion, Mr. Hulbert said: "Why, they can't expel you. They would not dare do it, for in the eyes of the public you six players are stronger than the whole Association." For a few moments I noticed that he was engrossed in deep thought, when suddenly he rose from his chair and said:

"Spalding, I have a new scheme. Let us anticipate the Eastern cusses and organize a new association before the March meeting, and then see who will do the expelling." It was an inspiration. I shared his enthusiasm, and thus was a new association conceived, and out of it all came the National League of Professional Base Ball Clubs.

We had daily conferences concerning this new project. In trying to fix upon a name for the embryonic organization, I recall that Mr. Hulbert said: "Let us get away from the old, worn-out title, "National Association of Base Ball Players," and call it "The National League of Professional Base Ball Clubs."

We spent considerable time in drafting a new Constitution for the League baby, and when it was finished we were quite proud of our work. That Constitution, with a few changes made from time to time to meet new conditions, has stood the test since 1876, and has resulted in making the National League of Professional Base Ball Clubs the leading organization in the annals of the sport.

In response to my expressions of enthusiasm over this new League Constitution and what it meant for the future of professional Base Ball, I recall the following characteristic remark of Mr. Hulbert:

"Why, Spalding, the wit of man cannot devise a plan or frame a form of government that will control the game of Base Ball for over five years."

And yet the principles engrafted in that Constitution have controlled the game for *thirty-five years!*

The next move of this active man, who had just broken into the ranks of Base Ball magnates, was to secure a secret meeting, at Louisville, with managers from Cincinnati, St. Louis and Louisville Clubs. I was present at that meeting, and Mr. Hulbert laid before the company the program we had mapped out. He went over the current history of the game, showed conditions just as they were, declared that gambling in every form must be eradicated at once and forever, and closed with the announcement that it was proposed to organize a National League of Professional Base Ball Clubs, under rules which should protect players and management and reduce the game to a business system such as had never heretofore obtained. There were present at this meeting Messrs. Charles A. Fowle, John J. Joyce, W. N. Haldeman, Thos. Shirley, Chas. E. Chase, Wm. A. Hulbert and A. G. Spalding. All the managers in attendance agreed to every proposition presented, and powers of attorney from Cincinnati, St. Louis, Louisville and Chicago were made out to Mr. Hulbert and Mr. Fowle, and they were clothed with full powers.

Armed with these credentials, Mr. Hulbert sent personal notices to accredited representatives of each of the Eastern professional clubs, viz.: President G. W. Thompson, of the Athletics, of Philadelphia; President N. T. Appolonio, of the Boston Club; President M. G. Bulkeley, of the Hartford Club; and President W. H. Cammeyer, of the Mutuals, of Brooklyn, that he would be pleased to meet them at his hotel—the Grand Central—in New York City, at a given hour—the time differing in each invitation—on the morning of February 2d, 1876. On the date appointed Mr. Hulbert was present at the place named to receive his company. One after another came until all had arrived. Then this aggressive Base Ball magnate from the West, who had never been present at a similar meeting in his life, went to the door of his room, locked it, put the key in his pocket, and, turning, addressed his astonished guests something after this manner:

"Gentlemen, you have no occasion for uneasiness. I have locked that door simply to prevent any intrusions from without, and incidentally to make it impossible for any of you to go out until I have finished what I have to say to you, which I promise shall not take an hour." He then laid before the assembled auditors the Base Ball situation in all its varied interests. He pointed out the evils of gambling that were threatening the very life of the game, reducing receipts, demoralizing players. He spoke of the abuse of " revolving," and paid his respects to the managers—some of whom were present—who were engaged in the reprehensible work of inducing players to violate their legal contracts. He showed that the National Association of Professional Base Ball Players had been either unable or unwilling to correct the abuses, in either of which events it was unfit for further control of the game. He closed his remarks by producing a constitution which we had prepared in advance for adoption by a new organization, to be then and there formed under the title of " The National League of Professional Base Ball Clubs." Section II. of this constitution declared the objects of the new League in the following unmistakable language:

First—To *encourage, foster* and *elevate* the game of Base Ball.

Second—To enact and *enforce* proper rules for the exhibition and conduct of the game.

Third—To make Base Ball playing *respectable* and *honorable.*

When Mr. Hulbert had finished, if there had been any fight in his auditors when he locked the door it had entirely oozed away. A Quaker prayer meeting could not have been more decorous than the proceedings from that time until the adjournment which soon followed.

Mr. Hulbert magnificently dominated the whole situation. The new man from the West had risen supreme and was absolute monarch in that assemblage. His " mailed fist " was strong enough to brush away any opposition that might manifest itself; but there was no opposition in sight. Mr. Hulbert nominated Mr. Morgan G. Bulkeley, of Hartford, as the first President of the National League of Professional Base Ball Clubs, and

MONUMENT OF WILLIAM A. HULBERT

when that gentleman would have waived the honor, on account of other conflicting engagements, Mr. Hulbert urged his acceptance as a tribute due to the East, where Base Ball had its origin and early development—and Mr. Bulkeley accepted. The selection of Mr. N. E. Young as Secretary of the League closed the eventful meeting, at which Mr. Hulbert demonstrated his skill and power as an organizer and ruler among men.

In closing this chapter, I wish to claim for William A. Hulbert that which is due to him as one who appeared in the history of Base Ball just at a time when such a man was needed, and as one who did more than any other among magnates to save and maintain the game in its integrity.

In December, 1876, before the National League had been a year in existence, William A. Hulbert was elected President, a position he held up to the time of his death. To him came the great struggle that attended the early years of the League. Upon his shoulders were loaded most of the heavy burdens of those days of formative and creative duty. Against him were directed the assaults of enemies of the League—and of the game. He was the recipient of the abuse of gamblers and of the innuendoes of their apologists.

The struggles he encountered cheerfully, for he was a born fighter; the duties he assumed willingly, for he was an industrious worker; the planning he undertook intelligently, for he was a master of business system, and the opposition of the rabble amused, while it injured him not at all.

William A. Hulbert was not a purist. He was never

charged with religious bigotry or fanaticism of any kind other than that which manifests itself in a great love for our national game. His name was not enrolled among the list of moral reformers. He thought this world was good enough for him—for anybody, and he enjoyed it in his own way. And yet this man stood like a stone wall, protecting the game of Base Ball in its integrity and turning back the assaults of every foe who sought to introduce elements of dishonesty, discord or degeneration. He demanded always clean management, a clean game, and the best interests of manly sport.

There have been other forceful men at the head of our national organizations, men of high purpose, good judgment and fine executive ability. But in all the history of Base Ball no man has yet appeared who possessed in combination more of the essential attributes of a great leader and organizer of men than did William A. Hulbert.

Mr. Hulbert continued as President of the National League until his death, at his home in Chicago, April 10th, 1882.

A monument was erected at his grave in Graceland Cemetery, bearing the names of the eight clubs then members of the National League.

God bless his memory.

I ask all living professional Base Ball players to join me in raising our hats to the memory of William A. Hulbert, the man who saved the game!

CHAPTER XVI.

WHEN GAMBLING CONTROLLED

CHAPTER XVI.

FIRST DETERMINED STRUGGLE AGAINST PREVAILING EVILS—
HOW GAMBLING AND POOL SELLING WERE ERADICATED
FROM THE GROUNDS AND FROM THE GAME.

1875-80

THAT the men who took upon their shoulders the task of organizing and maintaining the National League of Professional Base Ball Clubs realized the herculean proportions of the enterprise in which they were engaging is not to be believed; else they might never have undertaken it. They did know, however, that they would have opposition. They knew that an immediate and bitter struggle with the whole gambling fraternity would follow the inauguration of their plans; for the men who organized the National League were aware that gambling and Base Ball must be divorced. The union had never been legitimate. It had been forced upon the game by the weakness of its parents and the aggressiveness of its adventurous wooer. The alliance was an unholy one, and its offspring were bastards, all. The only hope for the future of the pastime was to separate it at once and forever from its evil consort. That of itself would mean a struggle; but the new sponsors welcomed the conflict, because it was a fight for the very life of the sport they loved, and they were willing to make sacrifice for it.

They knew also that there would be opposition from another source. Quite conscious were they that there were players, and good players, too, who would not take kindly to the proposed League organization. Such dishonest players were comparatively few in numbers—probably not exceeding five per cent. of those active in the professional game; but they constituted a mischievous and demoralizing element. The new leaders could not expect sympathy or co-operation in their fight against gambling from those who had been in collusion with gamblers. How to secure the confidence and loyalty of this small class, and at the same time retain the respect of the many clean-handed players, was one of many vexed problems that came before the new League organizers. So long as ball-players had been managing the affairs of the game the salary question was not so serious. It resolved itself into a division of the surplus—had there ever been any, after necessary expenses had been paid—be the balance what it might. But, under League control, with club management of teams and fixed salaries; with the essential declaration that players were to play ball and the management would do the rest, there loomed large upon the horizon of the Base Ball game a legal responsibility to be assumed—and by somebody who could be found on pay day.

With these and other problems confronting them, the League managers entered upon the discharge of their onerous duties earnestly and vigorously. One of the first things they did was to dignify the sport by advancing the membership fee from a paltry $10 per annum to $100 for each club. They made certain the possibility of remunerative gate receipts by requiring a bona fide population of at least 75,000 from any city seeking a franchise. They adopted a form of player's contract that would do away with or lessen the practice, so generally engaged in, of "revolving." They provided a penalty of expulsion for any player violating his contract, and any-one thus expelled was to be forever ineligible to reinstatement in any League club. They forbade bookmaking or liquor selling on any League ball grounds, and players were made subject to expulsion for being interested in any side-bet or for purchasing pools on any game. True, both preceding Associations had forbidden gambling and pool-selling in their constitutions; but neither had enforced nor successfully attempted the enforcement of provisions along this line. It was yet to be seen whether the National League would rise to the emergency its predecessors had so signally failed to meet.

The cities represented in the first circuit of the National League were Boston, Chicago, Cincinnati, Hartford, Louisville, New York, Philadelphia, St. Louis. The players of the respective teams were as follows:

Boston—Harry Wright, manager; J. E. Borden, T. H. Murnane, T. L. Beals, H. C. Shafer, A. J. Leonard, J. H. O'Rourke, J. F. Manning, F. T. Whitney, George Wright, John F. Morrill, Lewis Brown and T. McGinley.

Chicago—A. G. Spalding, manager; James White, A. C. Anson, Ross Barnes, C. A. McVey, J. P. Peters, J. W. Glenn, P. A. Hines, R. Addy, J. F. Cone, Oscar Bielaski and F. H. Andrus.

Cincinnati—C. H. Gould, manager; S. J. Fields, W. C. Fisher, C. J. Sweasy, H. Kessler, E. Snyder, C. W.

WHEN WHISKEY THREATENED

Jones, R. Clark, D. P. Pierson, A. S. Booth, Henry Dean and William Foley.

Hartford—Robert Ferguson, manager; D. Allison, W. A. Cummings, Thomas H. Bond, E. Mills, John J. Burdock, Thomas Carey, Thomas York, J. J. Remsen, J. Cassidy, Richard Higham and W. H. Harbridge.

Louisville—J. C. Chapman, manager; James A. Devlin, Scott Hastings, Charles N. Snyder, W. L. Hague, J. Gerhardt, Charles Fulmer, A. A. Allison, J. C. Carbine, George Bechtel, J. J. Ryan, W. H. Holbert, W. Somerville and H. Collins.

New York (Mutuals)—W. H. Cammeyer, manager; Robert Matthews, N. H. Hicks, Joe Start, James Hallinan, A. H. Nichols, E. Booth, W. H. Craver, James Holdsworth and Fred Treacey.

Philadelphia (Athletics)—A. H. Wright, manager; Alonzo Knight, W. R. Coons, W. D. Fisler, W. Fouser, D. W. Force, George Zettlein, E. B. Sutton, G. W. Hall, Levi Meyerle, David Eggler and Fergus G. Malone.

St. Louis—S. W. Graffen, manager; George W. Bradley, Lipman Pike, E. E. Cuthbert, J. V. Battin, R. J. Pearce, J. W. Blong, D. J. Mack, T. P. Miller, H. T. Dehlman, M. H. McGeary and John E. Clapp.

At the first annual meeting of the National League, held in December, 1876, a test of the quality of the management of that organization came in the fact that the Athletics, of Philadelphia, and Mutuals, of New York, clubs from the two largest cities represented in the League, relying upon the practice of former Associations in the way of condoning similar offenses, had declined to play their return games scheduled in the West, thereby forfeiting their membership in the League. They argued that these big cities were more important to the League than was the League to New York and Philadelphia. Very greatly to their surprise, both Athletics and Mutuals were summarily expelled! This left the League for 1877 to consist of six clubs only.

At this meeting of the League Mr. William A. Hulbert was elected to succeed Mr. Bulkeley as President, and N. E. Young was re-elected Secretary.

The championship pennant was won by Chicago, the teams closing the season in the following order: Chicago, Hartford, St. Louis, Boston, Louisville, New York, Philadelphia and Cincinnati. It is worthy of note in this connection that honors now were almost evenly divided, as between East and West, as shown by the alternating of the nines in the order of their standing in the race.

It should not be inferred that no other clubs than those composing the National League were in existence at this time. Reading, Pa.; Columbus, O.; Fall River, Mass.; Providence, R. I.; Binghamton, N. Y.; Syracuse, N. Y.; Indianapolis, Ind.; St. Louis, Mo.; Wilmington, Del.; Pittsburg, Pa., and many other cities, had formidable semi-professional teams that played regularly scheduled games.

The season of 1877 was one abounding in vicissitudes for the National League. Had its organization been no stronger; had its executives been no more determined than had been those of preceding Associations, the League would in that memorable year have joined the great majority, dying in infancy. As it was, the game made slow progress, not many new clubs were organized, while financial failures attended most ventures in a professional way. Not all League clubs lost money, but most of them did, and the gambling element was in high feather because of its assurance that the old order of things would soon be reinstated.

However, the League managers were immovable in their determination that the game should be kept clean and honest. Every case requiring discipline, whether of club or player, received it promptly, and in allopathic doses. So far as the executive heads of offending clubs were concerned, had they been rolling in wealth, no more unyielding temper could have been displayed by the League management. The effect was just what had been intended and hoped for. Confidence, always quick to take alarm in times of trouble and fly away, began slowly to return. It was evidenced in 1878 by an unexpected increase in the number of new clubs organized throughout the country, by unwonted interest and approval on the part of the press, and by revived activity at the turn-stiles.

This renewed interest in the sport was doubtless due in part to certain changes introduced in the game itself under League control. Players and managers had been alike agreed for some time that the use of a "lively ball," that is, one containing so much rubber as to cause the sphere to bound inordinately, was prejudicial to the best presentation of the game. It made the exhibitions too long. Nightfall saw many contests unfinished that had begun early in the afternoon. The use of the "lively ball" made the game uncertain. A batted ball would strike the ground at a distance from the fielder that would make its capture under favorable conditions easy and sure; but, because of some inequality of surface, or the presence of some impediment unseen, it would be deflected and with such suddenness and unlooked for rapidity that it was impossible to prevent its escape, or to check the base running epidemic that almost invariably followed a mishap of this kind. Moreover, the "lively ball" was accountable for such ridiculous scores that its abandonment was decided upon as a means of making the sport more interesting to spectators and less enervating to players. It is of record that, in one of its games, the Niagara team, of Buffalo, won by a score of 201 to 11.

So, in place of the "lively ball," yielding a score of three figures to the winners, a "dead ball," containing no elasticity whatever, was tried, with the result that many games of nine innings were played without a run on either side. It was about this time that the expression, "fell with a dull thud," began to find a place in our literature, and there can be no doubt as to its origin; for that is exactly how the "dead ball" struck the earth. In a game between Harvard University and a team from Manchester, N. H., played with a dead ball in 1879, the score stood 0 to 0 at the end of twenty-four innings, and this because of the nature of the ball used, rather than the superiority of the players using it.

Like everything else in the evolution of Base Ball, the ball had gone to the extreme limit of liveliness and to the extreme limit of deadness, and now, taking advantage of these tried-out extremes, saner reasoning prevailed, and the ball was gradually brought around to a happy medium; not too lively, not too dead, but just about right as to liveliness.

Finally, about the beginning of the decade of the 80's, a model ball in size, weight and constituent elements, practically differing but little from that now in use, was adopted, with most gratifying results.

In order to secure balls of uniform quality, as to constituent elements and grade of workmanship, the National League found it necessary early in its career to adopt an "Official League Ball," made according to stipulated specifications, and to be furnished under long term contracts. This plan has since been adopted by the American League, only official balls being used in either.

The year 1877 witnessed the birth of two minor organizations, both acknowledging allegiance to the National League. These were the International Association, composed of clubs in the United States and Canada, and the League Alliance, a strictly United States association.

The International Association, which lasted under that title through only two seasons, was composed of the Alleghenys, of Pittsburg; the Buckeyes, of Columbus; the Live Oaks, of Lynn; the Manchesters, of Manchester, N. H.; and the Rochesters, of Rochester, from the United States, and the Tecumsehs, of London, and the Maple Leafs, of Guelph, Ontario. The Tecumsehs won the championship.

In 1878 the International Association changed its clubs materially, the circuit being composed of the following cities: Allegheny, Buffalo, Hartford, Hornellsville, Manchester, Rochester, Springfield, Syracuse, Utica, and the Tecumsehs, of London, Ontario. The Buffalo club won the pennant.

In 1879 George Wright left the Bostons, with which club he had played so long, and, taking with him O'Rourke, went to Providence, where, under his management, the championship of the year was won by Providence.

The most sensational event of the period between the formation of the National League and the opening of the next decade was the expulsion from its ranks of four players by the Louisville Club in 1877. These men were A. H. Nichols, William H. Craver, George Hall, and James Devlin. The evidence of their guilt was so strong that, when confronted with it, Hall and Devlin confessed, implicating Nichols and Craver. Upon being summoned before the directorship of the club, all but Craver signed an order on the telegraph company for telegrams alleged to have passed between them and the sporting fraternity. Craver was at once expelled. Upon receipt of copies of the dispatches, showing conclusively the guilt of all, the other three were summarily dismissed, in disgrace, and never reinstated, although many appeals, in every conceivable form, were presented, backed by petitions, entreaties, and sometimes accompanied by threats. Louisville has, therefore, the credit of being the first club, under the National League, to expel members for crookedness. Indianapolis followed in 1878, by dismissing Nolan, a pitcher, for desertion.

This, then, was the first great victory won over gambling and the gamblers. It was the direct result of the determination on the part of the founders of the National League to eradicate this evil. Its effect was instantaneous and has lasted from that day to this. It has proven that, under the system of club management introduced at the time the National League was formed, it is possible to control the integrity of the game in every department by the simple exercise of firmness along lines of constant watchfulness and care, and by the inflexible administration of discipline.

As illustrating how general is the determination by everybody, everywhere, to keep the game of Base Ball free from the gambling curse, the following, from the San Francisco *Call* of April 25th, 1911, is in point. Three men were arrested by the police, charged with gambling on the grounds of a local club. The case was not made out, but the Judge, in releasing the men, said:

"I am dismissing these men because there is no proof here that they were gambling on the result of that game," said Judge Weller. "But I will do all that is within the power of this court to keep the game of Base Ball free from the stain of gambling. If the officers will bring to me men who have been caught redhanded at this thing, I will see that they are properly attended to."

I shall never forget a scene I witnessed one day in the office of President Hulbert, of the National League, as a sequence of the expulsion of the Louisville players. Mr. Hulbert's office was *en suite*, consisting of rooms connected by folding or sliding doors. I was sitting in the reception room and Mr. Hulbert was at his desk in the inner apartment, when the outer door opened and a sorry-looking specimen of humanity entered. It was midwinter and very cold, but the poor fellow had no overcoat. His dust-covered garments were threadbare and seedy. His shoes were worn through with much tramping, while the red flesh showing in places indicated that if stockings were present they afforded not much protection to the feet. Everything about the man's appearance betokened weariness and woe. His face was a picture of abject misery. The visitor passed me without a glance in my direction. His eyes were fixed upon the occupant of the farther room. He walked straight to the chair where Mr. Hulbert sat, and, dropping to his knees at the big man's feet, lifted his eyes in prayerful entreaty, while his frame shook with the emotion so long restrained. Then his lips gave utterance to such a plea for mercy as might have come from one condemned to the gallows.

The man was Devlin, one of the Louisville players. He had been a personal friend of Mr. Hulbert and, knowing that man's kindly heart, had felt that if he could only see him, face to face, his friendship and the memory of former days would cause him to relent in his purpose of punishment. How Devlin reached Chicago I never knew. There was everything in his condition and appearance to indicate that he might have walked all the way from Louisville. The situation, as he kneeled there in abject humiliation, was beyond the realm of pathos. It was a scene of heartrending tragedy. Devlin was in tears, Hulbert was in tears, and if the mists of a tearful sympathy filled my eyes I have no excuse to offer here.

I heard Devlin's plea to have the stigma removed from his name. I heard him entreat, not on his own account—he acknowledged himself unworthy of consideration—but for the sake of his wife and child. I beheld the agony of humiliation depicted on his features as he confessed his guilt and begged for mercy. I saw the great bulk of Hulbert's frame tremble with the emotion he vainly sought to stifle. I saw the President's hand steal into his pocket as if seeking to conceal his intended act from the other hand. I saw him take a $50 bill and press it into the palm of the prostrate player. And then I heard him say, as he fairly writhed with the pain his own words caused him, "That's what I think of you, personally; but, damn you, Devlin, you are dishonest; you have sold a game, and I can't trust you. Now go; and let me never see your face again; for your act will not be condoned so long as I live."

Among other acts of legislation at this era of the game was the adoption, in 1879, of the "reserve rule," under whose provisions each club was permitted to hold the services of five men. This rule has since had several amendments. The reserve rule has proven to be one of the fundamentals of successful Base Ball control, and it is now conceded by all familiar with management to be a requisite of professional ball.

In this year, also, the International Association, founded in 1877, ceased to exist, the Canadian clubs having both withdrawn, and in its place there arose the National Association of Base Ball Clubs, exclusively from Eastern cities, representing Albany, Holyoke, Manchester, New Bedford, Rochester, Springfield, Utica, Washington, and Worcester. This minor league only lasted two years, Albany winning the first championship pennant.

In 1879 was organized the first exclusively Western minor league, consisting of Davenport and Dubuque, in Iowa; Rockford, Illinois, and Omaha, Nebraska. The Dubuque club finished in first place.

Under the control of the National League, in the first years of its existence, many professional and semi-professional clubs came into being, but these, as a rule, were unattached to any league or association, played independently, and arranged games whenever and wherever they could. At that time National League clubs did not have regularly scheduled series, but depended upon local secretaries to arrange games for each club. The system providing for season schedules was not inaugurated until 1877—another of Mr. Hulbert's reforms.

The unattached clubs derived much of their revenue from exhibition games with National League teams, and it was not unusual for a League nine to visit a small city, sign up one or more of the best players of the local organization and take them away. I recall one instance where a League club visited St. Paul and took from the "Red Caps" of that city five of their finest players, practically breaking up the team! A great outcry, of course, was raised over this high-handed proceeding, and, while there was no League rule forbidding such action on the part of League clubs, it became evident to the far-sighted Hulbert that, unless this custom was stopped, it would reflect discredit upon not only the League but the game itself. He at once set about to institute a reform in this direction.

It so happened at that time that Mr. A. G. Mills, who was then living at Chicago, appeared on the field of Base Ball reform. In a published article over his signature he severely criticised the reprehensible practice above referred to of League clubs visiting cities, accepting their hospitality, and then stealing their players. In this communication, as I recall it, he outlined a plan showing how this abuse could be done away with and called upon the officials of the National League to put a stop to the pernicious custom.

Mr. Hulbert was very much impressed with the article of Mr. Mills, and, as it conformed to his own ideas on the subject, he immediately sent an invitation to the writer, asking him to call at his office, as he would like to consult with him on Base Ball matters. Mr. Mills accepted the invitation, and thus these two great Base Ball leaders met for the first time, and from thenceforward were close personal friends.

Mr. Mills evidently made a good impression on Mr. Hulbert, for just after this interview I called on the latter at his office, when he said: "I have found just the man we are looking for, and he has kindly agreed to help me in shaping up a plan that will prevent League clubs from robbing any more struggling clubs of their players."

I asked the name of the newcomer to the game, and when Mr. Hulbert told me, I replied: "That name sounds familiar. Why, A. G. Mills used to be the President of

OLYMPICS, WASHINGTON, D. C.

A. J. Leonard, l.f.   G. W. Hall, c.f.   H. W. Berthrong, r.f.

F. A. Waterman, 3 b.   C. J. Sweasy, 2 b.   E. Mills, 1b.

D. W. Force, s.s.   Asa Brainard, p.

H. F. Borroughs   D. L. Allison, c.   J. W. Glenn

the Olympic Club, of Washington, D. C., just after the war, and it must be the same A. G. Mills who tendered me an invitation to become pitcher of that team and offered me a position in the Treasury Department just after the Rockfords defeated the Nationals at Chicago, in 1867."

It proved to be the same A. G. Mills.

Out of this chance meeting, in 1876, between Hulbert and Mills, grew the original League Alliance, and then the Tripartite Agreement between the National League, the American Association and the Northwestern League, and then followed the National Agreement formulated by Mr. Mills when he became President of the National League upon the death of Mr. Hulbert in 1882. That strong document has been the bulwark of professional Base Ball, and with a broadened scope, through amendments to keep pace with the growth of the game, is the very foundation of organized Base Ball throughout America to-day.

An incident, somewhat embarrassing to me at the time, will serve to illustrate the indomitable energy of Mr. A. G. Mills in behalf of League interests. It occurred some time before he had become connected with the League in an official capacity, but bears directly upon the subject treated of.

As a former officer and player of the old Washington Olympics, Mr. Mills recognized the importance of some form of agreement whereby the interests of those who, under the new order of things, had capital invested might be protected against the whims, caprices and sometimes dishonesty of selfish, thoughtless and corrupt professional players and managers.

At the time I was the captain and pitcher of the Chicago Club, and believing that a document bearing my signature would have weight with the fraternity, Mr. Mills, who had been asked by President Hulbert to assist him, asked the privilege of attaching my signature to a circular letter he had written and which contained some essential matter bearing upon the importance of professional players standing by their contracts. It was a very urgent appeal to players, from one of their own number, and in the interests of the game, to remain absolutely loyal to the clubs with which they had signed, and under no circumstances whatever to play with any other organizations. To this document, of which several hundred copies were printed and sent by mail to managers and players, every one bore my name, though the real author was A. G. Mills.

Now, at this time in the history of Base Ball, it was not customary during the season's play to carry on trips around the circuit a lot of utility players, as at present. Ten or, at the most, eleven men constituted the limit. It was therefore of not infrequent occurrence, when players became ill or incapacitated through accident, to fill the team from the ranks of disengaged or surplus professionals in cities where visiting teams happened to be.

I remember that one day, our nine being scheduled to play at Boston, I found it necessary to go skirmishing for someone to take the place of a disabled man on our team, and met with a very sharp and unexpected rebuff.

"What?" said the player approached. "You ask me to play with your nine, when only yesterday I got a personal letter from you entreating me not to do the very thing you are now asking of me? I guess not. You can't catch me that easy."

And so it continued all season. Whenever I was in a particularly tight place, and seeking to fill the ranks of our crippled team, one of these circulars, written by Mills, but signed by me, would be thrust under my nose. Mr. Mills has told me that he issued five hundred of these, but it seems to me I saw more than that in my experiences during that season's play.

When I returned to Chicago from my barnstorming trips, I undertook to explain to Messrs. Hulbert and Mills some of the embarrassments occasioned by the literary bureau they were carrying on in Chicago under my name. However, I received but very little sympathy from either of the gentlemen; they seemed to regard it as rather a good joke. They knew, of course, that I was in sympathy with the objects they were seeking to promote, but they were certainly more deeply interested in their purpose than they were in my perplexities. Finally I said to them:

"It's all right, gentlemen. I am in this thing. I will continue to stand for the high moral precepts so beautifully expressed and of which you have made me the literary sponsor; but won't you do this much? Won't you please mail me an author's advance proof of the many letters you are sending out over my signature—not that I want to alter the magnificent phraseology in the slightest degree, but that when one of them is presented to me I may not appear so totally ignorant as now of the subjects of which I am supposed to be the author?"

I also suggested that it might be well to send a dictionary with each letter, as several of the players had complained to me that they could not understand some of the classical language emanating from my versatile pen, which college professors might successfully wrestle with, but which was somewhat ambiguous to the average ball player.

CHAPTER XVII.

H. D. McKNIGHT

CHAPTER XVII.

THE decade of the 80's began and continued an era of multiplied clubs and organizations. In April, 1881, three clubs from New York City, the New Yorks, Metropolitans and Quicksteps; the Athletics, of Philadelphia; the Atlantics, of Brooklyn; and Nationals, of Washington, several of them having been famous in former years, organized the Eastern Championship Association. Only three clubs finished the season. The Metropolitans made the best record, winning 32 and losing 13 games.

In the year 1882 William A. Hulbert, of Chicago, President of the National League, died of heart failure, at his home in Chicago.

In the same year Richard Higham was expelled on charges preferred by the Detroit Club, for collusion with pool-sellers.

In 1882 the Northwestern League, which later produced several major league players, was formed at Chicago. It comprised a circuit composed of the following cities: Peoria, Springfield and Quincy, Illinois; Bay City, East Saginaw and Grand Rapids, Michigan; Fort Wayne, Indiana, and Toledo, Ohio. Toledo won the pennant.

The Inter-State Association, another minor league, had its organization in 1882. Its clubs were from Brooklyn, Camden, Harrisburg, Pottsville, Reading, Trenton and Wilmington. Brooklyn won the championship.

The early years following the opening of the decade of the 80's witnessed a continuation of the struggle of the National League to maintain control of the game and preserve its integrity. Despite the fact that the League management had displayed an iron will as regards the eradication of old abuses; notwithstanding that, for the first time in the history of Base Ball, discipline had been strictly administered to refractory and dishonest players and to defaulting clubs; although protests against desirable innovations introduced by the League had failed to produce any effect in the way of causing their withdrawal, the backbone of opposition was not yet broken. There was slumbering discord among certain players. There was jealousy on the part of ambitious would-be magnates. There was the ever-present hostility of the gamblers, and there was open criticism of League methods by the class that is always " against the government."

In 1882 an organization was formed whose avowed purpose it was to rival the National League. This was the American Base Ball Association, and its leading spirits were H. D. McKnight, of Pittsburg, and Chris. Von der Ahe, of St. Louis. Mr. Von der Ahe was proprietor of a pleasure resort in the suburbs of his city, and he came to be interested in Base Ball from the fact that games constituted one among other attractions to his place.

The American Association made its appeal for public sympathy and support by proposing an admission fee of twenty-five cents to all games, instead of fifty cents, as charged by League clubs. It was claimed by promoters of the new association that League magnates were coining wealth through an unreasonable charge at the gates; that this exorbitant fee was prohibitive so far as the "poor laboring man" was concerned; that the League was making of Base Ball a rich man's game; that none but nabobs could see a game of professional ball any more. The effect of this competition was serious to the interests of the game in some ways. Unrestricted Sunday games in violation of law and the wide-open liquor traffic could not but be prejudicial. However, that "competition is the life of trade" seldom had a better exemplification, for business in both associations was immediately improved.

The defect in the argument in behalf of the institution of the new competitive organization was, that its premise was false. It was not true that League managers at the time of the formation of the American Association were making fortunes. On the contrary, many had been steady losers. But that was not all, nor was it the most serious difficulty. The old system of "revolving," based upon the natural antagonism of the rival organizations, neither of which at first recognized the rights, rules or existence of the other, was at once renewed, and under particularly trying conditions. A certain class of players, standing upon their alleged rights as American citizens to make the best possible bargain in their own interests, would go from one club to another, as prospects of a raise of salary presented themselves. And so distrust and general demoralization were present everywhere.

But the League management never faltered in its purpose. It kept its price of admission at fifty cents, though gate receipts at the beginning fell off. Did a player deserve discipline, he received it, though next day he joined a rival team. Was a club lax in its payment of fines or dues, it was promptly dropped from membership in the League. The liquor law was strictly enforced upon League grounds, and Sunday games were not permitted upon them.

The American Base Ball Association was organized with clubs in the following cities: Baltimore, Cincinnati, Louisville, Philadelphia, Pittsburg and St. Louis. Cincinnati won the championship.

The American Alliance, organized about the same time as a minor association of the American, had clubs at Brooklyn, Camden, Cincinnati, Harrisburg, Reading, Wilmington, Pottsville and Covington.

One year after the formation of the American Association, more trouble developed for the League in the organization of the Union Association, whose avowed mission it was to fight the reserve rule. This Association was born in 1883, at Pittsburg. Its first President was H. B. Bennett, of Washington. But at the following annual election Henry V. Lucas was elected to succeed Mr. Bennett. Mr. Lucas embarked in this enterprise on the declaration that the reserve rule was "an outrageous and unjustifiable chain on the freedom of players."

The cities embraced in the Union Association circuit

were Altoona, Boston, Baltimore, Chicago, Cincinnati, Philadelphia, St. Louis and Washington.

Mr. Lucas succeeded in securing promises and contracts from a number of prominent players; but most of them betrayed his confidence in one way or another. The season was a humiliating failure. Only the Washington Nationals, of all the clubs in the Union Association, made enough money to pay expenses. Frequent changes, caused by clubs dropping out, characterized the season and kept Mr. Lucas busy finding teams to fill their places. The Union Association finally disbanded in January, 1885, only two clubs being willing to enter a second contest. Mr. Lucas then retired, with his fortune dissipated and his combativeness destroyed. All players in the Union Association who had deserted the National League were expelled.

The following gentlemen are of record as having been prominent in the Union Association: W. Rilz, Altoona; I. W. Lowe and B. F. Matthews, Baltimore; Frank E. Winslow, George Wright and T. H. Murnane, Boston; A. H. Henderson and E. S. Hengle, Chicago; Justus Thorner, Cincinnati; Thomas J. Pratt, Philadelphia; Henry Lucas and Theodore Benoist, St. Louis; H. B. Bennett and M. B. Scanlon, Washington.

Most fortunate, indeed, was the National League that, when William A. Hulbert was suddenly removed by death from heart failure in 1882, one so eminently qualified as A. G. Mills was found to take his place. It needed just such a man to carry on the work of the League so ably begun. At the annual meeting of the League, held in

December of that year, Mr. Mills was elected President, and Mr. N. E. Young for the seventh time was chosen Secretary.

Mr. Mills was peculiarly equipped for the duties now put upon him, in that he was a player of marked capacity, before and during the Civil War, having been for years actively connected with the sport; a lawyer of splendid ability, as immediately demonstrated by the formulation of the National Agreement, a document that has stood the ravages of time and the wearing warfare of the courts; and an executive of sterling endowments in the way of administering affairs and managing men.

The National Agreement, made between the National League and the American Association, which latter body soon learned the necessity of some means of controlling the game, with amendments up to 1889, was in the following words:

THE NATIONAL AGREEMENT OF PROFESSIONAL BASE BALL CLUBS.

THIS AGREEMENT, Made between the Association known and designated as the National League of Base Ball Clubs, of the one part, and the Association known and designated as the American Association of Base Ball Clubs, of the other part, witnesseth, that

I. This document shall be entitled The National Agreement, and shall supersede and be a substitute for all other Agreements, similarly or otherwise designated, heretofore existing between the parties hereto.

II. (a) No contract shall be made for the service of any player by any club member of either party hereto for a longer period than seven months, beginning April 1st, and terminating October 31st, and no such contract for services to be rendered after the expiration of the current year shall be made prior to the 20th day of October of such year, nor shall any player, without the consent of the Club to which he is under contract, enter into any negotiation or contract with any Club, Club agent or individual for services to be rendered in an ensuing year prior to the said 20th of October. Upon written proofs of a violation of this section the Board of Arbitration shall disqualify such player for and during said ensuing year, and shall inflict a fine of five hundred dollars, payable forthwith into the treasury of the Board, upon the Club in whose interests such negotiations or contract was entered into.

(b) Every regular contract shall be registered and approved by the Secretary of the Association of which the contracting Club is a member, who shall forthwith notify the Secretary of the other Association party hereto, and the other Club members of his Association.

III. When a player under contract with or reservation by any Club member of either Association party hereto is expelled, black-listed, suspended or rendered ineligible in accordance with its rules, notice of such disqualification shall be served upon the Secretary of the Board of Arbitration by the Secretary of the Association from whose Club such player shall have been thus disqualified, and the Secretary of the Board shall forthwith serve notice of such disqualification upon the Secretary of the other Association party hereto. When a player becomes ineligible under the provisions of this Agreement, the Secretary of the Board of Arbitration shall notify the Secretaries of the Association parties hereto of such disqualification, and from the receipt of such notice, all Club members of the parties hereto shall be debarred from employing or playing with, or against, such disqualified player, until the period of disqualification shall have terminated, or the disqualification be revoked by the Association from which such player was disqualified, or by the Board of Arbitration, and due notice of such revocation served upon the Secretary of the other Association, and by him upon his respective Clubs.

IV. Upon the tenth day of October in each year the Secretary of each Association shall transmit to the Secretary of the other Association a reserve list of players, not exceeding fourteen in number, then under contract with each of its several Club members, and of such players reserved in any prior reserve list, who have refused to contract with said Club members, and of all other ineligible players, and such players, together with all others thereafter to be regularly contracted with by such Club members, are and shall be ineligible to contract with any other Club member of either Association party hereto, except as hereinafter prescribed.

V. Upon the release of a player from contract or reservation with any Club member of either Association party hereto, the services of such player shall at once be subject to the acceptance of the other Clubs of such Association, expressed in writing or by telegraph, to the Secretary thereof, for a period of ten days after notice of said release, and thereafter, if said services be not so accepted, said player may negotiate and contract with any other Club. The Secre-

A. G. MILLS

tary of such Association shall send notice to the Secretary of the other Association of said player's release on the date thereof, and of said acceptance of his services at or before the expiration of the ten days aforesaid. Provided that the disbandment of a Club or its expulsion from membership in either Association party hereto shall operate as a release of all its players from contract and reservation, but the services of such players shall at once be subject to the acceptance of the other Ciubs of such Association as hereinbefore provided.

VI. Each Club member of either Association party hereto shall have exclusive control of its own territory, and no Club shall be entitled to membership in either Association party hereto from any city or town in which a Club member of either Association party hereto is located. Provided, that nothing contained herein shall prohibit any Club member of either Association party hereto from resigning its membership in such Association during the month of November in any year, and being admitted to membership in the other Association with all rights and privileges conferred by this Agreement.

VII. No game shall be played between any Club member of either Association party hereto, or any of its players under contract or reservation with any other Club or ",team " while presenting in its nine any ineligible player. A violation of this section shall subject each offender to fine or expulsion in the discretion of the Board of Arbitration.

VIII. Each Association party hereto shall have the right to make and enforce all rules and regulations pertaining to the control, discipline and compensation of all players under contract with and reservation by its Club members, provided such rules and regulations shall in no way conflict with the provisions of this Agreement.

IX. A Board of Arbitration, consisting of three duly accredited representatives from each of the Associations parties hereto, shall convene annually at a place mutually to be arranged, and shall organize by the election of a chairman, secretary and such other officers and committees as to them shall seem meet and proper. They may make, and from time to time revoke, alter and repeal all necessary rules and regulations not inconsistent with this Agreement, for their meetings, procedure and the general transaction of their business. Their membership on said Board shall be determinable at the pleasure of their respective appointing Associations upon duly certified notice thereof. A quorum shall consist of at least two representatives from each Association, and all questions shall be voted upon separately by the respective delegations, and no such changes or additions shall be made unless concurred in by a majority of the delegates of each Association.

X. In addition to all matters that may be specially referred to them by both of the Associations parties hereto, the said Board shall have sole, exclusive and final jurisdiction of all disputes and complaints arising under and all interpretations of this Agreement. They shall also, in the interests of harmony and peace, arbitrate upon and decide all differences and disputes arising between the Associations parties hereto and between a Club member of one and a Club member of the other Association party hereto. Provided that nothing in this agreement shall be construed as giving authority to said Board to alter, amend or modify any section or part of section of the Constitution of either Association party hereto.

Ex-President A. G. Mills, of the Washington Olympics, in an article on the subject of the national game, said:

"When we behold what a revolution Base Ball has wrought in the habits and tastes of the American people we may well denominate its advancement a 'good work.' But a generation ago that large body of our people whose lives were not spent in the forest or on the farm was marked as a sedentary race, with healthful recreation denied to all but a favored few. Now, not the least of our claims to distinction among the peoples of the world is our general love of and devotion to healthful outdoor sports and recreations. The deterioration of the race has ended, and the rising generation is better equipped for the duties, the conflicts and the pleasures of life than were their fathers and mothers. And can it be doubted what has been the most potent factor in achieving this beneficent revolution? We have seen Base Ball steadily growing from its notable beginning before the war, accompanying our soldiers in the field, spreading like wildfire through the West, until now it is known and loved and practiced in every city and town within the borders of the United States. Base Ball is essentially the people's game, in that it is equally accessible to the sons of the rich and poor, and in point of exhilarating exercise to the player and healthy enjoyment to the spectator— whether played on the village common or the splendidly appointed grounds of the modern professional club—it satisfies and typifies the American idea of a manly, honest, entertaining recreation."

CHAPTER XVIII.

THE SPHINX SEES BASE BALL

CHAPTER XVIII.

1888–89

AN EVENT of considerable importance in its influence upon the American national game was the world's tour of Professional National League Base Ball Players in the winter of 1888-89. Base Ball had been advancing in popularity with such rapid strides in our own land during preceding years, that I felt the time had come when this great pastime should be introduced wherever upon the globe conditions were favorable to our peculiar form of outdoor sport. The first Base Ball tour abroad, it will be remembered, had been to the British Isles in 1874. It was quite natural, therefore, that, in mapping out this new enterprise, attention should be diverted to the opposite direction. It was known that many Base Ball lovers lived in the Hawaiian Islands, and that the British colonists of the South Pacific Isles, New Zealand and Australia, were nearly all devotees of field sports, for they had a racial love for outdoor games and enjoyed a climate that made their playing possible nearly the entire year. To the Antipodes, then, the tour was first proposed, and Mr. Leigh S. Lynch, who had wide experience as a manager of dramatic enterprises, was sent to Australia, via Honolulu and New Zealand, with instructions. His duty was to make arrangements, secure accommodations, schedule exhibitions, and prepare the public for the unusual visitation.

The securing of teams for this voyage in the interests of Base Ball missionary effort was not easy. It was proposed to take the players of the Chicago team, of which club I was then President, with one or two additions, as a whole, and no difficulty was experienced in interesting them; but the forming of an opposing nine, to be selected from the best players in other National League organizations, was beset with many obstacles. To openly ask for volunteers was out of the question, because it would be certain to result in a deluge of applications from undesirable players in the fraternity. To choose those best equipped to play the game meant the asking of many who could not go. It was absolutely essential that all who did go should be men of clean habits and attractive personality, men who would reflect credit upon the country and the game. Finally, when the ranks had been filled, it was found that several, on one pretext or another, were determined to withdraw, and it became necessary to fill their places hurriedly. Happily, however, capable men were available, and the corps lost nothing in playing capacity by reason of the action of those who dropped out.

The teams as completed for the voyage were composed of the following players:

Chicagos—Mark Baldwin and J. K. Tener (now Governor of Pennsylvania), pitchers; Tom Daly, catcher; A. C. Anson, first base and captain; N. F. Pfeffer, second base; Thomas Burns, third base; E. N. Williamson, short-stop; M. Sullivan, left field; J. Ryan, center field; Robert Pettit, right field.

All-Americas—John Healy, Indianapolis, and E. W. Crane, New York, pitchers; J. C. Earl, Cincinnati, catcher; G. A. Wood, Philadelphia, first base; F. H. Carroll, Pittsburgh, second base; H. Manning, Kansas City, third base; John M. Ward, New York, shortstop and captain; Jas. Fogarty, Philadelphia, left field; Ed. Hanlon, Pittsburgh, center field; Tom Brown, Boston, right field.

Other members of the party were: My mother, Mrs. Harriet I. Spalding; Mrs. Anson, Mrs. Williamson, Mrs. Lynch, Harry Clay Palmer, of the *New York Herald;* Newton Macmillan, of the New York *Sun,* and Mr. Good-friend, of the Chicago *Inter-Ocean.* George Wright and W. Irving Snyder also accompanied the party, Wright officiating as umpire at most games played.

Our special train, which consisted of two Pullman sleepers and a dining car, left Chicago for San Francisco on the 20th of October, 1888, following the close of the Base Ball season of that year. En route across the continent the teams played exhibition games at St. Paul, Minneapolis, Cedar Rapids, Des Moines, Omaha, Hastings, Denver, Colorado Springs and Salt Lake City. On the Pacific Coast, games were played at Los Angeles and San Francisco. Everywhere on this land journey the Base Ball Missionaries received splendid ovations.

On Sunday, the 18th of November, we sailed out through the Golden Gate, on the steamer "Alameda," bound for Honolulu, our first port of call. After a full

CHICAGO AND ALL-AMERICA WORLD TOUR TEAMS

Burns   Daley   Pettit   Sullivan   Baldwin   Tener   Healy   Carroll   Wood   Brown   Manning
       Williamson   Pfeffer   Anson   A. G. Spalding   Ward   Fogarty   Simpson
Mascot   George Wright   Ed. Hanlon   Earl

week on the Pacific, and a little more, with many pleasant experiences and a few of the other kind, the ball-tossing tourists reached Honolulu on Sunday morning, November 25th. Our time schedule, as given by the steamship company, had fixed the date for arrival at Honolulu for Saturday morning, the 24th, but the boat had failed to make time, and we found ourselves a day behind, which led to a serious complication.

A game of Base Ball between the great American teams had been announced for Saturday. It was now Sunday. Honolulu had the "lid on." What was to be done?

The American game had at that time, nearly a quarter of a century ago, taken a strong hold of the popular heart at Honolulu. Here was the home of Alexander J. Cartwright, founder of the first Base Ball club ever organized—Father of the famed Knickerbockers. Many Americans were there who had played the game at home, and the natives also were developing some skill at the pastime. The widely-heralded news of our coming, accompanied by the assurance that the game would be presented by its most celebrated and proficient exponents, had created interest among lovers of the sport and had aroused much curiosity on the part of the general public. Everybody wanted to witness the game; but, alas, it was Sunday. We were to leave late that evening; therefore it was Sunday— or never. Petitions came flooding in upon me for a Sunday game. I at once made an investigation, which satisfied me that the missionaries who were looking after the moral welfare of the natives had closed the doors against

Sunday entertainments good and tight. There was no doubt about it; Sunday ball was as "taboo" in Honolulu as had been a whole lot of things when the heathens were in full control of their island. I was importuned, almost with tears, to ignore the law. I was assured that the authorities were not likely to interfere in the face of such a popular clamor. A purse of $1,000 had been raised as a bonus for the game. That money was greatly needed just then, for we had embarked on an enterprise which would involve the expenditure of much cash.

We had counted on some gate receipts at Honolulu; but here was the law forbidding Sunday ball. There was only one thing to do. We obeyed the letter and spirit of the law, called the game off, and left a lot of disgruntled Americans and disappointed Kanakas, to say nothing of the much-coveted shekels.

I may as well take occasion here to define my views on the subject of Sunday ball playing. I am not, nor have I ever been, opposed to Sunday ball so far as the game itself is concerned. I believe in many of the arguments advanced in favor of the playing of League games on that day. I know it is the one day in the week when a great many of those who care for the game can have leisure, without too great loss, to witness the sport. I know it is a better way for the average American to pass Sunday afternoon than many others resorted to by the average American for entertainment on that day. I know that boys and men, by hundreds and thousands, who regularly patronize Sunday ball would be engaged in practices much more inimical to their wellbeing if no games were played on Sunday. I know the need of the money that is received for Sunday games by the management, especially of minor league clubs, whose gate receipts on weekdays are inadequate to meet expenses. All this I know, and yet I also know that it is of paramount importance that the laws of every city and state and country should be respected and upheld; that the youth of every community should be educated to honor and obey the laws. And so, whenever this problem presents itself for my decision, I first ask the question, "Is Sunday ball playing legal?" If it is, I say "Play Ball." If not, my answer is the same as that given to the petitioners at Honolulu. This rule obtained throughout our world tour. Wherever and whenever the law forbade, we played no games. Wherever and whenever the law allowed, we played games on Sunday.

Notwithstanding the mutual disappointment of visitors and visited at Honolulu as regards the failure to pull off a game of Base Ball, there was no law forbidding King Kalakaua, then on the Hawaiian throne, to entertain our party, which he certainly did in royal manner.

Sailing from Honolulu on Monday morning, November 26th, we were on the Pacific for over two weeks before reaching Auckland, New Zealand, on the 10th of December. Here a game was played to the great delectation of the New Zealanders, very few of whom had ever seen it, though many were proficient at cricket.

Leaving Auckland, we sailed direct for Sydney, Australia, where we arrived December 14th. We were now in "topsy-turvy" land for sure. It was the middle of December, and right in the midst of summer's heat, with

Christmas only ten days off and the fields ripe with the golden glow of harvest. We played at Sydney, Melbourne, Adelaide and Ballarat, being received everywhere with demonstrations of welcome, and much interest in the game was elicited at all points in the great island continent.

Originally our tour had been planned to end in Australia, retracing via Honolulu, as we had sailed; but before leaving the Pacific Coast I had been studying the situation and found that the distance from Australia around the world to New York was about the same as via San Francisco. During the voyage I had discussed the matter with the players, and as they were unanimously and enthusiastically in favor of the globe trip, we decided to return home that way.

Therefore, on the morning of January 8th, 1889, we left Melbourne homeward bound via Suez Canal, taking the steamer "Salier." Sixteen days later we arrived at the Island of Ceylon, and, upon landing at Colombo, we startled the natives of that far-off island of the seas by an exhibition of American ball playing, on January 26th, 1889.

Following this came the "flight into Egypt," with a game on the desert's sands in front of the Great Pyramids, and near enough to use one for a backstop. Afterwards the whole company was photographed *en groupe* on the Egyptian Sphinx, to the horror of the native worshippers of Cheops and the dead Pharaohs.

On the 19th of February, having reached the Bay of Naples, we went ashore, and under the shadow of Vesuvius showed the Italians how to play the great American game.

Rome was naturally our next point to visit, and there we played in the Villa Borghese, formerly the beautiful home of an Italian prince. The visit to Rome was one of the most enjoyable of the entire tour, so much was there to see of historic interest. King Humbert of Italy honored our game by his presence, and a number of American students at the great Roman College of the Catholic Church were in attendance. Following the visit to Rome, we played a game at Florence, and then departed for France.

One of the events of the European trip was the game played at Paris, within the shadow of the great Eiffel Tower, then under process of construction for the Exposition soon to occur. The American colony was out in full force at this game; but the Parisians did not seem to catch on to any appreciable extent, though many were present.

The reception of our company in England was one of the great triumphs of the world tour. This function took place at the club house of the Surrey County Cricket Club. It was the occasion of the first public welcome of the tourists to Great Britain, and there were present the Duke of Beaufort, the Duke of Buccleugh, the Earls of Sandsborough, Coventry, Sheffield and Chesborough, together with Lords Littleton, Oxenbridge and Hawke, beside Sir Reginald Hanson, Attorney General Sir W. C. Webster, with the Lord Mayor of London, the American Consul and others of note.

It is worthy of note that the English hosts of this

AMERICAN BASE BALL PARTY

and other occasions were astonished to see the professional American ball players enter into the spirit of these
receptions, not only attired in full evening dress, but with
a degree of familiarity with social requirements that was
quite foreign to professional cricketers.

The inaugural game in London was played at Ken-
nington Oval grounds, and though the day was a typical
London day in March, cold, wet and foggy, making ball
playing difficult and its enjoyment almost impossible, there
was a large crowd present to see the Americans. Soon
after the contest opened the Prince of Wales (afterwards
King Edward) and his brother-in-law, Prince Christian,
came upon the field. The game was suspended while the
American ball players gave three cheers and a tiger for
the Prince, which demonstration was heartily seconded
by the multitude, the Prince bowing his acknowledgments.

The party was escorted to the royal box, and, when
the game was resumed, at the request of one of the gentle-
men-in-waiting I took my place between the brother
princes to explain to them the points of the game, with
which, of course, they were not familiar. They asked me
numerous questions bearing upon the various plays as the
sport proceeded. The Prince of Wales became particularly animated in his appreciation of the activity of the
pastime.

"What's that for?" "Why is he doing that?" and
similar queries, came frequently from his lips.

Now it happened that day that the Prince, who was
short of stature, had a carbuncle or boil, or some sort of
swelling on his neck, making it very difficult for him to

turn his head. Standing at his side, I found it extremely awkward, from my height of six feet two, to keep him advised without bending low and talking in his ear. Under these circumstances, I did the perfectly natural thing for an American sovereign to do—just what I would have done had President Taft been witness of the game and needed instruction—which, of course, he would not. Stepping to one side, where I had observed an empty chair, I brought it over, placed it between their Royal Highnesses, sat down and resumed my comments in answer to their interrogatories.

As the game progressed, the scions of the great House of Guelph became more and more impressed, so that when Anson made one of his long hits and started for third, the Prince, with an ejaculation inspired by intense interest, slapped me on the leg and exclaimed, "That was a hard clip!" or something to that effect. And when Williamson, a moment later, on a swift grounder, right past first baseman, but far enough out so that Wood couldn't get it, reached his base by a pretty slide, I felt perfectly justified in returning the familiarity, and, tapping the late King of England on the shoulder, asked him, "What do you think of that?"

Now there have been a good many printed versions of this story. It may be, as claimed by some who were present, that all Britain held its breath while I took a seat in the presence of Royalty. I distinctly remember that Hon. Newton Crane, the American Consul, laughed immoderately that evening, as he and I drove together from the grounds, at what he termed my breach of "court etiquette." However, as I recall the incident after this lapse of years, I see nothing in it to cause me to blush. If I violated the code of court etiquette, I must plead that I was not at court, but at an American ball game. If I sat in the presence of Royalty, it is certain that Royalty sat in mine. If I tapped the future King of Great Britain on the shoulder, it was nothing more offensive than a game of tag, for he had first slapped me on the leg. If British Royalty honored us by its presence, which I am willing to concede, we repaid it by a splendid exhibition of our National Game. No, I am not able to see wherein honors were not quite even.

It was at this game that the Prince of Wales wrote his oft incorrectly quoted critique on the game.

The *New York Herald*—or rather, the London edition of that paper—had presented each spectator upon entering the grounds with a card, containing several questions calculated to draw out a consensus of English opinion on the game of Base Ball. The reporter of this paper explained to the Prince in my presence the object of these cards and expressed the wish that the Prince would give his opinion. The reporter, pencil in hand, stood ready to jot down the replies of the Prince when the latter said:

"Give me a card."

He then hurriedly wrote something and handed the card over to me that I might see how he had answered the questions. As I recall them from memory, his words were briefly as follows:

"I consider Base Ball an excellent game; but Cricket a better one."

Dignified courtliness, amiable courtesy, tactfulness and honest conviction are all forcefully presented in the hastily penned sentence of the Prince. They well illustrate the qualities that made King Edward famous as one of the world's great diplomats.

"The King is dead; long live the King."

It is estimated that at least 60,000 people witnessed the games of Base Ball played at this time in the British Isles at London, Bristol, Birmingham, Sheffield, Bradford, Glasgow, Manchester, Liverpool, Belfast and Dublin.

The welcome given our party on the return home by devotees of the game at New York was one of the great events of the remarkable tour. It was held at Delmonico's. A. G. Mills, President of the National League, presided. At his right sat A. G. Spalding, Chauncey Depew, Daniel Dougherty, Henry E. Howland, W. H. McElvey, and U. S. Consul W. Griffen. On his left were Mayor Chapin, of Brooklyn—the Mayor of New York was unable to be present; Mayor Cleveland, of Jersey City, Mark Twain, Rev. Joseph Twitchell, and officers of the New York and Manhattan Clubs. Among the guests were also members of the alumni of Harvard, Yale and Princeton Universities. Theodore Roosevelt, afterward President, was present at this banquet. As may readily be understood, the after-dinner speeches, from such a galaxy of talent, were replete with brilliant and witty thoughts.

Such, briefly, is the story of the world's tour of 1888-89. In all respects it was a splendid success. In a financial way, it cost in round figures the sum of $50,000, and the receipts were ample to pay all expenses. It presented exhibitions of the American National Game in foreign lands belting the globe. It created interest in the game in countries where it had never been seen before, and where from that day to this the sport has been growing in popular favor. It gave to the masses everywhere an opportunity to witness a pastime peculiarly American, and it showed to all the world that one may be at the same time a professional ball player and a gentleman.

Mike Kelly, in reminiscent mood, one day near the close of his great career gave out this interview to the New York *Sun:*

" The lightest I ever played ball was 157 pounds with my uniform on. I had India rubber in my shoes then. I was like I was on springs, and I was playing with the best ball team ever put together—the Chicagos of 1882. I bar no team in the world when I say that. I know about the New York Giants, the Detroits and the Big Four, the 1886 St. Louis Browns and all of them, but they were never in it with the old 1882 gang that pulled down the pennant for Chicago. Then was when you saw ball playing, away up in the thirty-second degree. That was the crowd that showed the way to all the others. They towered over all ball teams like Salvator's record dwarfs all the other race horses. Where can you get a team with so many big men on its pay roll? There were seven of us six feet high, Anson, Goldsmith, Dalrymple, Gore, Williamson, Flint and myself being in that neighborhood. Larry Corcoran and Tommy Burns were the only small men on the team. Fred Pfeffer was then the greatest second baseman of them all. All you had to do was to throw anywhere near the bag, and he would get it—high, wide or on the ground. What a man he was to make a return throw; why, he could lay on his stomach and throw 100 yards then. Those old sports didn't know much about hitting the ball either; no, I guess they didn't. Only four of us had led the League in batting—Anson, Gore, Dalrymple and myself. We always wore the best uniforms that money could get, Spalding saw to that. We had big wide trousers, tight-fitting jerseys, with the arms cut out clear to the shoulder, and every man had on a different cap. We wore silk stockings. When we marched on a field with our big six-footers out in front it used to be a case of ' eat 'em up, Jake.' We had most of 'em whipped before we threw a ball. They were scared to death."

CHICAGO WHITE STOCKINGS

Geo. Gore, l.f. Frank Flint, c. A. C. Anson, 1b. James McCormick, p. M. J. Kelly, r.f. Fred Pfeffer, 2 b.
Ed. Williamson, s.s. Abner Dalrymple, l.f. Thos. Burns, 3b. John G. Clarkson, p. Wm. Sunday, sub.

CHAPTER XIX.

JOHN M. WARD

CHAPTER XIX.

FIRST NOTABLE REVOLT OF PROFESSIONAL BASE BALL
PLAYERS—ORGANIZATION OF THE PLAYERS' LEAGUE—
WHY SUCH AN ORGANIZATION COULD NOT SUCCEED.

1889-90

IN TREATING of the sensational episode that ushered in the last decade of the 19th century I would not be misunderstood. I accord to most of the players who at that time suddenly abandoned the National League the utmost sincerity of motive. They argued that the people who patronized Base Ball paid to see *them* play. They were the star performers, the actual "producers" of the entertainment. They held, and truly, that no one would give up a farthing to the man at the box-office; nobody would part with a ticket at the turnstile; none would contribute a nickel at the grandstand, so far as the men presiding at those posts were concerned; and as for the owners of clubs, what did the public care for them?

The inference drawn by the players, and sought to be conveyed by them, was that they ought to manage the game themselves, have all the honor of its success, and reap a much larger portion of the proceeds of their skillful services. They claimed, moreover, that under the Reserve Rule and National Agreement they were deprived of their just rights as American citizens.

I did not believe then, nor do I now believe, that their contentions were based upon safe or sane business theory.

As one who has been connected with both ends of the Base Ball problem—with reasonable success I may fairly claim—it has ever been my fixed belief that, like every other form of business enterprise, Base Ball depends for results upon two interdependent divisions, the one to have absolute control and direction of the system, and the other to engage—always under the executive branch—in the actual work of production. The theory is as true in the production of the game of Base Ball as in the making of base balls or bats.

As a surface proposition, it was true, of course, that nobody would give up money to the " office force " of Base Ball for its services alone. But it was equally true that *the game* had to give up something to the men in these positions; for the man in the box-office, the man at the turnstile and the man at the grandstand are just as essential to the game's prosperity and perpetuity as is he in the pitcher's box or he on first base. And especially is the man absolutely essential who has a bank account to meet pay-rolls, ground rents and the multiplied expenditures on account of the game, which those not called upon to face them are too prone to overlook.

The National Brotherhood of Base Ball Players had been originally organized by John M. Ward in 1885. Its declared purpose, at the beginning of its career, was simply fraternal, and had to do rather with the relations between players, as such, than with those between players and the clubs to which they belonged. The effect of this organization, however, was to breed dissatisfaction; for its meetings afforded most excellent opportunities for the men to rehearse to one another their real or fancied grievances, and to plan and plot measures to secure relief.

After the world's tour, in 1888-9, when the prosperous season of '88 had ended, the Brotherhood of Players, finding fresh cause for complaint in the classification rule adopted by the League in 1888, and more reason for a hopeful outcome of their venture in the large attendance at games during the season just closed, issued a manifesto to the public.

It ought to be stated here that, previous to this time and in deference to protests against the Reserve Rule, the League had asked for a Committee from the Brotherhood to consider the subject and submit a rule to take the place of the obnoxious one. The Committee, consisting of Ward, Hanlon and Brouthers, after due deliberation, confessed, in a report made to the League, their inability to make any improvement. Indeed, in a published interview, in 1887, Mr. Ward had said upon this very subject:

"In order to get men to invest capital in Base Ball, it is necessary to have a reserve rule. Some say that this could be modified, but I am not of that opinion. How could it be modified? Say, for instance, that we began this season by reserving men for only two, three, four, or even five years. At the expiration of that period players would be free to go where they pleased, and capitalists who invested, say $75,000 or $100,000, would have nothing but ground and grandstand. Then again, players have agreed that this could be overcome by making the length of reservation vary. It could not, and would cause no end of dissatisfaction. It would be unfair to reserve one man for two years and another for five. The reserve rule, on the whole, is a bad one; but it cannot be rectified save by injuring the interests of the men who invest their money, and that is not the object of the Brotherhood."

But the manifesto issued Nov. 4th, 1889, declared:

TO THE PUBLIC.

At last the Brotherhood of Base Ball Players feels at liberty to make known its intentions and defend itself against the aspersions and misrepresentations which for weeks it has been forced to suffer in silence. It is no longer a secret that the players of the League have determined to play next season under different management, but for reasons which will, we think, be understood, it was deemed advisable to make no announcement of this intention until the close of the present season; but now that the struggles for the various pennants are over, and the terms of our contracts expired, there is no longer reason for withholding it.

In taking this step we feel that we owe it to the public and to ourselves to explain briefly some of the reasons by which we have been moved. There was a time when the League stood for integrity and fair dealing. To-day it stands for dollars and cents. Once it looked to the elevation of the game and an honest exhibition of the sport; to-day its eyes are upon the turnstile. Men have come into the business for no other motive than to exploit it for every dollar in sight. Measures originally intended for the good of the game have been perverted into instruments for wrong. The reserve rule and the provisions of the National Agreement gave the managers unlimited power, and they have not hesitated to use this in the most arbitrary and mercenary way.

Players have been bought, sold and exchanged as though they were sheep instead of American citizens. " Reservation" became for them another name for property right in the player. By a combination among themselves, stronger than the strongest trust, they were able to enforce the most arbitrary measures, and the player had either to submit or get out of the profession in which he had spent years in attaining a proficiency. Even the disbandment and retirement of a club did not free the players from the Octopus clutch, for they were then peddled around to the highest bidder.

That the player sometimes profited by the sale has nothing to do with the case, but only proves the injustice of his previous restraint. Two years ago, we met the League and attempted to remedy some of these evils, but through what has been politely termed " League diplomacy" we completely failed. Unwilling longer to submit to such treatment, we made a strong effort last spring to reach an understanding with the League. To our application for a hearing, they replied that " the matter was not of sufficient importance to warrant a meeting," and suggested that it be put off until fall. Our committee replied that the players felt that the League had broken faith with them; that while the results might be of but little importance to the managers, they were of great importance to the players; that if the League would not concede what was fair, we would adopt other means to protect ourselves; that if postponed until fall we would be separated, and at the mercy of the League; and that, as the only course left us required time and labor to develop, we must therefore insist upon an immediate conference.

Then, upon their final refusal to meet us we began organizing for ourselves, and are in shape to go ahead next year under new management and new auspices. We believe that it is possible to conduct our national game upon lines which will not infringe upon individual and natural rights. We ask to be judged solely by our work, and believing that the game can be played more fairly and its business conducted more intelligently under a plan which excludes everything arbitrary and un-American, we look forward with confidence to the support of the public and the future of the national game.

THE NATIONAL BROTHERHOOD OF BALL PLAYERS.

The revolutionary manifesto promulgated by the National Brotherhood of Base Ball Players, under date of November 4th, 1889, was answered by the National League, under date of November 21st, 1889, as follows:

TO THE PUBLIC.

The National League of Base Ball Clubs has no apology to make for its existence, or for its untarnished record of fourteen years.

It stands to-day, as it has stood during that period, sponsor for the honesty and integrity of Base Ball.

It is to this organization that the player of to-day owes the dignity of his profession and the munificent salary he is guaranteed while playing in its ranks.

The good name of this League has been assailed, its motives impugned and its integrity questioned by some of the very men whom it has most benefited.

The League therefore asks the public to inspect its record and compare the following statement of facts with the selfish and malicious accusations of its assailants:

The National League was organized in 1876 as a necessity, to rescue the game from its slough of corruption and disgrace, and take it from the hands of the ball players who had controlled and dominated the "National Association of Professional Base Ball Players."

No effort was made by the old Association to control its members, and the result was that contract-breaking, dissipation and dishonesty had undermined the game to such an extent that it seemed an almost hopeless task to attempt its rescue.

The League, upon its organization, abolished pool-selling and

EDWARD HANLON

open betting on its grounds, prohibited Sunday games and prohibited the sale of liquors. A better class of people were invited to attend the exhibitions, and a more systematic way of conducting the game was introduced. But the old customs and abuses were not to be crowded out without a struggle. At the end of the season of 1876, two of the strongest clubs, the Mutuals, of New York, and the Athletics, of Philadelphia, were arraigned before the League for violating their scheduled engagements. This was the first crisis the League was called upon to meet, and the world knows how promptly and vigorously it faced the issue by expelling those two prominent clubs, representing, as they did, its most populous and best-paying cities. The following season, 1877, was a disastrous one financially, and ended with but five clubs in the League, in one of which, Louisville, were players publicly accused of dishonesty. The League promptly investigated these charges, and when the four players of that club—Devlin, Hall, Craver and Nichols—were proven guilty of selling games, they were promptly expelled and have never been reinstated. These two steps, boldly taken, when the League was struggling for existence, settled the question as to a club's obligations to the League, and forever banished dishonesty from the ranks, stigmatizing the latter as an unpardonable crime.

The struggle for existence for the next three or four years was desperate, and at each annual meeting there occurred vacancies difficult to fill, because of the almost certain financial disasters threatening clubs in the smaller cities.

Finally, as a check upon competition, the weaker clubs in the League demanded the privilege of reserving five players who would form the nucleus of a team for the ensuing season. This was the origin of the " reserve rule " and from its adoption may be dated the development of better financial results. The system of reserve having proven beneficial, both to clubs and players, the reserve list was increased to eleven, and then to fourteen, or an entire team. Under this rule the game has steadily grown in favor, the salaries of players have been more than trebled, and a higher degree of skill has been obtained.

Out of, and as an incident to, " reservation," arose releases for pecuniary considerations. The right of reservation being conceded, the club's claim on the player's continuous services must be of some value. But, except in cases of disbanding or retiring clubs, that right has never been transferred without the player's coöperation and consent, usually at his request, and for his own pecuniary emolument.

In the exceptional case of the disbandment or retiring of a League club, the involuntary transfer of a player to a new club was the subject of complaint by a committee of the Brotherhood, in November, 1887. But, after several hours' conference with the League Committee, the former were obliged to admit that such involuntary transfer was essential to the welfare, if not the existence, of the

League, and, while it might work apparent hardships to one or two individuals, its abolition would imperil the continuance of full eight club memberships and the employment of perhaps thirty fellow players. The Brotherhood Committee, therefore, wrote into the contract they had formulated that 15th paragraph, by which each signing player expressly concedes such involuntary transfer of the right of reservation to his services from his club—if it should disband or lose its League membership—to "any other Club or Association," provided his current salary be not reduced.

And the necessity for such power of preserving the circuit of a League, by approximately equalizing its playing strength, is recognized by the new League, which the seceding players have temporarily organized; for they give this "extraordinary power" of transferring players, with or without consent, and with or without club disbandment, to a central tribunal of sixteen, whose fiat is final.

In view of these facts and concessions, the use of such terms as "bondage," "slavery," "sold like sheep," etc., becomes meaningless and absurd.

At the annual meeting of the League in November, 1887, the Brotherhood asked and received recognition upon the statement of its representatives that it was organized for benevolent purposes and desired to go hand in hand with the League, in perpetuating the game, increasing its popularity and elevating the moral standard of its players. They disavowed any intention or desire to interfere with the business affairs of the League, the salaries of players or the "reserve rule," simply asking that the contract be so revised that it, in itself, would indicate every relation between a club and its individual players.

This "Brotherhood Contract," then accepted and adopted, has never been violated by the League, either in letter or spirit, and we challenge proof in contradiction of this declaration.

To correct a misapprehension in the public mind as to the alleged "enormous profits" divided among stockholders of League clubs, it may be interesting to know that during the past five—and only prosperous—years, there have been paid in cash dividends to stockholders in the eight League clubs less than $150,000, and during the same time League players have received in salaries over $1,500,000. The balance of the profits of the few successful clubs, together with the original capital and subsequent assessments of stockholders, is represented entirely in grounds and improvements for the permanent good of the game, costing about $600,000.

The refusal of the Brotherhood Committee to meet the League in conference at the close of the season proves incontestably that the imperative demand for a conference in mid-summer, to redress grievances that have never yet materialized, was a mere pretext for secession.

They knew there was no urgency for the consideration of their claims, and knowing that the League could not, without sacrifice of time, money and other conflicting interests, convene its clubs in mid-summer, and anticipating and desiring a refusal, to cover the conspiracy, which it now appears was then hatching, they started the organization of a rival association while receiving most liberal salaries from their employers. Under false promises to their fellow players that they would only secede in the event of the League refusing them justice, they secured the signatures of the latter to a secret pledge or oath to desert their clubs at the bidding of their disaffected leaders. Upon the publication of their plot, September 7, 1889, they and their abettors denied, day after day, that there was any foundation for the story, and repeatedly plighted their words that the League should have a chance to redress their alleged grievances before they would order a " strike."

How false their promises and pledges, how evasive, contradictory and mendacious have been their every act and deed, from first to last, we leave to the readers of the daily and weekly press for verification.

An edifice built on falsehood has no moral foundation, and must perish of its own weight. Its official claims to public support are glittering generalities, that lack detail, color and truth, and the National League, while notifying its recalcitrant players that it will aid its clubs in the enforcement of their contractual rights to the services of those players for the season of 1890, hereby proclaims to the public that the National Game, which in 1876 it rescued from destruction threatened by the dishonesty and dissipation of players, and which, by stringent rules and ironclad contracts, it developed, elevated and perpetuated into the most glorious and honorable sport on the green earth, will still, under its auspices, progress onward and upward, despite the efforts of certain overpaid players to again control it for their own aggrandizement, but to its ultimate dishonor and disintegration.

By order of the National League of Base Ball Clubs.

> A. G. SPALDING,
> JOHN B. DAY } Committee.
> JOHN I. ROGERS,

PHILADELPHIA, November 21, 1889.

A careful perusal of these two manifestos, in which the issues that led up to the Brotherhood War of 1890 are well defined, will give to the student of Base Ball history a pretty good idea of the situation at the beginning of that memorable struggle, the counterpart of which

"DAN" BROUTHERS

will probably never again be witnessed in professional Base Ball.

On November 6th, two days after the promulgation of their manifesto, representatives from eight chapters of the National Brotherhood of Base Ball Players, viz.: J. M. Ward, New York; D. Brouthers, Boston; C. J. Buffinton, Philadelphia; E. Andrews, Brooklyn; E. Hanlon, Pittsburg; John Stricker, Cleveland; John Rowe, Buffalo; Fred Pfeffer, Chicago, met with E. A. McAlpin, Charles B. Cory, Henry M. Love, A. L. Johnson, M. Shire and John Addison, to form an eight-club Players' League in opposition to the National League. On the advice of their lawyers, however, the organization was deferred and not effected until January, 1890.

From the ranks of the National League clubs the following players seceded, joining the Players' League.

Boston—Kelly, Kilroy, Brouthers and Storey.

Brooklyn—Ward, Andrews, Seery, Bassett, Beerbauer, McGeachy and Tucker.

Buffalo—Wise, J. Irwin, A. Irwin, Mack, Carney, Keefe, Beecher, Rowe and White.

Chicago—Pfeffer, Baldwin, King, Boyle, Dwyer, Tener, Bastian, Bartson, Darling, Farrell, Williamson, Latham, Ryan and Duffy.

Cleveland—Snyder, Stricker, Sutcliffe and Radford.

New York—Ewing, Murphy, Welch, Keefe, Crane, O'Day, Conner, Richardson, Whitney, O'Rourke, Slattery and Gore.

Pittsburg—Hanlon, Staley, Beckley, Kuehne, Galvin, Miller, Morris, Fields, Dunlap and Maul.

Philadelphia—Wood, Thompson, Milligan, Cross, Hallman, Foreman, Buffinton, Farrar, Myers, Mulvey, Shindle, Griffin, Delehanty and Fogarty.

The players who remained, signing with the National League, were:

Boston—Clarkson and Ganzel.

Chicago—Anson, Hutchinson and Burns.

Indianapolis—McKean, Beatin, Zimmer, McAleer, Glasscock, Boyle, Somer, Rusie, Buckley and Denny.

Philadelphia—Decker, Clements, Schriver, Gleason.

Pittsburg—Sowders and Sunday.

Tom Daly refused to go to the city to which he was assigned, and joined the Brooklyn American Association club.

For two years the fight continued. It was intensely acrimonious. It did no good to any and infinite injury to many. It resulted in the death, in 1892, of the American Association, which for nine years had been pursuing a prosperous career. It caused serious financial loss to promoters of the National League and wrought ruin to the moneyed backers of the Brotherhood, while many Brotherhood players lost their all in the venture. It occasioned the utmost bitterness of feeling between players and club owners. It afforded opportunities for unscrupulous mischief-makers to ply their arts, and it utterly disgusted the public with the whole Base Ball business. It set Base Ball back from five to ten years in its natural development. It was a mistake from every standpoint.

But the Brotherhood War did accomplish two things:

First—It settled forever the theory that professional ball players can at the same time direct both the business and the playing ends of the game.

Second—It established the absolute honesty and integrity of professional Base Ball, for in such a fierce conflict, in which no quarter was asked or given by either side, if there had been any previous connivance for the selling of games between club officials, managers and players, it would certainly have come to the surface during those strenuous times.

A. G. SPALDING, OF NATIONAL LEAGUE "WAR COMMITTEE"

CHAPTER XX.

JOHN B. DAY, OF NATIONAL LEAGUE "WAR COMMITTEE"

CHAPTER XX.

THE BROTHERHOOD WAR — A CAMPAIGN OF ABUSE AND
FALSEHOOD ON BOTH SIDES—ONE CASE WHERE FIGURES
LIED—FATHER CHADWICK'S STORY OF THE STRUGGLE.

1889-90

TO describe in detail the battle royal for the control of professional Base Ball, which raged with unabating fury throughout its entire course, would require a book of double this size. No general ever planned campaign or conserved his forces with more painstaking care than did the commanders of the League and Brotherhood warriors. It was announced at the beginning that it was to be a fight to the death, and it was carried to a finish along these lines. In place of powder and shell, printers' ink and bluff formed the ammunition used by both sides.

If either party to this controversy ever furnished to the press one solitary truthful statement as to the progress of the war from his standpoint; if anyone at any time during the contest made true representation of conditions in his own ranks, a monument should be erected to his memory. I have no candidates to recommend for the distinction. As to my own case, I am sure that I can establish an alibi from the realms of truth. At any rate, if one on either side should now appear laying claim to the lonesome honor of telling the truth in those days, I could convict him by the testimony of many witnesses of having been guilty of disobeying "general orders."

General Sherman said "War is H—l," and he doubtless knew what he was talking about. At least I am prepared to endorse his views as applied to the Brotherhood War. Well, it's all over now, and forgotten by many, while only the pleasant and amusing incidents remain in memory. No one cared for the score of yesterday's game; nobody looked for the championship record of 1890. All eyes were centered on the question of attendance. Along with other practices peculiar to the Ananias Club, both sides then engaged in that of "faking" attendance reports. The Chicago papers, for instance, would appear every morning with figures—furnished by club officials—and reading something like this:

> "Brotherhood attendance—8,000."
> "League attendance—2,000."

Round figures are always suspicious, and the constant reiteration of these attracted my attention. I knew that the National League games at that time were drawing very meager crowds, and while at first I was aware that the Brotherhood games were more popularly attended, I was unwilling to believe that there was so much difference in the size of the crowds as appeared upon "the face of the returns." I waited a while, certain that the time would come when the Brotherhood fakirs would lay themselves open. The day came soon. The published attendance began to drop. From 8,000 it fell to 7,000; then 7,000 to 6,000. Of course, I knew what that meant, and had inspectors stationed at the Brotherhood grounds with instructions to count every one passing the turnstiles and report.   This was done for some time and the reports sent in.

Securing the services of a bright young Chicago reporter, who had a string of influential newspapers for which he syndicated Chicago specials, I placed in his hands the statistical information which had been procured as to faked attendance at Brotherhood games.   He published, side by side, the figures as given out by the Brotherhood managers and the *true* figures as sworn to by my agents.

The publication produced a profound sensation and resulted exactly as had been anticipated.   It discounted the claims made by the Brotherhood and impeached the integrity of their reports.   When explanations reflecting in a like manner upon the League's attendance were attempted no one paid any attention to them.   The Brotherhood had been put on the defensive.   The fact had been made clear that no dependence could be placed upon their statements, nobody cared to hear the pot object to the complexion of the kettle, and soon newspapers refused to publish attendance figures at all.   Thus was attention diverted from the pitifully small number of patrons who through all the struggle remained loyal to the League.

As showing the straits into which we were led in those days, I recall being present at a League game one day at Chicago when the attendance was particularly light. At the close of the contest, I was talking to Secretary Brown, when a reporter came up, asking:

"What's the attendance?"

Without a moment's hesitation the official replied: "Twenty-four eighteen."

As the scribe passed out of hearing, I inquired: "Brown, how do you reconcile your conscience to such a statement?"

"Why," he answered, "Don't you see? There were twenty-four on one side of the grounds and eighteen on the other. If he reports twenty-four *hundred* and eighteen, that's a matter for *his* conscience, not mine."

It was with very great satisfaction, therefore, that in the fall of 1890, at the close of that season, I received a delegation from the management of the Players' League, bearing a flag of truce. I was not President of the National League, but, as chairman of its "War Committee," I was fully authorized to treat with those who came asking for terms. Of course, I was conversant with existing conditions in both organizations. I knew that they were on their last legs, and I was equally aware that we had troubles of our own. We had been playing two games all through—Base Ball and bluff. At this stage I put up the strongest play at the latter game I had ever presented. I informed the bearers of the truce that "unconditional surrender" was the only possible solution of the vexed problem. To my surprise, the terms were greedily accepted. I had supposed that they would at least ask for *something*. Then, not to be outdone by the hero of Appomattox, whose terms I had appropriated, I agreed that we would furnish places for all the seceding players, under a reinforced National League of twelve clubs, which was duly organized for the following year, with these cities represented: Baltimore, Boston, Brooklyn, Chicago, Cincinnati, Cleveland, Louisville, New York, Pittsburg, Philadelphia, St. Louis and Washington.

I was President of the Chicago Club at the time of the Brotherhood War, and also Chairman of the "War Committee" of the National League. I naturally had a good deal to do with affairs, and was quite conversant with the inside workings of the scrap machine. Under these circumstances, and knowing that I might be charged with being a prejudiced historian, I have decided to introduce here a story of the causes that led up to the Brotherhood defection of 1890, from an account written by the late Henry Chadwick, the original manuscript of which I found in the library received from his wife after his demise in 1908, as follows:

"The chapter of League history covering the revolt of the League players, which was inaugurated in New York in 1889, is one which not only began a new era in professional club management, but it also exhibits some of the peculiar characteristics of the majority of the fraternity in a very striking light. The fact, too, that the secession movement had its origin in the New York Club's team of players, which club had petted its players for years, only emphasized the fact of the ingratitude for favors done which marks the average professional ball player.

"The revolt of the League players unquestionably grew out of the ambitious efforts of a small minority to obtain the upper hand of the National League in the control and management of its players. Added to this was the desire for self-aggrandizement which influenced a trio of the most intelligent of the players, headed by one man who was the master mind of the whole revolution scheme in connection with the Brotherhood, to its culmination in the organization of the Players' League; and it was the former organization which the leader of the revolt used as a lever to lift them into the position of professional club magnates.

"The methods adopted by the originator of the revolutionary scheme were of a nature well calculated to mislead the majority of the players. It would not have done to openly seduce the leaders of the League from their club allegiance; so it was deemed necessary

JOHN I. ROGERS, OF NATIONAL LEAGUE "WAR COMMITTEE"

to first combine all of their players under the banner of the Brotherhood organization, the ostensible objects of which were the mutual benefits of its members, and to aid those who needed aid from sickness or misfortune. This was a very plausible plan, and apparently devoid of guile; but, in building up the Brotherhood, care was taken to bind its members by an ironclad oath—something unnecessary in the case of an organization designed exclusively to serve benevolent purposes. This oath, in fact, was the carefully disguised seed of the revolt, from which was developed the full-grown plant of the Players' League.

"Once having gathered the League players within the fold of the Brotherhood, the chief conspirator soon began to draw aside the mask of his disguise, and securing the coöperation of the more intelligent of his confreres in aiding the revolt, a quartette of leaders assumed the direction of affairs. These 'big four' of the great strike, correctly estimating the weakness of character and lack of moral courage of the average Brotherhood member, knew that he would be loath to break the oath of allegiance to the Brotherhood, however willing he might be to violate his National League obligations, and they went quietly to work on this basis to complete their plans looking to the ultimate declaration of war upon the National League and the establishment of the rival Players' League.

"It is a fact that cannot be gainsaid that fully two-thirds of the members of the Brotherhood, up to the close of the League campaign in 1889, had never contemplated the disruption of the National Agreement and the organization of a Players' League as the outcome of the Brotherhood scheme, or they would not have joined it. Naturally enough, the players' sympathies were with the success of the Brotherhood as an association of players for benevolent objects. But not until they had been influenced by special pleadings, false statements and a system of terrorism, peculiar to revolutionary movements, did they realize the true position in which they had been placed, and then a minority, who possessed sufficient independence and the courage of their convictions, returned to their club allegiance in the National League.

"A step in the progress of the revolt, which the leaders found it necessary to take, was that of securing the services of such journalists in each League club city as would lend their pens as editors of Brotherhood organs. This movement was deemed essential in order to bring a special influence to bear on such capitalists among the wealthier class of patrons of the game as were eager to join in a movement calculated to gain them a share in the 'big bonanza' profits of the money-making League clubs. Another use these organs and writers were put to, in forwarding the interests of the leaders, was that of denouncing every player who was independent enough to think for himself in the matter of revolt as a deserter or a 'scab.' Of course, this system of terrorism had its effect on the weaker class of the Brotherhood, and the result was that only a few refused to become slaves of the ' big four.' And thus was started the League of Professional Ball Players.

"The original plan of organization of the Players' League embraced coöperation by the players in the matter of gate receipts and profits; and one of the inducements held out to players to secede from League clubs was the alluring one of sharing in the proceeds of the season's games. The bait proved to be a tempting one and it was readily taken. But after the Players' League had been started, and the bulk of the players had committed themselves by contract to the revolt, the leaders, in order to secure the required financial aid of sympathetic capitalists, seceded from their plan of coöperation, and a change was made in the new League's constitution, the feature introduced being that of obliging each player to depend upon the gate receipts for the payment of his salary—after all necessary expenses outside the salary list had been paid. This new clause proved distasteful to several players who had taken the oath of allegiance to the Brotherhood, but who had not legally signed Players' League contracts, and these men were not slow in returning to the National League after discovering the trickery they had been subjected to by the leader. But others, lacking in moral courage, and who still had faith in the movement to make them magnates instead of $5,000 a year slaves, remained obedient to the Brotherhood taskmasters.

"The leaders had originally declared that their war was against the National League and that only; but when their plan of campaign met with its first failure, resort for recruits for their revolutionary army was had to the ranks of the American Association, and the early disruption of this organization was due to the influence exerted by the revolt. This was the return made to the Association for the neutral position they had occupied in the differences which had occurred between the League and the Brotherhood. Had the Brotherhood followed the honorable course of holding a conference with the League at the end of the championship campaign—the only appropriate time for such a conference—there is no questioning the fact that every grievance, real or imaginary, alleged by the Brotherhood would have received due consideration by the League, and all enactments calculated to antagonize the best interests of the players would have been removed from the League's statute books, for it was too plainly to the interest of the National League to place their club players in the position of making their interests and welfare identical with those of the League management."

Now and then, in the course of these reminiscences, I have had occasion to speak of the loyalty of professional ball players, one to another, and of the quality of their integrity as a rule. A conspicuous illustration of these traits occurred during the Brotherhood imbroglio. I must plead in extenuation of the part I played in this incident that, as before stated, the revolt of the players had precipitated a struggle of intense bitterness. As time passed on, and the interests of both the National League and the Players' League were placed in jeopardy, feeling became fierce. It was, indeed, a war to the death.

The League was determined to win if it took every dollar that had been made and saved; and the Players were willing to resort to anything to achieve success or spare themselves the humiliation of defeat. Meanwhile the public had become utterly disgusted with both sides to the controversy, and all clubs were losing money right and left.

With these conditions present, there came a time in the life of the contest when the National League managers believed that an assault should be made with a view of breaking through the ranks of the Brotherhood in the hopes of capturing some of their players. Let it be remembered that there was no *agreement* of any kind between the contending forces, but that *disagreement* on every point was rampant. No scruples were entertained regarding the securing of players in any way from the opposition by either side. The League, having been robbed of nearly all its men, was perfectly willing to engage in any act that would sow discord in the ranks of the Brotherhood and secure a return of some of the stars.

MICHAEL J. "KING" KELLY

To me was delegated the task of approaching the enemy with a view of making a capture. I was given a *carte blanche* in the matter, with instructions to pay the price necessary to produce the result. I didn't fancy the job a little bit. The enterprise was not at all to my liking. I tried to beg off; but it was no use. It was urged with force that I had been a player, knew all the boys, and could gain a hearing where no one else could, and that hopes of success would be greater with me than with any other.

So I reluctantly consented, and determined to go after big game. I sent a note to Mike Kelly, the "King,"— then at the zenith of his popular career—whose sale I had manipulated at Chicago, to whom I could talk unreservedly, and whose defection from the ranks of the enemy would cause greater consternation than that of any other, I thought. I invited Kelly to meet me at my hotel. He came. We passed the usual conventional civilities, talked about health, the weather and kindred exciting topics, until at length I opened the ball with the question.

" How are things going with the game, Mike?"

" Oh, the game's gone to ———."

" What? You don't mean to say that the managers are getting discouraged?"

" Aw, ——— the managers!"

" Why, what's the matter?" incredulously.

" Everything's the matter; everybody's disgusted; clubs all losing money; we made a ——— foolish blunder when we went into it."

I thought the time was ripe. Placing a check for

$10,000 on the table, I asked, "Mike, how would you like that check for $10,000 filled out payable to your order?"

"Would Mike Kelly like $10,000? I should smile."

"But that's not all, Mike. Here's a three years' contract, and I'm authorized to let you fill in the amount of salary yourself."

His face blanched. "What does this mean? Does it mean that I'm to join the League? Quit the Brotherhood? Go back on the boys."

"That's just what it means. It means that you go to Boston to-night."

"Well," said he, "I must have time to think about this."

"There is mighty little time, Mike. If you don't want the money, somebody else will get it. When can you let me know?"

"In an hour and a half," he answered.

"What are you going to do, meanwhile? Consult a lawyer?"

"Lawyer? Naw; you're good enough lawyer for me," and, saying that he would be back in an hour and a half, he left the room.

At the appointed time I was awaiting him—and he came, true to appointment. I didn't see much of encouragement in his face. His jaw was set, and there was a bright sparkle to his eye that somehow seemed to augur ill for the success of my mission.

"Well, Mike, where have you been?" I asked.

"I've been taking a walk," he answered. "I went 'way up town and back."

"What were you doing?"

"I was thinking."

"Have you decided what you're going to do?" I asked.

"Yes," he replied without hesitation; "I've decided not to accept."

"What?" I ejaculated. "You don't want the $10,000?"

"Aw, I want the ten thousand bad enough; but I've thought the matter all over, and I can't go back on the boys. And," he added, "neither would you."

Involuntarily I reached out my hand in congratulation of the great ball player on his loyalty. We talked for a little while, and then he borrowed $500 of me. I think it was little enough to pay for the anguish of that hour and a half, when he was deciding to give up thousands of dollars on the altar of sentiment in behalf of the Brotherhood.

From 1876 to 1899 the National League of Base Ball Clubs occupied the unchallenged position as the great major organization, to which all minor leagues looked for advice and protection. But in 1899, owing to financial conditions growing out of the Spanish-American War, the game was not profitable, and the League managers, mistaking the true cause of the trouble, attributed it to the carrying of so many clubs, and decided to return to the eight-club system, dropping Baltimore, Cleveland, Louisville and Washington from the League, though holding League franchises in those cities.

This was just exactly what had been hoped for by a certain bright young enthusiast who was at that time

dominating the affairs of the Western League. Mr. B.
Bancroft Johnson saw his opportunity and was not slow
to avail himself of it. He at once proceeded to the organization of a new rival to the National League, which he
named the American League. This organization, made
easy by the dropping of four cities from the roster of the
major League, was rendered still easier by the abrogation
on the part of the National magnates just at that time of
the Reserve Rule.

Thus was introduced into Base Ball history a new and
formidable rival to the National League, and one which
has prospered ever since its introduction into the arena,
under the capable management of one of the ablest and
most consistent Base Ball men the game has ever produced.

The cities of Baltimore, Cleveland, Louisville and
Washington, dropped from the National League, were not
at once seized upon by President Johnson, who had loftier
ambitions; but he immediately perfected an eight-club
league, with the following cities represented:

Baltimore, Boston, Chicago, Cleveland, Detroit, Philadelphia, St. Louis, Washington.

With these cities, each having excellent teams, the
American League began the first decade of the 20th
century.

CHAPTER XXI.

WHEN THE GAME REACHED SILVERTON

CHAPTER XXI.

THE STORY OF "FREEDMANISM"—HOW IT WAS PROPOSED
TO SYNDICATE BASE BALL—ATTEMPT TO KILL THE
NATIONAL LEAGUE IN THE INTERESTS OF SORDID
MAGNATES.   1900–01

SOME years before the opening of the 20th century the National League had begun to lose prestige with the public. This loss of caste was not due to a failure on the part of the League to correct abuses. It had achieved wonders in that respect. It had absolutely driven out gambling and gamblers. It had made players to so regard their interests that not one of them cared or dared to be seen talking with a gambler. Indeed, at one time this dread became so great that players would and did personally assault members of the crooked fraternity who attempted to engage them in conversation on the streets. It had done away with the drinking evil—so fully as the appetites of men can ever be controlled by discipline—and at one time a dozen capable players had been expelled, without hope of reinstatement, for overindulgence in liquor. The trouble now was not with gamblers or with players, but with club officials, generally termed *magnates*, and it will be readily understood how difficult a matter it was to deal with them. Especially was it hard to reach cases where there was no actual violation of Base Ball law—just personal cussedness and disregard for the future welfare of the game.

Soon after the American sport became established as a national pastime, and was showing for its promoters a balance on the right side of the ledger, a certain clique came into the League for purposes of pelf. They at once let it be known by their acts that they were in Base Ball for what they could get out of it. They were absolutely devoid of sentiment, cared nothing for the integrity or perpetuity of the game beyond the limits of their individual control thereof. With these men it was simply a mercenary question of dollars and cents. Everything must yield to the one consideration of inordinate greed. It will not be difficult to understand that any man who dominated such a faction as has here been described, while he might have a pleasing personality, would nevertheless be a standing menace to the perpetuity of the game.

I do not know how better to characterize the monstrous evil which at this time threatened the life of Base Ball than to denominate it "Freedmanism"; for Andrew Freedman, owner of the New York franchise, absolutely held sway over one-half the League interests and was the incarnation of selfishness supreme. Surrounding himself by a coterie of men willing to follow such a leader; dictating policies that were suicidal as to the League of which these men were an important integral part, it is no wonder that this destructive element in those years worked havoc to our national pastime.

The special phase of aggressive onslaught against League interests that called me from an unofficial position, as simply an honorary member, into an active struggle to protect the game from enemies in its own household, was

Mr. Freedman's move to syndicate Base Ball. But, prior to this time, Freedman's personal course had become so obnoxious to most of those connected with the game that nobody outside his own following could endure his eccentricities of speech or action. He would apply to other members of the League, in ordinary conversation, terms so coarse and offensive as to be unprintable. Taking umbrage at some personal newspaper criticism, he would openly declare his intention of ruining the game. My brother, Mr. J. Walter Spalding, who was a Director of the New York Club (owned by Freedman), was compelled to resign in order to retain his self-respect. Even those who were associated with Freedman in the enterprise which called me into the struggle complained to me of his ungentlemanly bearing whenever he met with opposition from any source, while those opposed to him and to his methods pleaded with me to re-enter the field, urging that my presence was needed to force this undesirable magnate from the ranks.

The following, from the columns of a New York paper at about this time, will serve to show the peculiar personal quality of the man:

" After remaining away from the Polo Grounds since the Fourth of July, when he had a row with ex-Umpire Heydler, Andrew Freedman, President of the New York Base Ball Club, visited the field on July 25th, with the result that there was another muss which disgusted 3,000 spectators. This time it was not the umpire against whom Freedman made his attack, but one of the Baltimore players, 'Ducky' Holmes, who was a member of the New York team last year. The score was 1 to 1 when the first half of the fourth inning began and the teams were playing sharp ball. With one out and McGann on first, Holmes went to the bat and struck out. He was in the act of walking back to the bench when a man in the grandstand cried out: 'Holmes, you're a lobster. That's what you left

here for.' Holmes retorted. Umpire Lynch noticed that Holmes was talking to the crowd, and ordered him to keep quiet. The player promptly
obeyed.   Then Clarke, of the Baltimores, made a hit and, when
Nops struck out, the visitors took the field.   As they did so, Freedman hurried from his private box in the grandstand down onto the
field, and almost ran to the bench where Joyce and the New Yorks
were making preparations to go to the bat.   Umpire Lynch saw
Freedman and went over to him, at the same time asking what was
the trouble.   'Lynch, I want that man Holmes thrown out of these
grounds,' exclaimed Freedman, white with rage.   'He's insulted me.'
Lynch claimed he did not hear the alleged insult and refused to
remove Holmes.   Freedman, still in a rage, secured the services of
a detective and a policeman, whom he ordered to eject Holmes.
Umpire Lynch called, 'Play Ball,' but Freedman declared that the
game could not go on if Holmes were left in the game, and then
Lynch gave the game to Baltimore by a score of 9 to 0.   The crowd
cheered the decision, and then a large contingent surged around
Freedman, demanding the return of their money and yelling at him
at the top of their voices, calling him a cheat and threatening him
with bodily harm if he did not return their money.   Freedman was
at first disposed to refuse; but the threatening attitude of the crowd
finally forced him to submit.   As he moved away he was hissed by
over a thousand people.   One man yelled, 'You ought to be expelled
from the League.   You're killing Base Ball in New York deader
than a herring.'   This sally was received with marks of approval
and more hissing.   Holmes was escorted off the grounds, but was not
arrested."

Another of many contemptible acts of ineffable mean-
ness on the part of Freedman was his treatment of Mr.
Henry Chadwick. In the course of his duties as sporting
editor and writer on sporting topics, Mr. Chadwick took
occasion to point out certain flagrant abuses in the management of the New York Club, whereupon Freedman
wrote a letter to Chadwick, accusing him of ingratitude
in criticising the New York Club while he was a recipient
of its "bounty." It seems that the League had voted
Mr. Chadwick a life annuity of $600 for what he had
done for the game, and Freedman was not above assuming credit for the fact and berating the good old gentle-

man as a pauper. With fine spirit, Mr. Chadwick published Freedman's letter, in which he declared that if other League managers were of Freedman's mind he would not accept another penny. To the credit of the gentlemen be it said that every one wrote, disclaiming any sympathy with Freedman's view of the case.

In August, 1901, a secret meeting was held at the home of Andrew Freedman, at Red Bank, N. J. There were present representatives from the New York, Boston, Cincinnati and St. Louis Clubs. Managers of the Chicago, Brooklyn, Philadelphia and Pittsburg Clubs were neither invited nor expected.

At this meeting the National Agreement, drawn by A. G. Mills, and which had been for so many years the cornerstone of the Base Ball edifice, withstanding all the storms that had beaten upon it, was abrogated, that a Trust might be formed which should thereafter control the interests of the game. The nature of this proposed radical change in League Base Ball control may be gleaned from the following excerpt from the files of the New York *Sun*, under date December 11, 1901:

"This scheme contemplates the organization of the National League Base Ball Trust, to be divided into preferred and common stock, the preferred stock to draw a dividend of 7 per cent., all of which is to belong to the National League, as a body; the common stock to be used in payment for the present eight League Clubs, as follows:

"New York to receive about 30 per cent.
"Cincinnati to receive about 12 per cent.
"St. Louis to receive about 12 per cent.
"Boston to receive about 12 per cent.
"Philadelphia to receive about 10 per cent.
"Chicago to receive about 10 per cent.
"Pittsburg to receive about 8 per cent.
"Brooklyn to receive about 6 per cent.

" The management of the company is to be placed for a term of years in the hands of not more than five men, to be selected by the stockholders and designated as a Board of Regents. From this board of managers a President and a Treasurer are to be chosen, though the Secretary need not necessarily be a member of the Board of Regents. The salary of the President must not exceed $25,000 per year, and the Treasurer not over $12,500. As the eight clubs will lose their identity by being merged into and becoming a part of the National League Trust, the different clubs will be under the direction of the managers, who will each receive a salary of $5,000 per year."

Of course, this newspaper clipping, startling as it was, did not convey to the world in general what it did to some of us who had long been identified with the game, both as to its playing and its management. To us it meant the immediate syndicating of Base Ball along lines identically the same as those which have disgraced control of the theatrical business in America for many years. It meant the introduction of a system whereby one man or a half-dozen men, working with him to a single purpose, might dominate the entire business—and with villainous brutality. It meant the blacklisting of players without cause; the boycotting of cities without excuse. It meant, in short, what has been aptly termed " Syndicate " methods, and the general demoralization of our national sport in its every interest.

It was at this juncture that the managers of the Chicago, Philadelphia, Pittsburg and Brooklyn Clubs appealed to me to come to their aid. Before I arrived at the Convention, without my connivance, knowledge or consent, the name of A. G. Spalding had been placed in nomination for the Presidency of the National League. I did not desire that office. I had quite enough on hand to engage all my time and attention without the added cares and responsibilities attaching to the office for which I had been named.

But I was terribly in earnest in my desire that Freedmanism should not obtain ascendancy in the League, and so I found myself an interested spectator of the proceedings of the National League Convention on Wednesday, December 11, 1901, and immediately thereafter I was in one of the sharpest Base Ball battles of my life. Let it be remembered that at the formation of the National League I had engaged in a struggle against abuses that had grown up under the mild, pacific, fostering influences of the two National Associations of Amateur Base Ball Players and Professional Base Ball Players. I had fought with President Hulbert to stamp out gambling and pool-selling. Later I had been engaged in ridding the game of players who were in collusion with the gambling fraternity. Still later I united with those who found it necessary to free Base Ball from a lot of irresponsible, unreliable drunkards, who, although good players, were a disgrace and hindrance to the game.

Now, for the first time, I was face to face with a situation full of graver menace than any of the others had been, because those who were seeking its ruin now were men of real power, men of ability, men of acute business instincts—an enemy that knew how to fight.

In all the former battles for the life of our national sport the men who stood for the preservation of Base Ball in its integrity had won. Every form of abuse had been so completely eradicated that public confidence had been regained, the press of the country was united in its declaration that the game was clean; that gambling had been kicked out; that pool-selling had been kicked out; that drunkenness had been kicked out; and now I was determined that so far as I had the power to help the upright managers of the League, Freedman and Freedmanism should be kicked out. As to the proper control of Base Ball the man was impossible; he must go.

Perhaps in no other way can I so well define my position at that time as by republishing here the substance of the address made by me at the Convention to which I had been called, to prevent, if possible, the syndicating of Base Ball. After the roll-call on that day, I addressed the Chair, asking, as an honorary member of the League, the privilege of a hearing. This courtesy having been granted me by the presiding officer, without objection from anyone present, I proceeded with my remarks substantially in the following words:

" Mr. Chairman and Gentlemen:

"I claim the right of addressing a few words to this League. I find myself placed in a somewhat awkward position by the announcement that has been made in the press the last few days, connecting my name with the nomination for the presidency of this League. I at first looked upon it as my annual newspaper nomination; but I find that the papers still, without my request or permission, are using my name, and declare that it has been brought before this Convention. I learn that it was; that I have been nominated here. I don't know who nominated me. He had no authority to do it. I didn't know he was to do it. I have heard that it came before the Convention in a regular manner, and have learned that there has been some discussion about it.

"I repeat that I now find myself placed in a very embarrassing situation, and I believe that I am entitled to insist upon this League coming to an early vote on that question. I don't ask you to vote for me. I don't care if you vote eight to nothing against me. I simply claim that as a member of this League in years gone by—as an honorary member now—as a gentleman who has a personal reputation to maintain, I have a right to demand that you cast your votes on my nomination and get it out of the way.

"If you will stop and think a minute, you will see that I am placed in a somewhat peculiar position before the public. I might say in this connection that a very prominent president of one of the League clubs (Mr. Soden), a gentleman for whom I have the highest regard and in whom I have the utmost confidence, asked me as a special favor to refrain from making any comment or withdrawing my name, as it might injure the National League; might be used as a club by the American League, with whom you are at war. I told him I would do so.

"Now, I find that, being nominated, my name is foot-balled around quite generally; in the press, in this room, everywhere, in a way that to me is not satisfactory.

"I am told that this is the last day of the National League. Rumor declares that it will not outlive the day. Gentlemen, I was present at the birth of this organization. ' I saw it when its eyes were first opened to the light of day, twenty-six years ago next February, in this city. If it is to be buried to-day—if this is its last day—I ask, gentlemen, the privilege of closing its eyes in death. I claim that not only as a privilege but a right.

"I also want to be here to take away the body, that an autopsy may be held to determine the cause of death. I also claim that I have a right to say something about where it shall be buried, and I may have something to offer as to the design of the monument that is to be erected over it.

"This National League has two fathers: One, William A. Hulbert—God bless his memory—and the other—myself. Twenty-six years ago this month I spent thirty days in Mr. Hulbert's house with him, writing the first constitution; and I claim, because of that; because of the fact that I have been unanimously elected an honorary member of this body, I have the right to speak in its councils.

"We have a very sick patient here—as I read in the papers—a very sick patient. I think it is time that somebody asked some questions to find out what has brought it to this condition. Emaciated in form, pulse weak, heart fluttering; and yet we see a few motions of the muscles that indicate that life is not extinct. Gentlemen, as an honorary member of this League, if it is to die, I propose to stay by that corpse until it is buried. I sincerely hope I am misinformed.

"I object to any more daggers being thrust into that body in my presence. At least I have the right to demand that. Let us stand by this body that seems to be at the point of death for a few minutes and see if we cannot fan it into life; see if we cannot do something that will bring it back and save the reputation that has been twenty-six years in making—a reputation, gentlemen, that you need to be very careful and guarded how you throw away.

"This League has a great reputation. I have known something about its early career, its middle career, and have kept watching it. What was it for? What was the organization of this League for? To perpetuate, establish and maintain the *integrity* of Base Ball. What is this Base Ball that we talk about? I do not want to take much of your time, but let us take a few moments to answer this question.

"Base Ball is a distinctly American sport, suitable to the American character, played under rules known to every American boy ten years of age. And here is the National League, the guardian of that sport. To be the guardian of a nation's sport is no mean honor. I sometimes wonder if you realize the responsibility. Here, in your bickerings and your financial schemings, everything is subordinated to those features.

"The game first appeared back in the forties. In the latter part of the fifties it became known in New York, New England and Philadelphia. When the soldiers from those sections went into the army they took with them this new game of Base Ball. It was played in camps of both armies. At the end of the war it was disseminated throughout the United States, and there was a furore of Base Ball. So, gentlemen, Base Ball has a patriotic as well as sentimental and business sides.

"This National organization, which has stood for so many years, I hope may not expire to-day. I beg of you, think before you stab it to its death.

"Of course, as this game became popular all over the country, there was needed some form of organization. The first organization was the National Association of Amateur Base Ball Players, composed of clubs all over the Nation. That soon got into trouble because a man would come with two hundred proxies and elect himself president. The man who had the next number would be treasurer, and so on. You can imagine how long such an arrangement could last. It answered the purpose for the time being, but it was found inadequate. The next step was the semi-professional, or veiled-amateur era, as you might term it. From that came the full-fledged professional player, represented in the old Cincinnati Red Stocking Club in 1869. I was among those original professional players, and in a small way did what I could to relieve a certain odium that existed between amateurism and professionalism. A professional League was organized, and here sits the first secretary of that professional League. It served its purpose.

"We were new at legislation, and one thing after another crept in. We had the gambling instinct to contend with. The first thing we knew, the gamblers had us by the throat. I have seen players go up and buy pools before the game commenced, generally on their own club, but they often would have a friend buying double the amount on the other. It became so intolerable that Base Ball was a stench in the nostrils of every decent man, and it was almost a disgrace to say that you were a professional Base Ball player. Mr. Hanlon will bear me out in that. Mr. Reach played in those days and he can bear me out. The public was interested in the game, but the gamblers would not permit it to be played except under their direction.

"I had the honor to be captain and pitcher of the original Boston Base Ball Club. I look back to that period as covering four or five of the pleasantest years of my life. We won the championship right along. Our crowds, large at first, kept getting smaller. The last year we played in Boston we never lost a game on the home grounds and we hardly had as many spectators as players.

"I went to Chicago with three other players of the Boston Club. Excuse me, gentlemen, if I digress here. The rules provided at that time, in this first professional association, that if a ball player signed a contract with any other club except the one he was with before the season was closed he was expelled. I took certain chances there of being expelled, but the gentleman who has done more for Base Ball than any man who has ever lived said to us: 'Boys, I'll attend to that; your salaries go whether you are expelled or not. I defy this Association to expel you players, because you are stronger than the Association; and, furthermore, there are iniquities in this Association that need correcting.' The result of that was—the meeting did not take place then until March—Mr. Hulbert and myself, in his house, where I spent thirty days, in December, 1875, decided to organize a new association.

"So this National League was born in rebellion, and I take pleasure in saying that I was one of the rebellious parties. I was looking over the other night the original constitution that we wrote— several drafts were made of it, and we re-wrote it—and when we got through with that we had a pretty nice structure; and, gentlemen, as I look at it to-day, you could get very many good points from that old constitution of 1876, making allowance, of course, for the improvements of the game. You can find some very good ideas there. At any rate, the contrast between the constitution of '76 in this National League and the one of 1901 before us is very marked.

" It was customary for the Eastern Clubs to go West and the Western Clubs to go East, and back again, two trips each year. In those days the expense of traveling back and forth was enormous. Previous to the organization of the League, the New York and Philadelphia Clubs had got the Western Clubs to come East twice; they had gone once, and when it came the following year, they said, ' We don't go.' They were given to understand when they came into the National League that no more nonsense of that kind would be allowed. The first year we ran against the New York and Philadelphia people trying the same thing on the National League. At the annual meeting Mr. A. G. Mills appeared as State's attorney for the National League and demanded the expulsion of these two Clubs. It was one of the most pathetic scenes I ever witnessed. I saw the President of the Philadelphia Club in Mr. Hulbert's room, with tears in his eyes, saying: ' I beg of you not to expel us; we will enter into any bonds; we will do anything.' Mr. Hulbert said: ' No; we are going to expel you to-morrow.' The same thing was done with the New York Club, which was run by Mr. Cammeyer, a great personal friend of Mr. Hulbert. Mr. Hulbert said: ' No; we are going to expel you.' They were brought into the room, charges were made, and the vote was unanimous against them. The New York Club walked out; the Philadelphia Club did the same thing. We didn't stop to consider gate receipts. What did we take into their places? Worcester and Troy! Think of that!

" I have been in the National League when we did those things. The following year we found four players selling games when we were organized to protect them and prevent it. They were guilty. One player came to Chicago, appeared in Mr. Hulbert's office with tears in his eyes, down on his knees in prayer, and begged him not to expel; that his family was starving. Those were pathetic times. I remember Mr. Hulbert going into his pocket and giving the man fifty dollars. He said: ' Devlin, that's what I think of you personally'; but, damn you, you have sold a game; you are dishonest, and this National League will not stand for it. We are going to expel you.'

" I have lived in those days. I have seen the result of such action. The New York and Philadelphia Clubs were expelled and you are enjoying the fruits of it; it gave a standing to this national sport. The expelling of those players has preserved the integrity of professional Base Ball, and you have not had a case since. Later we expelled ten of the most prominent players in America for drunkenness. That has helped to remove drunkenness from Base Ball.

"Now we seem to be up against a new condition. I don't know just what is the cause of it, but when I read in the papers that the National League is not expected to live the day out, I cannot resist coming up here to at least enter a protest against letting it expire. It seems to me that you have had a sort of consultation of physicians. I don't know just who can be called the head physician; who wrote the prescription; I don't know what apothecary made up the dose, but I know that some poisonous preparation has been given to this old body that lies prostrate here to-day, and I accuse the man who did it, and I accuse all the rest of you who permitted it. If this body dies, I charge you with its death.

"I would feel that I was not doing what I ought to do as an honorary member of this League if in these days of distress I did not raise my voice in solemn protest against any further efforts in the same direction. I have no personal feeling against any man in this room. In fact, I can say that some of the best friends I have in the world are here. But when it comes to the question of personal friendship for one of you, or two of you, or all of you combined, I think more of the National League than I do of any one of you or of all of you.

"I hope that some kind of argument, some words that I may utter here, will bring you to a realizing sense of the situation. The eyes of this Nation are upon you, and somehow or other the people have an idea that you are a band of conspirators, talking nothing but gate receipts. You have got into a fight with the American League; you have lost players, I understand; I certainly judge from the papers that you have lost their support, and I am told that some have violated the confidence that was reposed in them by this League.

"I accuse you of having violated a trust in having abrogated the National Agreement. The most damnable thing that was ever done in Base Ball was the way that was done. I don't know and care not who the members of the Board of Arbitration may be, and I care not whether or not you had a right; I say it was damnable to take away the very foundations of this whole business. I feel an especial interest because the first National Agreement in effect was one that bore my name in '77.

"Now, it appears that peculiar things have been going on here, and I don't know just what all this commotion is about. I don't really get onto it; but I find myself in an embarrassing position before the public, as standing for the presidency of this League; and while I have been told that it won't do for me to say anything, I can't wait any longer.

"My name is mentioned here in connection with the presidency. I understand it was brought before this meeting. Who is the man who presented it? Whoever he was, he had no authority from me to do it. I never knew he intended to do it. I regret his having done it if he did not have some intimation that it might be carried to a vote.

"I am not seeking the office, and I don't ask you to vote for me; but I do ask you to get it out of the way in any way you please; vote it eight to nothing, seven to one, or five to three against me, or any way; but, gentlemen, I feel that I am entitled to have it settled, and settled to-day.

"Mr. Chairman, I won't detain you any longer. I would ask that a vote on the presidency of the League be taken now. I thank you, Mr. Chairman, for your kindness."

CHAPTER XXII.

WHEN SYNDICATISM WAS KILLED

CHAPTER XXII.

1901–02

THE premature publication of the article on "The Trust Scheme" created a profound sensation. My speech in the Convention did not pour oil upon the troubled waters. The entire Base Ball world was stirred to its depths. The would-be Syndicate had to do something to turn back the tide of public indignation sweeping in from all quarters. The press of the whole country had gone into a discussion of the subject. Everywhere the scheme was denounced as outrageous; and so the Trust was forced to emerge from the cover into which its members had crept when the storm broke. The first sound from that quarter was the bland announcement that the Convention was prevented from transacting its customary business by the deadlock occasioned by Mr. Spalding's efforts to have himself elected President of the League! I met this charge by inviting members of the press to meet me at my hotel, where I told them such facts as were pertinent to the situation. I said to them that I was not in any sense a candidate for the office of President of the National League; that I didn't want it, and that if elected I would resign unless Andrew Freedman got out at once!

After the publication of the interviews growing out

of this meeting, the Convention got down to business and occupied its sessions in voting a tie of four votes each for Mr. N. E. Young, as President-Secretary-Treasurer of the League, and four for myself. The monotonous details of the prolonged sessions of the Convention at this date have lost their interest. Suffice to say that twenty-five ballots were taken without result, when representatives of the four Trust clubs left the hall without adjournment or permission. Mr. N. E. Young, President of the League, retired soon after, first instructing the stenographer to take no further notes of anything that might subsequently transpire.

It was at this time, about 1 o'clock a. m., December 12th, 1901, that friends of the League administered a restorative which caused the sick patient to " sit up and take notice," while that part of the American public interested in the subject of Base Ball looked on with renewed excitement. It seems that during the preceding session, and prior to the withdrawal of the Trust delegates, Mr. Rogers, representing the Philadelphia Club, had been asked to preside. Now, on motion, that gentleman was recalled to the chair.

From this time on the proceedings were characterized by the most perfect harmony, and business was dispatched without delays of any kind. A teller being needed to take the place of Mr. Knowles, who had left the hall, Mr. Hurst, the stenographer, was appointed to that office.

Upon the calling of the roll for the twenty-sixth ballot, Chicago, Philadelphia, Pittsburg and Brooklyn voted for A. G. Spalding for President-Secretary-Treasurer. There being no response to the call of the clubs of New York, Boston, Cincinnati and St. Louis, the Chair declared that Albert G. Spalding, having received four votes as President-Secretary-Treasurer—and there being no votes against him—was duly elected to succeed Mr. N. E. Young.

The Convention then took a recess, at 1.30 a. m., to reconvene next day at 2 p. m.

After my rhetorical effort of the preceding day, I had withdrawn from the Convention hall and devoted the afternoon to newspaper interviewers, who were in evidence by the score, until dinner hour, following which, wearied with the trying incidents of the day, I went to bed. About 2 o'clock a. m., Messrs. Reach, Rogers and Hart called me up, asking:

" Have you heard the news? "

" Why, no. What news? "

" You've been unanimously elected President-Secretary-Treasurer of the League."

" Have I? What wrought the miracle? "

The case was then fully explained to me, and the humor of the situation was at once borne in upon my mind. Here was I, "unanimously elected" by four votes in an organization that had eight votes, four of which were absent without leave.

Catching the spirit of what now seemed to me a huge joke, I determined, in the interest of Base Ball, to seize the advantage, and play the political game for all there was in it. If I was President-Secretary-Treasurer—the Pooh Bah of the League—certainly I was entitled to the records, the treasures, the archives of that body. More-over, I had been disturbed in the midst of pleasant dreams. Why should the gentleman—my opponent—who imagined himself in possession of all the offices in the Base Ball kingdom, be permitted longer to rest in the solace of that delusive dream? Therefore, at about 4 a. m., I repaired to the hotel where Mr. Young and his son, Robert, were domiciled, and first broke in upon the slumbers of the younger Young. I told him that affairs were becoming very serious in the National League.

"Oh, yes," he said, "I know it. Father is nearly dead, Mr. Spalding. He can't stand another day like this. He's all broken up."

"But," said I, "to-day's nothing to what to-morrow will be. I've been unanimously elected President of the League, and I'm going to raise Cain to-morrow. Where's your father?"

"He's in the next room. I'll call him."

The elder Young soon appeared, rubbing his eyes. He had been in a turmoil of confusion for several days, and had just fallen asleep. He certainly looked ten years older than when he had arrived from Washington. I felt heartily sorry for the old gentleman, and a bit ashamed of myself for disturbing him. I then explained the situation to father and son, and demanded possession of the trunk containing the "archives." I showed Mr. Young that it would at once relieve him of further annoyance and anxiety; that I was in fact the only genuine dyed-in-the-wool executive of the League, and that the papers followed the office.

But Mr. Young seemed to be no more thoroughly convinced than was I of the legitimacy of my claim. That he was willing to be relieved of the office, with all its multiplied titles and cares and responsibilities, I felt absolutely certain; but how would he explain to the League if he gave up the papers to a false claimant? What could he do if the courts should find him guilty of having turned over the "archives" to an impostor? He was willing, however, to give the trunk over to the keeping of his son, Robert, to be held in trust by him until my title should be made clearer. I saw that further argument would be wasted upon the old gentleman, and went away. But I didn't go far away. I only went as far as my hotel. Securing the services of a burly porter, whom I knew I could trust, I told him to follow me to the Fifth Avenue Hotel, and, at a signal, to take a trunk that I would point out to him and convey it to my quarters. I then returned to Robert's room, and while in the midst of a most vigorous plea in behalf of the father's peace of mind, showing how the strenuosity of the situation was wearing him to a frazzle, my friend, the porter, bore away the trunk with its more or less valuable contents.

I was now quite prepared to carry out the program of grim humor thus successfully inaugurated. Therefore, when the time came to reconvene, after recess, I was present at the Convention room. I saw that representatives from all the loyal clubs were on hand, and I also observed Mr. Knowles (representing the New York Club with Mr. Freedman) present in the corridor outside the door, evidently watching things. I asked Mr. Rogers to bring the meeting to order and call me to the chair. He did so. I didn't lose much time. I was afraid Knowles might get away, and I needed him in my business for a few moments. I then made one of the briefest addresses of my life. I said:

"Gentlemen, I accept this office. Thanks. Call the roll."

The calling of the roll elicited responses from Chicago, Philadelphia, Pittsburg and Brooklyn. I said New York had a representative present, but not responding to the call. I should recognize Mr. Knowles, who was standing outside, as present, constituting a quorum. We then proceeded with the regular business, which was soon transacted. During the progress of this session I stepped to the door and accosted Mr. Knowles, urging him to come closer to the Chair, as I found it difficult to make my voice heard at so great a distance. Mr. Knowles stuttered and stammered a few words of denial that he was present *as a delegate*, and then shot down stairs at a gait that would have enabled me to play checkers on his coat-tails had I been interested to pursue him.

The newspapers were by this time full of the all-engrossing subject. All I had to do was to speak four words to a reporter, and it was good for a column in his paper. A sentence was sufficient for a page of Base Ball literature. On the morning following my induction into office I was besieged by an army of reporters.

"What are you going to do next?"

"What about Freedman?"

"How are you going to get rid of Freedman?"

These were a few among hundreds of similar interrogatories forced upon me. I told the reporters that I would call another meeting for next day, to be open to the public, to which I would issue a challenge to Andrew Freedman to appear and engage with me in an open discussion of the Base Ball situation. I would then show them how Mr. Freedman was to be disposed of. "In the meantime," I added, "Mr. Freedman is out of it. I have read him out."

Next day all newspaperdom was on hand—and then some. I called the meeting to order, explained that it was not a regular League affair, but a meeting at which Mr. Freedman and I were to engage in a joint debate concerning League matters. I then asked Mr. Freedman to come forward. There was no response.

"Has anyone seen Mr. Freedman?" I asked. "Have you seen him?" I said to a prominent newspaper man.

"Not on your life," was the reply.

"Will somebody kindly step to the doorway and ascertain if Mr. Freedman is awaiting an invitation to come in?"

Those present smiled, then grinned, then laughed, then shouted.

Very seriously I explained my great surprise and disappointment that the President of the New York Club was not present to represent the cause of the proposed new Base Ball Trust. Doubtless something serious must have occurred to prevent him from taking advantage of such a splendid opportunity to exploit his enterprise. However, I felt that, being there, I ought to say something in behalf of a game its enemies were seeking to kill. I did say something.

But Andrew had not been napping. As I was about to leave the room, a dapper little fellow took hold of my coat sleeve and handed me a paper of portentous appearance.

" What's this? " I demanded.

" It's a summons, Mr. Spalding. You've been enjoined."

I tossed the paper over to my lawyer, with the remark, " Now, it's up to you," and left the room. How I dodged the minions of the law during the next two months, to prevent being dragged before the courts, would not be of public interest, and is therefore omitted from these reminiscences.

I may be pardoned, however, for referring to an incident in connection with this case which occurred at that time. Hon. Thomas B. Reed, the great statesman and parliamentarian, had established an office in New York. I called upon him for counsel. Like most great men, he was a lover of our national game, and I found him deeply interested in the controversy then waging in New York. He had kept close watch of proceedings and needed not much in the way of explanation when I came to state the case. I said to him:

" Mr. Reed, I have come to consult you professionally. I want to present a case for your consideration, and then ask your opinion as to two points." After briefly going over the facts as they were, referring to my election and to my ruling as to Knowles, I asked:

"First—Am I President of the National League?

"Second—Was I within the practice of parliamentary usage in counting a quorum under the circumstances?"

The great lawyer had a merry twinkle in his eye as he replied:

"Mr. Spalding, I will answer your second question first. You were unquestionably within strict parliamentary practice in counting Mr. Knowles as present. I recall an even more deeply strained case in my own experience. The opposition were filibustering over a measure in the House and seeking to obstruct business by breaking the quorum. They thought they had practically succeeded; but from where I stood I was facing a mirror so placed that clearly reflected in it was the image of a member from Arkansas. We needed just that one vote for a quorum. Upon roll-call, when the gentleman's name was reached, and the Clerk was about to mark him absent because of no response, I demanded that he be counted as present. I could see him all the time, marching back and forth in the corridor. Objection was made to the effect that the member was absent and could not be counted. Some controversy arose, which attracted the curiosity of the man outside. I watched him closely. He approached nearer and yet nearer. Finally, he stuck his head inside the opening and, quick as flash, I turned and shouted, 'There he is, now.' Before he could catch the point and dodge away he had been seen by half the members present. Mr. Spalding, your ruling was perfectly correct. But," he added, with a laugh, " You are no more President of the National League than am I. My knowledge of arithmetic does not enable me to make four votes a majority in an organization the total voting force of which is eight."

I was now regularly, legally and most emphatically enjoined from acting as President-Secretary-Treasurer of the League, and this condition lasted throughout the winter. Nothing could possibly be done in the way of perfecting arrangements for next season's play. In New York State I couldn't even express an opinion on the subject of Base Ball without being in contempt of court. I therefore spent most of my time in other States, where, without contempt of court, I could express my contempt of all men and all measures calculated to injure the game.

Finally, it became absolutely necessary to do something. The time when ball games ripen was nearly at hand, and the sport was restrained with me. I sent for Mr. Hart, then President of the Chicago Club, to visit me at my home at Point Loma, California. Upon his arrival he gave me satisfactory assurances that Mr. Freedman was ready to step down and out so soon as it could be made to appear that he was not forced out "under fire," as he expressed it. I told Mr. Hart that, if he was positive such an arrangement could be brought about, I would place in his hands my resignation, to be used at such time as would be most desirable for the ends aimed at. Armed with my resignation from an office to which I had never been legally elected, Mr. Hart returned. Mr. Freedman soon sold his interests in the New York Club to Mr. John T. Brush, and the incident was closed.

I have been informed that Mr. Freedman subsequently declared that he had won the battle; that "Spalding had been defeated in his aspirations to become President of the National League."

In view of the fact that I never wanted the **Presidency** of the League; in view of the further fact that I would not have accepted it save as a sure expedient for ridding the game of Freedmanism; in view of the still further fact that I repeatedly declared that if elected I would resign as soon as Freedmanism was eliminated by the ousting of Freedman; in view of the most important fact of all, that Andrew Freedman did get out, thereby making "Freedmanism" impossible, I am quite willing to let those interested in the great American game decide as to who won the battle.

If anyone needs any aid in arriving at a decision, the following among many similar paragraphs from a few of the leading papers of the country published at the time may serve the purpose:

Editorial from the New York *Evening World*, December 17, 1901:

"The Evening World violates no confidences in making the statement that the public is saying to A. G. Spalding, 'More strength to your arm!' in his efforts to put Andrew Freedman out of the Base Ball business for keeps."

Editorial in the Boston *Evening Record*, December 14, 1901:

"A. G. Spalding has been chosen President of the National League. That will mean a good deal for Base Ball according to straight-out business principles and regard for decent methods, because Spalding has made up his mind first of all to get rid of Freedman. The only way to make a fair start is to cut the thing right out at the roots by cutting Freedman out."

Editorial from the *Boston Herald*, December 18, 1901:

" The situation in the National League of Base Ball men is very badly complicated. Those who compose its directions are equally divided, four clubs being on one side and the same number on the other. As regards the right and wrong of their respective positions, the division also is about the same. Mr. Spalding, of Chicago, is entirely right in his effort to turn Mr. Freedman, of New York, out of Base Ball direction. Mr. Freedman has been the most serious injury to the sport of any man who ever engaged in it. His influence there has always been malign—in fact, if it continues, it is the opinion of the most intelligent men on the subject that he will bring about the ruin of the National League. Mr. Spalding is, therefore, to be applauded and encouraged in his efforts to get rid of Freedman."

Editorial from *Harper's Weekly*, December 28, 1901:

" A. G. Spalding's election as President of the National League is a distinct forward movement in Base Ball affairs, which have been and are yet in anything but a satisfactory condition. Mr. Spalding stands for clean sport, and his connection with the national game is so well known that it is superfluous to speak of it in this column. Freedman's influence, on the other hand, has been bad. New York, the greatest sporting city in the world, and loyal to the game to the very core, has been subjected to the most wretched management in its Base Ball affairs. It is unfortunate that Mr. Spalding, upon assuming the Presidency of the National League, must enter upon a law suit, but perhaps matters will straighten out ere the season opens. There is one thing to be remembered, however, and that is: Mr. Spalding will have the American public back of him, which Mr. Freedman, even if triumphant in the legal battle, never can hope for. Without the support of the public success is impossible."

CHAPTER XXIII.

Copyright, 1905, by Chickering.

BYRON BANCROFT JOHNSON

CHAPTER XXIII.

1900-10

ALTHOUGH minor leagues had been recognized and
protected long before—the National League having
fostered the first Northwestern League, organized in
1883—and the Eastern League, formed in 1884, having
received the protection of the National Agreement—and
notwithstanding the fact that numerous minor organizations were constantly coming into being, all feeling the
need of and seeking protecting care, it was not until early
in October, 1901, that the lesser leagues took action to
combine for self-protection; forced to do so, no doubt, by
the uncertainty of affairs of the two Major Leagues,
which at this time were at each other's throat in a deadly
strife.

The abrogation of the old National Agreement by Mr.
Freedman and his confreres at the historical secret Red
Bank meeting in 1901 cemented the minor leagues in a
closer bond than had theretofore existed, and the formation of "The National Association of Professional Base
Ball Leagues," at a postponed meeting held on the 24th,
25th and 26th of October, 1901, was therefore most
timely and important.

The objects of the new National Agreement, adopted

by the association of minor leagues, are set forth as follows:

" 1.—To perpetuate Base Ball as the National Game of America, and to surround it with such safeguards as to warrant absolute public confidence in its integrity and methods.

" 2.—To promote and afford protection to such professional Base Ball leagues and associations as may desire to operate under its provisions."

As one of its fundamental features, the new Association provided for a governing body, denominated " The National Board of Arbitration," to consist of five members, to be chosen by the Leagues represented in the Association. The first members of this Board were: M. H. Sexton, of Rock Island, Ill.; James Whitefield, of Kansas City, Mo.; W. H. Lucas, of Portland, Oregon; J. H. O'Rourke, of Bridgeport, Conn.; and T. H. Murnane, of Boston, Mass.; with J. H. Farrell, of Auburn, N. Y., acting as Secretary. The first President of this Association was P. T. Powers, a most energetic and competent official.

In 1902 the new American League, of which Mr. B. B. Johnson was President, determined to drop Baltimore from its circuit and replace it with New York. Consequently, since the two big leagues were at war, a raid was made by the American League upon players of the pioneer organization, with the result that no difficulty was found in capturing a team for the metropolis. Mr. Brush, however, who had bought out Freedman's interest in the New York National League Club, did not believe that the American League could secure available grounds, and he was disposed to temporize with the situation.

When the National League met in annual session in New York, in December of that year, its members were startled by the announcement that not only had grounds been secured, but that an "all star" team had been signed to play upon these grounds.

It did not take the managers of the older league long to realize that the time had come for peace with its rival, if peace was possible. Mr. Brush alone of all the club magnates was opposed to treating with the ambitious young league. Mr. Brush, however, was overruled, and a committee was appointed to call upon representatives of the American League, then present in the city, with overtures of peace. As the American League representatives were at New York upon another mission, they asked for time to lay the plans for a treaty before their League at a special session to be called for that purpose. The meeting referred to was held early in January, 1903, and a committee with power to act was appointed. The National League committee was retained, but no powers were given it except to confer and report. This resulted in further delay; but finally, after considerable sparring, a treaty of peace was agreed to which was subsequently ratified, and the two major leagues were now in a position to adopt mutual protective rules, which they did, under the title of a New National Agreement, in 1903.

This agreement was entered into between the National League of Professional Base Ball Clubs and the American League of Professional Base Ball Clubs, known as Major Leagues, as parties of the first part, and the National Association of Professional Base Ball Leagues

AUGUST HERRMANN

as party of the second part. The provisions were quite similar to those of the abrogated Agreement originally drafted by Mr. A. G. Mills, under which the National League had so long flourished, except that they also included a most important new feature, in a National Commission, to be composed of President of the National League, President of the American League, and a third member, to be chosen by the two above-mentioned officials.

The National Commission was to have power to inflict and enforce fines or suspensions or both upon either party to the agreement who are adjudged by it to have violated the terms of the agreement. It was provided that whenever the National League and the American League shall claim the services of the same player the right to the player in controversy shall be established by the Chairman of the Commission, who alone shall determine and declare the decision. It was provided that in case of controversy between a National League Club and a Minor League Club over the same player the case shall be adjudicated by the President of the Commission and the representative of the American League. In case of contention between an American League Club and a Minor League Club the question is to be settled by the President of the Commission and the National League representative. It was further provided, that in case the Chairman of the Commission and the representative of a League working with him in the adjudication of any case cannot agree, then the decision of the Chairman shall be final.

The first officials of the National Commission were H. C. Pulliam, President of the National League; B. B. John-

son, President of the American League; and August Herrmann, of the National League, chosen by the others as
Chairman of the Commission. These gentlemen served
until the death of Mr. Pulliam, in July, 1909, who was
succeeded by Thomas J. Lynch, the Commission as at
present constituted consisting of Messrs. Herrmann,
Lynch and Johnson.

Most fortunate, indeed, was the selection of August
Herrmann as third member of the National Commission.
Honest, earnest, ever devoted to the interests of the game,
he has brought to bear upon all cases brought before that
body for adjudication a mind unprejudiced, a judgment
keenly analytical and fair, and a will unswervable from
the cause of justice. Much of the credit for the splendid
record of the National Commission belongs to August
Herrmann, who has stood through his incumbency of a
trying position above criticism as an impartial and
upright official. It is to be hoped that his services may
be long retained as Chairman of the Commission that he
has honored.

Thus has been established a Supreme Court of Base
Ball. It has thus far worked admirably. It will continue so to act as long as men are at the head of the
National Game who are willing to subordinate personal
ends and aggrandizement to the good of the sport. Let
us hope that condition will last henceforth and forever—
that the people may never lose confidence in this ideal
tribunal.

In the evolution of Base Ball, it took many years for
those in control of the game to learn the very simple

lesson, known well to every man engaged in commerce, that "competition is the life of trade." It needed just such a man as B. B. Johnson, and just such a League as he has established, to provoke the kind of public interest that now attaches to the game of Base Ball. It requires just such competition as is annually presented in the post-season contests to give zest to the sport. So long as the National League was alone upon the field it occupied a position akin to that of the Old Knickerbockers. Had that ancient organization never encountered opposition, the chances are that there would never have developed a national game. And so it needed the American League, with the Boston Americans' victory of 1903, to make the National League managers realize that they had not all the ball players on earth—that there were others. And when the Chicago White Sox in 1906 again took the national pennant from the pioneer League, it served as nothing else could have done to stimulate interest in the sport in every quarter. Since the two big Leagues are now engaged in a generous rivalry, each conceding that the other has its legitimate place in the field, both are to be congratulated that wise counsels have prevailed and that at last a Supreme Court has been established upon sound legal and business bases that promises to simplify the conduct of the game in future by guaranteeing justice in all cases where arbitration is found necessary.

The need of co-operation between Leagues was never better illustrated than during the Freedman controversy. The two Leagues were at that time engaged in a fratri-

H. C. PULLIAM

cidal war. And yet B. B. Johnson was big enough and broad enough to extend his aid in ridding the game of Freedmanism at that time, and had the full moral support of the American League. A smaller-minded man would have seen in that case an opportunity to twist the knife blade that had been inserted into the body of his rival and helped the enemies of its own household to kill it out- right. But he was not that kind of man. Throughout that entire struggle he stood by me most royally, and I am glad of this opportunity thus publicly to express my appreciation of his unselfish, patriotic efforts to preserve the integrity of our National Game.

It was not a great while after the coming together of the two big Leagues in a mutual understanding until a series of World's Championship games was proposed. So long as a bitter fight had been in progress this was impossible, of course. But, in 1903, the Boston and Pittsburg teams, winners of the American and National League pennants, respectively, met for an after-season schedule of games. To the very great surprise of the friends of the National League, who, up to that time, had regarded the players of the American League as not in the same class as those of the older organization, Boston took five games to three won by Pittsburg, and immediately the fortunes of the American League advanced by leaps and bounds. The contest of 1903 had established the equality if not the superiority of the players in the new League.

In 1904 there was no World's Championship series, the New York team, winners of the National League pennant, declining, for some reason, to meet the Boston winners of the American League pennant. This fact only sharpened the desire of the public for another contest. The wish was gratified in 1905, when the New York Champions met and defeated the Philadelphia Athletics, of the American League, winning four out of five games played.

In 1906 the tables were turned, and the Chicago White Sox, of the American League, defeated the Chicago Cubs, of the National League, winning four games to two of the series. The public was now beginning to look upon the World's Championship as a sort of hippodrome, cut and dried, to go one year to one and the next year to the other League. However, Captain Chance, of the Chicago National Cubs, upset that theory by winning the world's series over the Detroit Tigers, of the American League, two seasons in succession, capturing pennants in both 1907 and 1908, and the Pittsburg National League Club winning from the Detroit American League Club in 1909, and the Athletic American League Club winning from the Chicago National League Club in 1910.

Of scarcely less interest than the World's Championship contests were those between leaders in both the National and American Leagues in 1908, Chicago, New York and Pittsburg teams crowding each other in the National race, and Detroit, Cleveland and Chicago alternating throughout the season for the first place in the American League.

In 1909 the race in the National League was between Pittsburg and Chicago, Pittsburg winning. In the American League, Detroit, Philadelphia and New York led, Detroit finishing first.

In 1910 Chicago and New York were at the front, the Cubs winning the National pennant, and in the American League the Philadelphia Athletics won from New York.

It was in April, 1908, that Henry Chadwick, for more than fifty years connected as a writer on Base Ball matters with publications of New York and Brooklyn, died at his home in the latter city.

From the time of his arrival in America, at the age of thirteen years, Henry Chadwick was closely identified with our national game. As a lad, he saw it played by its earliest exponents. He was personally acquainted with members of the first Base Ball club ever organized. He knew all the members of the two famous quartets of clubs in New York and Brooklyn. He attended and made records of games played before the first Association of Base Ball Players was formed. He devised the first system of scoring and recording contests on the ball field.

In young manhood he became an authority on the playing of the game, and was personally instrumental in the working out of many improvements in the game itself. Aside from his acknowledged gifts as a writer of pure and forceful English, Mr. Chadwick possessed a peculiar penchant for statistics. To this attribute of Mr. Chadwick more than to any other source is attributable the perfectly accurate records covering the entire professional field and for which the game is to-day indebted.

But it was not to Mr. Chadwick's love for Base Ball,

"FATHER" CHADWICK

great as it was; not to his ability as a writer, forceful and graceful as his literary efforts were ever acknowledged to be; not to his accuracy as a statistician, perfect as were his achievements along those lines; but to his indomitable energy and sublime courage in behalf of the integrity of Base Ball that our national game is most indebted for its high standing in the estimation of the American people.

Coming upon the stage of action at a time when the gambling and pool-selling evils were threatening its very life, he threw himself with all the force of an ardent nature into the struggle. He saw the managers of the early associations temporizing with the abuses referred to, encouraging them by continued toleration; but never for an instant did he falter in his demands for a clean game. He made enemies by the hundreds; he received the personal abuse of unscrupulous newspapers and their correspondents; he called upon his head the anathemas of all who were guilty, and the sneers and jibes of the weak and vacillating. He demanded the eradication of gambling. He exhorted strict temperance in the ranks of all ball players and advocated extreme measures in dealing with habitual inebriates. He insisted upon fair treatment of umpires, seeking always the enactment of rigid rules protecting them against rowdies, whether on the field, in grandstand or on bleachers. During the early evolution and development of the game, he was for many years Chairman of the Committees on Rules in the leading Associations. In that position his efforts were uniformly for rules looking to the upbuilding of an edifice of sport that should withstand the shocks of all time.

CHADWICK MONUMENT

As to his personality, I was for many years intimately associated with him and knew the fine old gentleman well. I cannot better express my estimate of him now than I did at the time of his death in these closing words of my contribution to his memorial tributes:

"I don't believe he had an enemy in the world, and I am sure I voice the sentiments of everyone interested in Base Ball and clean athletic sports when I say that he was an honor to the game he loved so well and for which he did so much."

April, 1909, witnessed the unveiling in Greenwood Cemetery of the monument erected to the memory of this fine old gentleman. It is a beautiful stone, and for ages will tell the story of how a good man's worth is esteemed by those who knew it and felt its influence.

The following, from the pen of John B. Foster, appeared in the New York *Evening Telegram* of April 22, 1909:

"On the eastern side of Greenwood Cemetery, near the driveway which circles from the Ninth Avenue entrance, is the grave of Henry Chadwick, the 'Father of Base Ball.'

"The plot is in a newer portion of the beautiful burying ground. The trees have not begun to grow above it yet, but the flowers have, and there are banks of pansies and violets around the mound underneath which sleeps the dead writer.

"Organized Base Ball, and the men who are connected with organized Base Ball, contributed to the monument to the dead. Yesterday it was unveiled. Very appropriately, the unveiling was done by Miss Leonora V. Caylor, daughter of another veteran writer on the national game, O. P. Caylor, formerly of the editorial staff of the *New York Herald* and also of that of the *Cincinnati Commercial Tribune* and the old *Sporting Times*.

"The monument which has been erected to the memory of Mr. Chadwick is a plain and simple gray granite shaft, quite massive in dimensions. On its top there is a huge Base Ball carved in granite and on three sides of the shaft there are bronze tablets which tell the story of his life and the story of the sport toward which he contributed so much. One tablet gives his age and across it, in letters which will last ages, there is the well-known inscription, 'Father of Base Ball.' The other tablets show bats crossed with the mask and the glove, which are part of the implements of the national pastime.

"Mrs. Chadwick, who is ninety years of age, was present yesterday with her daughters and listened to the ceremoni·s at the side of the grave. The Rev. Dr. T. E. Potterton, of the Church of Our Father, began with prayer, after which Miss Caylor pulled the cord which held a national flag in folds over the monument. Mr. William Hudson, of the *Brooklyn Eagle* editorial staff, a personal friend of the dead writer, delivered the oration, and Charles H. Ebbets, President of the Brooklyn Base Ball Club, in behalf of organized Base Ball, presented the monument to Mrs. Chadwick.

"Miss Florence Richter, daughter of the editor of *Sporting Life,* designed the monument, which was warmly praised by those who were present yesterday at the dedication ceremonies."

"THE OLD TIME BASE BALL F

George Wood	J. H. O'Rourke	John E. Manning	S. Henry Hooper	J. J. Hurley	Mertie M. Hackett	Clarence W. Sm
Worcester 1880	Boston 1873 to '78-'80	Boston 1873-'79	Harvard 1875	Boston 1866	Boston 1883-4-5	Harvard 1886
T. H. Bond	Walter S. Barnes, Jr.	Dr. S. A. Hopkins	T. H. Gray	Walter H. Hackett	T. McCarthy	
Boston 1877-'81 Committee	Harvard 1884 Committee	Iowa University 1877	Harvard 1867	Boston 1885	Boston 1885, '92-'95	
T. H. Murnane	H. C. Schafer	Wm. H. Hawes	Thos. F. Gunning	J. W. Rollins, Jr.	Webster Thayer	John A. Lowell
Boston 1876 Committee	Boston 1871	Boston 1879	Boston 1883-4	M. I. T. 1879	Dartmouth 1880	Lowells 1861
Frank Barrows	John F. Morrill	A. G. Spalding	Geo. A. Sawyer	John F. Kent	Ivers W. Adams	Col. Geo. A.
Boston 1871	Boston 1876 Committee	Boston 1871-'75	Harvard 1877	Harvard 1875	First Pres't Boston Club 1871	Harvard 18

CHAPTER XXIV.

BOSTON, SEPTEMBER 24, 1908

| Rufus S. Woodward | | C. P. Nunn | Geo. W. Foster | Jas. A. Gallivan | Samuel E. Winslow | | Walter I. Badger | Wm. F. Garcelon |
| Amherst 1881 | | Harvard 1879 | Harvard 1887 | Harvard 1888 | Harvard 1885 Committee | | Yale 1882 Committee | Harvard L. S 1895 Committee |

| ard | Charles F. Bearse | Geo. M. Richardson | Wm. H. Folsom | Louis A. Frothingham | Wm. H. Coolidge | Col. E. C. Benton | J. J. Hallahan |
| | Boston Jrs. 1872 | Beacons 1879 | Harvard 1881 | Harvard 1893 | Harvard Committee 1881 | Chairman of Committee | Announcer |

| T. Fearing | F. W. Blair | A. H. Latham | Rev. C. F. Carter | | Adams Crocker | | Chas. D. Burt | Master Horace Murnane |
| Harvard 1882 | Amherst 1881 | Harvard 1874 | Yale 1878 | | Harvard 1885 | | Harvard 1882 | (T. H. Murnane's son) |

| Fred. W. Thayer | Samuel J. Elder | Jas. A. Tyng | H. C. Beaman | | Wm. Nash | | Frank Whitney |
| Harvard 1878 | Yale 1873 | Harvard 1876 | Harvard 1885 | | Boston 1885-'95 | | Boston 1876 |

ball, to be played at some intermediate spot on or before July 4th," which was passed by a strong majority. A committee was appointed of J. T. Claflin, senior class; Walker, junior class; H. D. Hyde, sophomore, and T. Tomson, freshman, to make arrangements for the game. A challenge was immediately sent and accepted for thirteen picked men of each college to meet on June 27th. A delegation from Williams was to meet that from Amherst at Chester Factories and draw up the rules and regulations for the game. Mr. Hyde, of Amherst, met the two Williams delegates, but nothing was agreed on. On Mr. Hyde's return, negotiations were carried on by mail for two weeks, till at last it was amicably settled that each party should use its own ball, and it must always be caught on the fly, sixty-five runs to be the limit of the game. The Pittsfield Base Ball Club offered its grounds for the game, and July 1st was appointed as the date.

There was to be but one drawback to the game. All Williams College was to be present, including the faculty, while Amherst allowed only the players to go.

It is interesting to note the manner of selecting the team for this game. The men were "chosen by ballot from the students at large." There was no long period of daily practice and no elimination from the squad at various times.

On Thursday afternoon Amherst's seventeen picked men started for Pittsfield. They arrived in Pittsfield eager for battle. Soon the Williams boys began pouring into town until it seemed as if Williams must be deserted. Old men and women, young men and maidens, proprietors

CHAPTER XXIV.

BASE BALL IN COLLEGES, ACADEMIES AND PUBLIC SCHOOLS—
FIRST RECORDED INTERCOLLEGIATE GAME—BASE BALL
AND EDUCATION GO HAND IN HAND—NOTABLE REUNION
OF OLD COLLEGIANS AND PROFESSIONALS.

1859–1910

WITH Dr. Oliver Wendell Holmes declaring that he
played a game called Base Ball while at college—
and he graduated at Harvard in 1829—and from other
published facts, it is certain that the game (then generally known as "Town Ball" or the Massachusetts game
of Base Ball) was known in the leading colleges many
years before the breaking out of the Civil War. But the
first recorded intercollegiate game took place in 1859,
just two years before the struggle of the 60's began.

This game was between Amherst and Williams, and
was played at Pittsfield on July 1, and was won by
Amherst by a score of 66 to 32. There are now hanging
in the Amherst College trophy room the two balls which
were used in this game, which bear the following inscription: "The veritable balls used in the first game of intercollegiate Base Ball ever played, July 1, 1859, Amherst
vs. Williams, won by Amherst."

This is how it came about. At a meeting of the college, directly after morning prayers, at which Mr. Sneed,
of the senior class, presided, Mr. Claflin made a motion
that "Amherst challenge Williams to a friendly game of

345

of female schools with their pupils—the great square of the ball ground was surrounded five or six deep.

The appearance of the teams on the field must have been very amusing, although there was some attempt at uniformity of dress, as "the Williams team were all dressed alike and wore belts marked Williams, but the appearance of the Amherst team was decidedly undress. The only attempt at a uniform was the blue ribbon which each man had pinned on his breast."

It seems that the question of professionalism entered even into the first game, as it was "rumored that the Amherst thrower was the professional blacksmith who had been hired for the occasion." A bystander remarked that "the story must be true, as nobody but a blacksmith could possibly throw for three and a half hours as he did."

The Amherst ball weighed two and one-half ounces and was about six inches in circumference. It was made by Henry Hebard, of North Brookfield, and was considered a work of art at the time.

The Williams ball was about seven inches in circumference, weighed about two ounces, and was covered with light colored leather, so as to make it seen with difficulty by the batters.

About 11 o'clock the game started, with Amherst having the first inning, and at the end of the second round the score stood: Amherst, 1; Williams, 9. This success called out from the Williams students a long, universal clapping and cheering whenever one of their comrades gained a tally. Amherst grew desperate and at the end of the third round stood even; at the end of the fourth

NOT LIKE THIS IN THE OLDEN TIME

round Amherst led, and continued to do so until the end of the game, sometimes having three tallies to one for Williams.

After four hours of steady playing, in which twenty-six rounds had been played, with no intermission and with unabated interest on the part of the spectators, the game was decided finished, and Amherst was declared the winner by the score of 66 to 32.

The batting order of the teams was as follows:

AMHERST TALLIES		WILLIAMS TALLIES	
J. T. Claflin (C.)	7	H. S. Anderson (C.)	2
E. W. Pierce	5	H. T. C. Nichols	2
S. J. Storrs	7	R. E. Beecher	3
P. E. Tower	7	J. E. Bush	4
M. B. Cushman	4	J. H. Knox	4
J. A. Evans	5	S. W. Pratt, 2d	2
E. W. Fenn	6	A. J. Quick	3
H. D. Hyde, thrower	4	B. F. Hastings	4
J. A. Leach	5	J. L. Mitchell	3
H. C. Roome	5	C. E. Simmons	4
H. Gridley	5	G. P. Blagden	1
T. Tomson	6	H. B. Fitch	0
L. R. Smith, Umpire.		G. A. Parker	0
		C. R. Taft, Umpire.	

Referee, W. R. Plunkett, President Pittsfield Base Ball Club.

In his interesting book, "Old Boston Boys and the Games They Played," published in 1908 by Brown, Little & Co., Boston, Mr. James d'Wolf Lovett writes: "About this time we lent our aid to the class of '66 in organizing the first club at Harvard under the New York rules." This would seem to indicate that theretofore, in common with most other clubs in that section, Harvard had been playing under the New England rules, which differed materially from the New York game under the Knickerbocker rules.

Continuing, upon the same subject, Mr. Lovett says: " The prime movers in starting this game at Harvard were George Flagg, Frank Wright, Arthur Hunnewell, Tom Nelson, Eugene Greenleaf, Frank Harris, Ned Sprague, George Parker, Putnam Abercrombie, Charles Fiske and others. Thus was the pioneer Base Ball club of Harvard College duly organized."

We may safely assume that all the colleges of the New England States knew the game before the Civil War period, and that those of all the Atlantic States had teams soon after the struggle, in the furore for Base Ball that followed upon its heels. The statistical columns of the Guides contain the records of the hard-fought contests of every year since the game has been established in the great educational institutions of the land. Every season has witnessed fine exhibitions in contests between college teams, and not a few of the best League professionals have graduated from colleges to enter the game as a vocation.

There are now fully half a hundred or more regularly organized teams in connection with the leading Universities of this country. Among them are Alabama, Amherst, Arkansas, Army, Beloit, Brown, Bucknell, Carlisle, Chicago, Columbia, Cornell, Dartmouth, DePauw, Fordham,

Georgia, Georgetown, Harvard, Holy Cross, Illinois, Indiana, Lafayette, Maine, Michigan, Minnesota, Navy, New York, Northwestern, of Evanston, Ill.; Northwestern, of Watertown, Wis.; Pennsylvania, Princeton, Purdue, Rochester, Seton Hall, Southern California, Syracuse, Texas, Vermont, Virginia, Wisconsin, Washington and Jefferson, Washington State, Wesleyan, West Virginia, Westminster, Williams and Yale.

That education and Base Ball go hand in hand had notable exemplification at Boston in the fall of 1908. The story, as given below, is from Boston papers:

(*The Globe*, Sunday, September 20, 1908.)

"OLD-TIMERS WILL HAVE GREAT GAME.

" PROFESSIONALS AND COLLEGE MEN TO WEAR OLD UNIFORMS—NOVEL GATHERING TO BE HELD THURSDAY.

" One of the old masters would have the opportunity of a lifetime could he come back to this mundane sphere for but one afternoon, next Thursday, and sketch the animated picture that will be presented at the American League Ball Park, when members of the old-time Boston National League world-beaters will meet for a friendly bout their old college rivals. Then the crimson of Harvard, the blue of old Yale, with the green of Dartmouth, will meet in a kaleidoscope of color.

" This first meeting of old professionals with genuine college amateurs will be a red-letter day in the history of our national pastime.

" The professionals will wear the same style and color of uniforms worn by the Boston Club in the 70s, while the collegians will appear once more in the same style and color of the uniforms worn by the rah rah boys during their days in college.

" No player will be allowed to take part in the game who has played ball for the last twenty years, while age or early service will be no handicap to a player taking part in the mighty contest. In fact, the more ancient, the more honor and glory for the individual.

" John F. Morrill, famous in his day as a player, captain, and finally manager of the Boston Club, has given much time to make the event a success.

"OUR CHOICE"

"Among those sure to be here for the game will be A. G. Spalding, who pitched nearly every game for the Boston Champions during the first five years of their existence, and who was one of the original members of the club in 1871.

"Mr. Spalding arrived East from California last Thursday, and wired at once from New York to Mr. Morrill, sending his measurement for a uniform for the occasion.

"George Wright, one of the original members of the team, is due to arrive in Boston from California to-day and should be in good shape to enter the contest.

"James H. O'Rourke, a second-year member of the team, still playing ball, has accepted the invitation to join the old fellows, objecting, however, to being considered an old-timer.

"John Manning, who started out with the team in '74, as young as ever, is already on the ground working for new glory.

"Harry Schafer, one of the original third-base men, will be there in his old-time style, as young as ever in mind and heart.

"Frank Whitney, a member of the '76 team, will come on from New York. Among others who have promised to be on hand wearing the grand army badges of the old Boston Club will be Jerry Hurley, William Haws, Robert Wheelock, John O'Rourke and Thomas Bond, one of the really great pitchers of the country for Boston for several years. Charley Snyder from Washington, Murtie Hackett, Dr. Thomas Gunning from Fall River, Thomas McCarthy, one of the real kings of the diamond, John Burdock, if possible, and several others. As guests John M. Ward and John Chapman will be on hand. Among those who will take a long chance will be the writer.

"Col. Sam Winslow has full charge of the college end of the meeting, and reports everything going along swimmingly. The colonel was a prime favorite at Harvard about '85, when the old college had a ball team that made the boys sit up and take notice. Walter I. Badger, the old Yale second baseman; William Coolidge, who covered second for Harvard at the same time, and Fred Thayer, the captain of the great Harvard team of '77, have lined up the old guard from their colleges in the most enthusiastic manner. Bigelow Carter and A. Hubbard will wear the blue once more on the ball field, J. Rollins of Tech, and the greatest amateur catcher of his time, George Richardson, and a large number of college men will be out to offer their services to make the meeting a grand, all-round success.

"The gate receipts will go to charity, and Col. Benton and Col. George B. Billings have given much of their valuable time to make the event one long to be remembered.

"A banquet at the Algonquin Club after the strenuous day's work is down on the program, where the old games will be won over again and Base Ball made better for the meeting of the men who were instrumental in building up a national sport."

(*Boston Transcript,* September 25, 1908.)

"AN HONEST OLD-TIME GAME.

"PROFESSIONALS DEFEAT AMATEURS OR COLLEGIANS IN BASE BALL CONTEST OF EXCEPTIONAL CHARACTER—SUCCESSFUL BANQUET IN THE EVENING.

"There was nothing of the burlesque order in the remarkable game of Base Ball played on the Huntington Avenue grounds yesterday by forty-three old-time professional and amateur players. It was a game in which men famous on the diamond in the seventies and eighties took part, and by instinct their old cunning, dulled a bit by long lack of practice, came back to them for the afternoon, and they played the best Base Ball of which they were capable. For seven innings men with gray hair, men with little hair at all, men grown rotund and men grown thin, assumed the old Base Ball gait, laid for infield and outfield flies, and handled the willow at the bat as only men to the diamond born can. For six innings the score ran evenly, the amateurs, or collegians, getting two runs in the first, the professionals one in the third and two in the fourth, and the amateurs tying the score in the sixth with two more runs added to the one they had pounded out in the fifth. In the seventh inning the professionals fell on Smith, Harvard, '86, and by timely work at the bat secured two runs. As the amateurs were blanked in that inning and the game was called, the final score was: Professionals 7, Amateurs 5.

"Practically every one of the celebrities of decades ago who had promised to take part showed up. To mention all the achievements and past affiliations of each would require columns of space; suffice it that A. G. Spalding, who used to pitch for Boston thirty-seven years ago and probably is the best known man in the Base Ball world, was there, and, in a clean white flannel uniform occupied the pitcher's box for several innings. Next to him was Colonel Samuel E. Winslow, who was captain of the Harvard team of '85, which took the collegiate championship by winning twenty-six games and losing one; and after him Walter Badger, Yale's old foot ball and Base Ball player of the early eighties. The two latter acted as captains of the amateur teams yesterday. Mr. Badger played throughout the game; but it was Colonel Winslow who received the cheers of the crowd of six thousand people when, the first and only time up at the bat, he dropped a beauty in short center and made possible the **tying**

.'un. He had only one chance in right field and that was to chase a rolling ball clear to the back fence. His throw in was a work of art.

"The majority of college players were old Harvard men, but there were several from Yale, Dartmouth, M. I. T., Amherst and the University of Iowa. Twenty-seven men were used on their side, while the professionals had sixteen men. Everybody had a crack at the ball or a chance in the field. There were three umpires, Hon. Louis A. Frothingham, candidate for the Republican nomination for lieutenant governor and an old Harvard Base Ball captain himself; Hon. James A. Gallivan, another Harvard man, and Joe Kelley, manager of the Boston Nationals. It was odd to note under what rules the old-timers played. They moved the pitcher's box nearer the plate at least ten feet; the pitchers threw an underhand ball; the batsmen called for a high, low or fair ball, and they had to have it; they had a chance to have nine balls called before they took a base; they ran the danger of being out on caught foul tips; and the catchers could catch foul flies on the bounce and still have their man out. Also, to effect a double play, the catcher could drop the ball after a third strike, pick it up, touch the home plate, and then nail a runner between bases, scoring a double play. All of these things, with the personalities and the histories of the players, with men with megaphones to announce everything, and with the First Corps Cadet Band to break the innings with tunes appropriate to the individual players, made a very interesting afternoon.

"In the evening a banquet at the Algonquin Club was attended by all of the participants in the game and a few invited guests. Governor Guild and Hon. Louis A. Frothingham were compelled to send letters of regret. Colonel Everett C. Benton, chairman of the committee in charge of the event, introduced Colonel Winslow as toastmaster, and he called on Mr. Spalding for the first speech. The latter said he was glad he had come three thousand miles for the game, for Boston was the only city where such an event could be carried through successfully. He referred to the fact that the national game got its first real start in this city. 'Just as Boston was the cradle of liberty for the Nation, so also was it the cradle in which the infant game was helped to a healthy maturity,' he added. 'The work of the early Boston teams, with Harry Wright—God bless him—Messrs. Adams, Porter, George Wright and other Nestors of Base Ball, left its impress for all that is good in the national game. Base Ball is fast getting a foothold in the remote parts of the world, and the time is surely coming when it will be the universal field sport of the world.'

"John Lowell, the oldest Base Ball player in the party—he was seventy-one years of age July 29 last, and in honor of whom the famous Lowell Base Ball team was named—told of the difficulties the players of those days had in getting practice, and said that the young men in commercial life who played carried their bases from the clubhouse in Bowdoin Square to the Common at 5 o'clock in the morning, played until 7 o'clock and then went to their day's work.

"Samuel J. Elder, Yale, '73, who was the closing speaker of the evening, said that Base Ball was typically American, just as Cricket was typically English. The two games illustrated in an exceptional manner the habits and the sentiments of the two nations.

"'In England the principal Cricket matches in which the championship of the country is at stake often take three days to finish. They go about it in a leisurely, dignified way, the spectators bringing with them their luncheon, and the players often taking tea during the game. Imagine Mike Kelly or any of the idols of Base Ball taking tea during a game! In America we have our hour and fifteen or thirty minutes. It is swift, sharp, keen play. It is decisive, and the same fan who hustles from his office, hangs on to the rail of a car, then gets to the game and enters into it with the keenest zest, is in as great a hurry to get home when the game is over. Base Ball is not only a great pastime, but it is a great salvation, just as is anything that gets people out into the open.'

"Others who spoke were John F. Morrill, Boston, '76-88; George Richardson, Beacon Base Ball Club; Webster Thayer, Dartmouth, '79; C. H. Taylor, Iver W. Adams, first president of the Boston Base Ball Club; Charles Porter, successor to Mr. Adams; Joseph J. Kelley, manager of the Boston Nationals; Timothy H. Murnane, and Walter I. Badger, Yale, '82."

All the larger cities have Public School Athletic Leagues, with regular Base Ball organizations auxiliary thereto. The influence of these is being rapidly extended throughout the country, and now many cities of 50,000 population and upwards are organizing leagues in the ward schools, playing regularly-scheduled matches for trophies, presented sometimes by local friends and sometimes by patrons of the game who are interested in a more general way.

What the outcome of this new movement may be no one may safely predict. Since the government has endorsed Base Ball as a National Game, to be fostered and encouraged as a means for building up a healthful, contented and well-disciplined Army and Navy; as the national administration has found that it pays to provide bats, balls, bases and all the paraphernalia of the game to our soldiers and sailors, is it too much to expect that the time will come when these concomitants of our national pastime may be regarded as just as essential to the equipment of a well-appointed school as globes, maps, chemicals and astronomical apparatus?

Perhaps the following able editorial from the columns of the Newark, N. J., *Evening News*, of September 10th, 1908, answers the question:

"BASE BALL FOR BOYS.

"The Trenton experiment of providing Base Ball for boys under proper supervision is noteworthy because of its success from practically every reasonable point of view. The experiment consisted of devoting a large proportion of one of Trenton's public parks to the use of Trenton's youthful ball players. A large number of 'diamonds' were laid out and a fund was provided whereby balls and bats were purchased. Then, to prevent disputes and disorder, umpires were also selected whose judgment could be relied on and whose decisions were final.

"A Junior Base Ball League was organized and prizes were awarded for the champion players. No less than 153 teams of about a dozen boys each were formed and admitted to this league, and the summer's series of championship games began last June. Out of that number 147 teams completed the series and still remain in the organization, ready and eager to begin another series next summer. Four months ago a majority of the Trenton people would probably have said that not half the Junior League teams would last the season through, but an American boy can no more be separated from Base Ball than he can from the dinner table when he's hungry.

"This 'boys' movement' has taken such a firm hold in Trenton that last week 6,000 citizens attended an athletic meet near that city, given for the benefit of the movement, and $1,000 was netted with which to promote and maintain the Base Ball fields and other playgrounds next year. And the beauty of it is, that there has been clean, harmless Base Ball under reliable auspices, the boys have been kept out of danger, mischief and immoral associations, and the police records show a very marked decrease in the number of juvenile arrests. Not a single arrest for disorder was made during the entire summer at the ball grounds, though many hotly disputed points had to be settled.

"Trenton boys are exactly like the boys of other cities. They love Base Ball. If they can't play themselves they will dig holes in the board fences, climb trees, sit astride chimneys and take all manner of risks to see others play. If they can't play in the parks they will play in the streets, and if there's no place at home they will run away to play. Trenton seems to have successfully solved the problem of what to do for the boys, and is now trying to find out what to do for the girls. It all goes to show that children must play. It is their privilege by nature, by right and by necessity."

CHAPTER XXV.

LINCOLN'S NOTIFICATION

CHAPTER XXV.

1860–1910

ATTENTION has been called heretofore to the baptism of Base Ball as "Our National Game" during the Civil War. But even before that unhappy era it held among its devotees one who was soon to become Commander-in-Chief of Army and Navy.

It is recorded that in the year 1860, when the Committee of the Chicago Convention which nominated Abraham Lincoln for the Presidency visited his home at Springfield, Illinois, to notify him formally of the event, the messenger sent to apprise him of the coming of the visitors found the great leader out on the commons, engaged in a game of Base Ball. Information of the arrival of the party was imparted to Mr. Lincoln on the ball field.

"Tell the gentlemen," he said, "that I am glad to know of their coming; but they'll have to wait a few minutes till I make another base hit."

The authenticity of this incident I have no reason to question. The facts as here presented were conveyed to me in a letter under date of December 18th, 1908, from Mr. John F. Morrill, of Boston, which letter is in my possession. The truthfulness of the story was further established by another communication from Mr. Waldo M. Claflin, of Philadelphia, who had it from a personal and intimate friend of Mr. Lincoln himself, Mr. Alexander P. Brown, of Philadelphia.

The interest of former President Roosevelt in athletics, and his special predilection for Base Ball, are too recently and too generally known to require emphasis here. While President, Mr. Roosevelt, in his capacity as Commander-in-Chief of Army and Navy, used his official efforts upon frequent occasions to secure the playing of Base Ball at Army and Navy stations, by garrisons and crews, urging that it was the best available means of preserving the *esprit de corps*, and an excellent avenue for the administration of discipline. He has ever stood for Base Ball as the out-of-door game *par excellence* of the American people, and no wonder! For he is himself the very incarnation of all that goes to make a great ball player.

Quite recent dispatches by the Associated Press report President William H. Taft and Vice-President Sherman as frequent, highly-interested spectators at Base Ball games at the Capital. Here is one of them:

"WASHINGTON, April 19, 1910.—President Taft went to the Base Ball game to-day, saw Washington beaten, 8 to 4, by the Boston Americans, was initiated into the mysteries of the 'spit ball,' shared a five-cent bag of peanuts with Vice-President Sherman, wished hard for Washington to win and said sadly that he hoped he was not a hoodoo.

"President Taft arrived at the beginning of the second inning. The Vice-President, a dyed-in-the-wood fan, had gone directly to the grounds from the Senate chamber.

"Mr. Sherman kept a detailed score of the game, supplying the President with such statistical information as he asked for, and caused some one in the party to remark that if he ever lost the job of Vice-President, he might get a place on Ban Johnson's scoring staff.

"The President was disappointed in Washington's failure to win, but he said he enjoyed the game and hoped to get to the park frequently.

"The President was the center of interest up to the sixth inning, when Washington got the bases full, with no one out. Then the ruling passion put the chief executive temporarily in eclipse and the faithful rooters nearly yelled their heads off for Delehanty to 'Hit 'er out!' and for Charley Street to 'Biff it in the eye!' Two runs resulted from the combination of bats and cheers.

"Mr. Taft was as interested as all the rest. He knows Base Ball thoroughly and is up on all the finer points of the game. The day was ideal for the national game."

As long ago as when the late Hon. Paul Morton was Secretary of the Navy, in 1905, for the purpose of obtaining correct information and data as to the status of Base Ball in that branch of the public service, I wrote a personal letter to that official, and received the following interesting reply, which is here published for the first time:

"NAVY DEPARTMENT.

"Mr. A. G. Spalding,   "Washington, March 9, 1905.
    "Point Loma, Cal.

"*Dear Sir:*—I am in receipt of your letter of the 2d instant in reference to Base Ball in the Navy. The enlisted men of the Navy have been playing Base Ball as far back as the memory of anybody in the Department goes and it is the chief amusement of the men on whatever station they may be. For years the game was carried on by subscription on the part of the officers and men, but in 1903 my predecessor, Secretary Moody, issued an order, a copy of which is enclosed, which provided the necessary material for the sport at the expense of the Government. With the facilities thus given, the game has been even more general than it had been in former years, and wherever two or three vessels are together, and the weather is favorable, Base Ball games are arranged between the ships, and between representative nines of the ships and land crews, which attract general attention wherever they are played.

"I am advised that on the Asiatic Station during the last several years regular series of games have been played between teams representing the different vessels of the squadron, and these games were attended by thousands of people, natives of the ports at which the vessels happened to be lying. The games between the teams representing the vessels of the North Atlantic Squadron are features of

EX-SECRETARY OF U. S. NAVY PAUL MORTON

the winter maneuvers in the West Indies, and whenever opportunity offers in the summer and fall cruises the tests are carried on.

"Many games are played between teams representing vessels of the Navy and posts of the Army whenever a vessel of the Navy happens to be stationed in the vicinity of one of the shore posts. The officers who have the responsibility of the administration of the enlisted personnel of the Navy recognize Base Ball as one of the very best influences in connection with the discipline of the ship, not only for the men who actually engage in the game but for the very much larger number of men who are interested spectators. The spirit of the crew of each ship in behalf of their Base Ball team runs very high and there is a healthy rivalry stimulated, not only to develop the best possible teams but to keep the good conduct classes of the vessels large, so that each vessel may have the largest delegation of 'rooters' at the games. The possibility of being debarred from going ashore to witness a ball game is probably a most efficient influence towards preserving discipline and good conduct on ships during the Base Ball season.

"The officers take an active interest in the game, and the training of the ship's team is directed by an officer who has played ball at Annapolis and who generally acts as captain of the team.

"The influence of the game, as far as I am able to ascertain, is most beneficial and it is heartily encouraged by the Department as a means of giving the men rational enjoyment and to make them contented with the service. It is claimed by officers who have had charge of Base Ball teams that where a team has been kept together for a considerable period of time Base Ball playing is developed that would do credit to professionals.

"While foot ball is also encouraged as one of the sports of the enlisted men, it has never secured the popularity and has never been developed to so high a point as has been the fact with Base Ball.

"I trust that the above will be of interest to you and that it will answer the purpose of which you write.

"Very truly yours,   "PAUL MORTON,
                          "*Secretary, U. S. Navy.*"

As regards Base Ball in the Army, it is pleasant to note the fact that the national game is by far the most popular form of sport known to our national defenders, the rank and file of the regular army; but it will be readily understood that, under our system, in times of peace not many men are stationed at any one point in our country, and hence but little is heard of the games played at small

forts and the few presidios. Wherever troops are stationed, however, contests between nines composed of soldiers and civilians resident in the vicinity are of frequent
occurrence.

Speaking of Base Ball in the army, a non-commis-
sioned officer of the Twelfth Regiment, U. S. A., said
recently:

"Yes, the game is a great one among the boys, even in the far
West. While I was a bit too old to play, I saw plenty of Base Ball
there before coming East to Chickamauga and Tampa at the beginning of the Spanish War. Our regiment, the Twelfth Infantry, is
the acknowledged champion of the Army. I don't believe the
Twelfth's team has ever been beaten, and it has met some strong
opponents, too, among the Southern League Clubs. When they are
practicable, trips to other posts are frequently made, and in an out-
of-the-way garrison a rattling good Base Ball game is no ordinary
event. Everybody turns out to see the play. Our colonel—the one
we had before the war—he has since been made a brigadier general—
was a thoroughbred sport and entered into the spirit of the game
with as much vim as the newest recruit. In fact, Base Ball is the
game throughout the entire Army and I don't know what the boys
would do without it. In the winter there is regular gymnasium exercise at most posts, but it isn't like a nip and tuck tussle on the
diamond."

The United States Army and Navy have been very
important factors in the advancement and development of
the game of Base Ball. While the game did not originate
in the Army or Navy, these important departments of our
government were the media through which the sport, during the Civil War, was taken out of its local environments—New York and Brooklyn—and started upon its
national career.

The returning veterans, "when the cruel war" was
"over," disseminated Base Ball throughout the country
and then established it as the national game of America.

At the breaking out of the war, in 1861, the New

York Volunteers took their Base Ball implements with their war accoutrements and camp equipage to the front, and then first introduced the game into Army and Navy. Of these volunteer troops, New York ball players were among the very first to enlist. That quality of manhood which made them good ball players also inspired them to respond promptly to President Lincoln's call for men. Naturally, their exodus from the Empire State made it difficult to keep the game going, as evidenced by the fact that over two-thirds of the organized clubs disbanded or ceased playing between the beginning and end of the war.

This wholesale disbandment of clubs at that era has sometimes been construed as indicating a waning interest in the game, and at that period there were many who voiced the sentiment that the sport was doomed. But the real cause of the trouble should have been recognized in the fact that the best ball players were born fighters, and hence ideal material for soldiers. There were many causes of discouragement to all forms of pleasurable pastime during those gloomy years, and Base Ball suffered perhaps more than any.

But though Base Ball languished at its New York birthplace, not so in Army and Navy. While the special duty of soldiers and sailors was to shoot and kill, little did the men of either army realize that what was to them simply a camp pastime would come to be in later years the national game of their country.

Although Base Ball was taken up by the volunteer soldiery as a simple camp diversion, all its players soon became infatuated with it—and so must everyone who comes under its spell. The game continued to gain in popularity among "the boys" as the war progressed, and almost every regiment, and many crews, had Base Ball teams; and, when occasion offered, games were fought out, in generous rivalry, on Southern fields.

No one seems to know just how Base Ball found its way into Confederate lines; but, as many Southern youths had been in attendance at Northern colleges before the war, it is conjectured that this may have been the avenue of its introduction. Whatever may have been the means by which it got there, no one denies that it was there in full glory before the end of the war.

Thus it will be seen that Base Ball has its patriotic side—thanks to the soldiers and sailors of the Civil War—and this, together with its distinctive American character and spirit and its peculiar adaptability to the American temperament, have caused it to go on from year to year, gaining in power and popularity, until to-day it is the leading field sport of the world.

CHAPTER XXVI.

BASE BALL IN ALASKA

CHAPTER XXVI.

BASE BALL IN AMERICAN COLONIES — STORY OF LEAGUE
GAMES IN THE LAND OF THE MIDNIGHT SUN — BASE
BALL POPULAR IN ALASKA, HAWAII, PORTO RICO AND
THE PHILIPPINES. 1894–1910

THAT Base Ball follows the flag is abundantly proven
by facts set forth in these pages. It has been
played by our soldiers and sailors wherever they have
carried the stars and stripes. But no one seems ever to
have conceived the idea of taking teams of "All-America"
pennant winners to give exhibitions to polar bears and
seals on arctic ice during the short days that prevail in
December in the land of the "midnight sun." And yet
no less a personage than Brigadier General Frederick
Funston, the famous hero of the Philippine War, writing
in Harper's *Round Table*, in 1894—three years before he
won his fame and his high commission—describes a league
season of Base Ball in Alaska under most remarkable
conditions. Here is the story:

"On the 29th day of March, 1894, a party of eleven Tinneh
Indians and myself, after a twenty days' snowshoe journey across
the bleak tundras and mountain ranges of Northeastern Alaska,
reached Herschel Island, in the Arctic Ocean, sixty miles west of
the mouth of the Mackenzie River. Here, in a little cove, locked
fast in the ice, were the steam whalers Balæna, Grampus, Mary D.
Hume, Newport, Narwhal, Jeanette and Karluck, all of San Francisco. Some of these vessels had been out from their home port three
years. The preceding October, after one of the most successful seasons in the history of Arctic whaling, all had sought shelter in the
only harbor afforded by this desolate coast to lie up for the winter.
The ice-packs coming down from the North had frozen in all about

371

Herschel Island, so that as far as the eye could reach was a jumble of bergs and solid floe, but behind the island where the ships lay the salt water had frozen as level as a floor. The nine months that the whalemen were compelled to lie in idleness, while not enlivened by social gayeties, were far from monotonous. With lumber brought up from San Francisco there had been built on shore a commodious one-room house, whose most conspicuous articles of furniture were a big stove that roared day and night, a billiard table and a number of benches and chairs. This was the clubroom of the sixty or seventy officers of the fleet, and here they congregated to play billiards and whist or sit about through the long Arctic evenings, while the wind howled outside, smoking and spinning yarns of many seas, or of boyhood days at New Bedford, New London and Martha's Vineyard. There were veterans who had whaled on every ocean, and had been in nearly every port on the globe; men who recollected well the raid of the cruiser Shenandoah when she burned the fleet on the coast of Siberia thirty years before, and who had been in the Point Barrow disaster, when nearly a score of ships were crushed in the ice floe. The sailors and firemen of the fleet did not have the privileges of this house, but contented themselves with games and amusements of their own. They had an orchestra that played long and vociferously, and there was an amateur dramatic troupe that gave entertainments during the winter. But it was on the great national game of Base Ball that officers and men most depended to break the tedium of their long imprisonment and furnish needed exercise.

"A large number of bats and balls had been brought up from San Francisco by one of last summer's arrivals, and as soon as the ships had gone into quarters seven clubs were organized and formed into a league to play for the 'Arctic Whalemen's Pennant,' which was a strip of drilling nailed to a broomhandle. One nine was composed entirely of officers, another of seamen, a third of firemen, a fourth of cooks and waiters, and so on—the seven nines constituting the 'Herschel Island League.' A set of written rules provided that the series of games should begin after a month's practice and continue throughout the winter, and that all must be played on schedule time regardless of weather. Another provision was that on the diamond all ship rank was obliterated, and a sailor could 'boss' even venerable Capt. Murray without fear of reproof. No sooner had the harbor frozen over than the diamond was laid out and practice begun. Salt water ice is not quite so slippery as that from fresh water, but great care had to be used by the players.

"After a season of practice, during which there was much speculation as to the merits of the various nines and no end of chaff and banter, the first game of the series was played, and in the brief twilight of an arctic December day, with the mercury 38° below zero, the 'Roaring Gimlets' vanquished the 'Pig-Stickers' by a score of

62 to 49. All winter, regardless of blizzards and of bitter cold, the games went on, three or four each week, until the schedule was exhausted, and by this time the rivalry was so intense that playing was continued, the clubs challenging each other indiscriminately. The provision in the by-laws that a club refusing to play on account of weather forfeited its position caused one game to be played at 47° below zero, and often during blizzards the air was so full of flying snow that the outfielders could not be seen from the home-plate. Even after the sun had disappeared for the last time and the long arctic night had begun, games were played in the few hours of twilight at midday, but were usually limited to four innings, as by 2 o'clock it would be too dark to see the ball.

"All the whalemen were dressed in the Esquimau fur costume, only the face being exposed, and on their hands wore heavy fur mittens. These clumsy mittens, together with the fact that one was apt to fall on the ice unless he gave a large part of his attention to keeping his feet underneath him, made good catching practically impossible. 'Muffs' were the rule, and the man who caught and held the ball received an ovation, not only from the whalers, but from the hundreds of Esquimaux who were always crowded about the rope. With the ball frozen as hard as a rock, no one was apt to repeat an experiment of catching with bare hands. One of the center fielders was a corpulent Orkney Islander, whose favorite method of stopping a hot grounder was to lie down in front of it. The Esquimaux considered him the star player of the fleet. Sliding was the only thing done to perfection, the ice offering excellent facilities for distinction in that line; and there was always a wild cheer when a runner, getting too much headway, knocked the baseman off his feet and both came down together. The scores were ridiculously large, seldom less than fifty on a side, and sometimes twice that. On the smooth ice a good hit meant a home run.

"A most amusing feature of the games was the interest shown by the Esquimaux. With the fleet there were nearly a hundred of these people from Behring Strait and Point Barrow, and there were several villages in the vicinity of Herschel Island. These latter were Kogmulliks, the largest Esquimaux in existence, and the presence of the fleet had drawn them from all along the coast. Men, women and children became typical Base Ball cranks, and there was never a game without a large attendance of Esquimaux, who stood about, eyes and mouths wide open, and yelled frantically whenever there was a brilliant catch or a successful slide. At first dozens of them would break over the line and try to hold a runner until the baseman could get the ball, and it was only by vigorous cuffings that they were taught that the spectators' duties are limited to cheering and betting. They borrowed the paraphernalia and tried a few games of their own, but rarely got beyond the first inning, usually winding up in a general mêlée and hair-pulling. One of their umpires, who insisted on allowing a nine to bat after it had three men out in order to even up the score, was dragged off the diamond by his heels. They are naturally great gamblers and bet among themselves on the results of the whalers' games.

"A fact that impressed me very much at one of the games that I saw was that the crowd of several hundred people watching our national sport at this faraway corner of the earth, only twenty degrees from the pole, and thousands of miles from railroads or steamship lines, was more widely cosmopolitan than could have been found at any other place on the globe. From the ships were Americans, a hundred or more, men from every seafaring nationality of Europe—Chinese, Japanese and Malays from Tahiti and Hawaii. The colored brother, too, was there, a dozen of him, and several of the players were negroes. Esquimaux of all ages were everywhere, while the red men were represented by the eleven wiry fellows who had snowshoed with me from their home in the valley of the Yukon. One day I noticed that in a little group of eleven, sitting on an overturned sled watching a game, there were representatives of all the five great divisions of the human race.

"There are no men on earth who are more hospitable and more thoroughly good fellows than these whalers of the Arctic Ocean, and it was hard to leave them; but we finally got away and started on the long tramp over the snowy wastes toward the Yukon. Just before we left a notice was posted in the clubhouse which, with many 'whereases,' 'aforesaids,' and other legal formula, recited that the 'Auroras' thought they knew something about ball, and hereby challenged the 'Herschels' to meet them on the diamond within three days."

The New York *Sun*, in an article published over ten years ago, tells how the game even then had made its way to our colonies, only a few years after the insurrection in Hawaii and the Spanish War had given us our island possessions. Here is the article:

"Westward and eastward the national game is taking its way. Cuba has already taken up Base Ball, and has gone so far as to send a team of players to this country. In Porto Rico the American soldiers gave a few exhibitions of the national pastime, and on the Fourth of July our men in khaki were running around the bases, and incidentally abusing the umpire. The returns from Guam are not yet in, but Governor-General Leary is a typical American and may be depended upon to do the proper thing by the game. It is in Hawaii, however, that Base Ball has become most quickly acclimatized, and if the Kanakas persist in their pursuit of the game, we may soon expect to see a team of Hawaiian players traveling through the United States, somewhat after the fashion of the Australian Cricketers in Great Britain. Indeed, why may we not look forward to a succession of visits from 'colonial' players, from Cuba and Porto Rico, from Hawaii and the Philippines? Someone has said that in the British military expeditions to the four corners of the earth, the Cricket bat goes with the cannon, and while the United States has no lands or tribes to conquer, it is only to be expected that Base Ball, along with Boston beans and beefsteaks, will invade our new possessions.

"That Base Ball is popular in Hawaii is evident from the amount of space devoted to the accounts of the game in Honolulu and elsewhere. *The Pacific Commercial Advertiser* of Honolulu contains, in its issue of July 24, an interesting account of a match game for the '99 Base Ball pennant. Three teams were contending for the mastery—the Stars, a name which recalls our famous teams of two decades ago, the Artillery team and the Kamehamehas, a fine, resounding title, abbreviated for convenience's sake to Kams. The Artillery team dropped out of the contest early, discouraged by fairly lost games and no victories. On July 22 the Stars and the Kams met. If the Stars had won, the pennant of '99 and the acclaim of the populace would have been theirs, but the Kams played brilliantly, won the game and tied the series. All Honolulu was looking forward to the following Saturday, when the deciding game would be played.

"That the players in Hawaii have a good knowledge of the game is clear from the *Advertiser's* account. 'The Stars were first up,' says the Base Ball reporter, 'and before three men were out two had crossed the rubber. But the Kams more than evened things up when they came in. An error was made. Jackson lost control of the ball for a moment, the collegians slugged it, and the small boy at the scoreboard hung out the figure 4. The Stars came back with 2 in the fourth, the Kams were put out and the score was again even. In the fifth the Stars flew out in one, two, three order, and the Kams made 2. In the seventh both pulled in two runs, leaving the Kams two ahead. In the final inning the Stars tried for one of their old-time finishes. With but one man out and two on bases their chances seemed bright. A double play by Mahuka, however, did the trick and the game was over.' A very creditable game, creditably reported, with just enough of the familiar Base Ball slang to give verisimilitude and to show that the Hawaiians have 'caught on.'

"The make-up of the Hawaiian teams is suggestive of the Hawaiian-American alliance. Among the players on both sides we find distinctively native names, Mahuka, Makanani, Kaanoi, Kekuewa; and names of the Anglo-Saxon type, Crowell, Wise, Leslie, Moore,

BASE BALL IN OUR INSULAR POSSESSIONS

Porto Rico—Philippines—Hawaii

Gorman, Thompson, Willis and Davis, with one admixture, Toyo Jackson. It is gratifying to observe that these teams played the game well and fairly, and played what is known as 'clean ball.' The Hawaiians have not yet became Freedmanized. May they never be! And this interesting incident of the day is thus recorded by the Hawaiian reporter: 'Senator J. S. McCandle had paid for the privilege of admitting all soldiers free, and many of the boys in blue and brown availed themselves of the opportunity.' Our hat is off to Senator McCandle, of Honolulu."

Mr. H. G. Merrill, writing on Base Ball as played in Porto Rico, says:

"Base Ball has gained quite a strong hold on the natives in many of the towns of Porto Rico. A letter from Mr. Spinosa, a prominent player and sportsman, tells of a recent game in which the winning run was made amid great excitement. The score was 5 to 4 in the ninth inning with three men on bases and two out, the batsman having two strikes called on him. The catcher thought to catch the base-runner napping at first base and threw the ball wild, so that the winning run came in. It was a Sunday game witnessed by a large crowd, and Mr. Spinosa wrote: 'Some of us desecrated the Sabbath in our expressions of the play. The San Juanites were so highly elated that they challenged the regular Santurce team to a game and I intend to give them the worst drubbing they ever dreamed of—25 to 0 or something like it.' The Americans on the island are making Base Ball highly popular with the intelligent class of natives and have coached them so well that many of them play the game in surprisingly good style."

Up to date information from our island possessions is to the effect that in all the colonies acquired in recent years Base Ball teams are rapidly multiplying in numbers, the players everywhere are swiftly gaining proficiency, while the game itself is advancing with giant strides in public favor.

Throughout Cuba, Porto Rico and Hawaii regularly scheduled league games are played, exciting deep interest and attracting great throngs of spectators. The same is true of the Philippines. Wherever our soldiers and sailors go the game is immediately introduced, the natives acquiring it with avidity. As a result of the introduction of Base Ball into our island colonies, many American professionals are finding winter employment, both as coaches and players, while here and there the appearance of a Spanish name on the published score card of games played at home shows that first-class professionals are being developed in the islands.

A correspondent, writing from Havana to a New York paper not long ago, gives the following account of a game he witnessed:

"I have seen some notable games of Base Ball, but never anything that approached a contest in Havana about three years ago for the championship of the Island of Cuba. For two years the Matanzas and Havana Clubs had struggled for the mastery, and this was to be the decisive game. There were 20,000 people on the ball grounds, and when I drove out the clubs had been playing three hours and a half, and had not yet reached the third inning. They had had four umpires and the grounds were lined with police. The excitement of the people was beyond description. Everybody on the grandstand was hoarse from violent screaming, and when the third inning came to a close with a home run on the part of the shortstop of the Havanas, the populace crowded over the balustrade and almost smothered the player with caresses. They began all over again the following day under rigid police rules and the curbing of the excitement wherever it was possible, and the game was brought to a satisfactory close. The Havanese have picked up the slang of the American ball field. It was very odd to hear the incessant jabbering of Spanish interrupted by such phrases as 'home run,' 'foul tip,' 'fair ball,' 'take your base,' etc. The excitement of the players was no less intense than that of the spectators, but despite all the frenzy which characterized the game it was noticeable that the Cubans played mighty good ball."

Ever since the occupation of Cuba, at the beginning of the war with Spain, the natives have exhibited an ever-increasing interest in the sport. At Havana league games frequently attract crowds of ten thousand spectators. The players in the big Cuban league are very skillful, ranking with our first-class players except in the art of batting. The games are conducted with systematic regard for the maintenance of good order, much more deference being paid to the umpire and his rulings than is true in our own major league contests. No liquors are sold within Cuban league grounds, the man with a " thirst " being compelled to go a long distance for relief. Betting, however, is a habit so ingrained in the Cuban character that it will be a long time before that evil is eradicated from the game. Professional players do not receive salaries there as here, but seventy-five per cent. of the gross receipts of each game goes to the competing teams, of which the winners receive 50 per cent. and the losers 25 per cent. Under this system professional players in the strongest teams get about $100 a week.

For the following I am indebted to a recent number of *Van Norden's Magazine*. It is taken from an article written by Wadsworth Haynes:

" Then there is the Canal Zone, where the ' dirt is flying,' according to Mr. Taft, and where the canal engineers and workers from the United States have formed a regular league for the greater glory of the national game. There was Base Ball in the Zone as far back as when the French were trying to make the ditch, but it did not flourish. The last reports from Panama gave a seven-team league, in which Empire and Culebra were the big rivals, both being recruited from men working in the heart of the big cut, only a mile apart.

" ' Active operations ' are going on in the Philippines. Mr. George W. Moore, writing from Luzon some time ago, said: ' When I went over to Masbete the game was not known to the Filipinos, but after I had explained its possibilities they took to it with great enthusiasm. Before long we had many students who were able to play as well as the average American youths. Soon they began to organize teams in the various towns in the provinces, and now we have a regular Base Ball season in Masbete.

" ' As for fans, the Filipinos have the Americans backed off the

boards. (Mr. Moore may be forgiven. He did not see the National
League post-season games last year.)   It is nothing for the spectators to swarm on the diamond to express their appreciation of
some brilliant play. At one game 5,000 persons were on the field
congratulating a player, and it was nearly an hour before the game
could be resumed. Everybody in town turns out for the games, and
there is a spirit of rivalry that reminds one of the league games in
the United States.

"'An American umpire would have an easy time of it in Luzon,
for the players never treat the arbiter of the game to the criticism
and sarcasm that he receives in America. The umpire's decisions
are always received without kicking, and the official is accorded a
respect that would seem impossible to the men who decide the games
in the United States.' O, happy umpires in Luzon! Probably if
Merkle had failed to touch second base there the fact would have
been thought unworthy of comment."

CHAPTER XXVII.

A "BASE BALL CUP TIE FINAL" CROWD AT TOTTENHAM, LONDON, ENGLAND

CHAPTER XXVII.

1888–1910

IT must be conceded that efforts to introduce Base Ball into England have not met with the full degree of success that American lovers of the game had hoped and prophesied. Although, as heretofore chronicled in these pages, the game had been presented by strong teams in 1874 and again in 1889, it was not until about eight years ago, in 1903, that regular Base Ball clubs began to be organized in England. This long delay was due, doubtless to two facts connected with the exhibition given in 1889. The day upon which that game was played was characterized by a typical London fog, rendering it very difficult for the crowd to note the fine points of the game, and not easy for players to present the sport in the most attractive way. But even at that, Base Ball was played in such a skillful, scientific and altogether energetic manner as to discourage our British cousins from undertaking it at once. Perfectly satisfied with cricket, and not feeling the need of a new sport, the American pastime was soon forgotten.

However, it is impossible to keep Americans from playing their national game, and it happened that certain of our countrymen living at the time in England got

383

together for practice, and, on the occasion of a visit of Buffalo Bill's "Wild West," played a game with his cowboys. This game — played in the rain — attracted a large concourse. It was won by the cowboys by a score of 13 to 5.

Although this game was played at London, it was in the North and Midland counties that the sport first took on regularly organized form in the way of scheduled games between contesting teams. This was because of the fact that Base Ball in England seems to appeal rather to the mining and factory men than to the denizens of the metropolis.

It is not known just how many clubs are playing the American game in England to-day; but probably twenty-five would cover the entire number.

The strongest supporters of the game in England are the large American business firms, such as the Messrs. Fuller, the great confectioners; Messrs. Dewar, of whisky fame; J. Earle, of the Remington Typewriter Co., and many of the first music-hall artists here, Americans by birth; and last, but no means least, Mr. Francis W. Ley and H. Newton Crane, for many years American Consul at Manchester, and more recently a practicing barrister in London. These gentlemen assist the game, both in a monetary sense and by personally attending the games and bringing their friends. One of the music-hall "mummers" is said to have spent close upon £2,000 ($10,000) pushing the game forward. The amount of their subscriptions it would not be politic to state, but it can safely be said that they all give about the same sums. There are practically no English manufacturers supporting the game. Of course it has not paid its promoters, but they did not take it up as a money-making scheme, nor with any idea of benefiting their pockets. The assistance they have given has been solely through a love of the game, and of pushing it in England, and bringing it before the English public as a sport worth studying and playing. The public at present do not know enough of the game to criticise it.

The progress of the American national game in British provinces has been slow but sure—except in Canada, where it gained a footing in its early days, rose rapidly, and has for many years been regarded as the National Game, fairly outclassing lacrosse and all other forms of field sport in popular favor. It was impossible that it should have been otherwise. The term "American," though frequently employed as referring to possessions of the United States alone, covers all the continent, and that which has been long considered strictly our own bids fair soon to become the Game of All-America, for it will not be many years before Base Ball will have supplanted bull-fighting in Mexico, in a measure, as it has cock-fighting in Cuba, while it is likely to drive out the field sports of all South America, so rapidly is it gaining in popularity in the little republics there.

The Canadian people, in spirit and temperament, are very like our own. Though Britons, they have absorbed Yankee characteristics from being brought into commercial competition with business men of the United States. As a result, just as British field sports were found too slow for us, they have failed also to keep pace with the vigorous, wide-awake instincts of our neighbors to the North. Canada, in proportion to her population, is just as full of Base Ball fans as is our own country. They play ball, talk ball, and speculate on results of pennant races and league contests just as we do.

The chief drawback to the game in Canada is the presence of a sparse population in a widespread territory. This means a country of magnificent distances, with long and expensive railroad jumps for league teams, and a consequent discouragement to the investment of capital in professional clubs.

And yet, notwithstanding all the hindrances, wherever there is a congested population in Canada the game flourishes. Toronto, Montreal and Hamilton are centers of Base Ball interest and enthusiasm in the East, while in all the smaller cities adjacent to these are strong teams of high-class players. In the Far West, Winnipeg, Vancouver, Victoria, in fact, all cities of consequence, maintain clubs. It is quite noticeable, too, that when Canadians have a team in a league whose schedule crosses the border the pennant is not always left on this side of the line. British Americans had a way, long years ago, of annexing Base Ball trophies, as exemplified by the victory of the Tecumsehs, of London, in 1877, and only four years ago, in 1907, the Toronto Club defeated Buffalo for the Eastern League pennant.

In a recent able and comprehensive paper on Base Ball in Canada, Mr. J. P. Fitzgerald, of Toronto, has some exceedingly interesting facts. He shows that some of the best material in the big States leagues came from over there. He mentions Arthur Irwin, Tip O'Neill, Bob Emslie, Dr. Pete Wood, saying that these were all old-timers who made good when the game was young. But now the good ones, like bargains at a country auction, are "too numerous to mention." Catchers Clarke, of Cleveland; Gibson, of Pittsburg; McLean, of Cincinnati, and Archer, of Chicago, are all "Canucks." Pitchers Grohan, Hardy, Graney and Hollingsworth all claim Canada as their native heath. Congalton, of Boston; O'Hara, of Baltimore, and Jimmy Cockman, of Newark, belong across the border.

The opposition of Britons everywhere to professionalism in the realm of sport has militated to some extent against the quality of the game in Canada, for the reason that ambitious youngsters, as soon as they prove fit, come to the States, where, if they are up in the game, they find ready employment at good salaries.

The trip of the Chicago and All-America teams to Australia, in 1888, planted Base Ball seed in a fertile soil, where the sport has been growing in popularity ever since. It is difficult for one who has not visited the provinces of Great Britain to understand how slow the people of those countries are to take on any new thing, especially anything that had not its origin and development in the mother country. The peoples of Australia, New Zealand and Tasmania are nearly all of British derivation. Either English, Scotch, Welsh or Irish, they know little else than that which they have derived from British sources. Taught from infancy to revere and play the sports of their native land, or the land of their fathers, and religiously believing that Great Britain is the greatest country on the face of the earth, they look, and quite naturally, it must be admitted, somewhat askance at innovations in that line emanating from other shores. So strong and elemental is the tie which binds in this respect, that we find the peoples of the Antipodes sending their wool to England to be made into hats, caps, clothes, and then returned as the manufactured article, to be bought at high prices, and, after the twofold voyage across the seas, to be worn by the people of those far-distant possessions. Accustomed to pay tribute to the mother country in this way, Australians have seemed never to think that they might themselves reap the benefit of their natural resources, and at the same time give employment to thousands of skilled workmen, by establishing manufactories of their own. I refer to this matter—quite foreign to the text—to explain why a sport that has in a short time made such headway in America has been so slow to advance in the great island continent of the South Pacific.

And yet, while Base Ball has not supplanted cricket in Australia, and probably never will, it is making fine progress and becoming exceedingly popular wherever played. There are teams in Brisbane, Sydney, Melbourne, Adelaide, Ballarat, and many other prominent cities of Australia.

Following is an extract from a letter written by Mr. Harry W. Hedley, an Australian, shortly after the world's tour of the American ball players in 1888. It will be of interest as giving the opinion of one who was certainly

not prejudiced in favor of our pastime as against those
of his own country:

"Permit me to acknowledge receipt of your very interesting
and instructive letter on Base Ball which appears in this week's
Leader, copies of which I hope you will duly receive by this post,
and to thank you for your reference to my very cursory treatment
of the subject written after seeing the game played by its able
exponents, whose visit to us last Summer will always remain a
pleasant memory with Australians who made their acquaintance.
That the game in its thoroughness and "go" is essentially characteristic of Americans can quickly be seen, and as an old cricketer
I recognize in it many features the study and practice of which
would, I feel sure, benefit our cricketers in connection with their
own national game. Some thirteen years ago, when I was captain
of one of our suburban cricket clubs (St. Kilda), we had a caterer,
an American, C. S. Jewett, who introduced Base Ball to us, and
we played several enjoyable games with the American Christy Min-
strel troupes who visited Melbourne, but I need hardly tell you that
when I saw men like Anson, Ward and others on the diamond, and
talked ball with such as A. G. Spalding, George Wright and my
jovial friend, Harry Palmer, I discovered for the first time how
very little I had known previously of your great game. Some of
our cricketers who have taken to it have developed fairly good form,
and Harry Simpson has done his utmost to thoroughly establish the
game in Australia, but I have no desire to paint a picture in unduly
roseate colors, and am therefore constrained to admit that it has
hardly taken the hold upon our public which seemed probable immediately after the departure of the Chicago and All-America teams,
and while their remarkably skillful displays were fresh in the memory of our people. I may tell you, however, that we Victorians have
during the past few years been suffering from a terribly strong over-
dose of horse racing, five and six days' racing continuously in every
week, and week after week, without intermission of any "off" season.
I am happy to say that there is a prospect of racing reform being
extensively carried on with a view to materially curtailing the number of meetings, and when that desirable consummation has been
reached I hope for an increased interest to be displayed in other
field sports which (cricket and Base Ball included) have suffered
from the general attention paid to the turf with its more exciting
attraction in the shape of betting. Our great Winter game, as
you are doubtless aware, is football, neither Rugby nor Association
rules, but a game played under rules of Australian origin. Being
an Englishman by birth, though an Australian by the acclimatiza-
tion of nearly a lifetime, I have no prejudice in comparing our game
of football with the other two named. The Australian game was,

in fact, evolved from the other two, and is, I have no hesitation in saying, a pronounced improvement upon both. Our footballers are all young fellows, who either attend the schools and colleges or work at their trades—artisans, clerks and others, clerks and tradesmen preponderating—and all our matches are played on Saturday afternoons, the Saturday half holiday being an established institution with nearly every class of the community.

"Base Ball, I am certain, will not supplant or even rival either football or cricket in public esteem in this country, but I quite agree with you and with Spalding, Palmer and others who think they may become kindred sports."

That Mr. Hedley's prophecy was not too bright, the following recent letter from Mr. Leonard I. Lillyman, showing conditions of the game in Australia at the time of the visit of our fleet, in 1908, will amply attest:

"Twenty teams play regularly in Sydney in Base Ball and there are a like number in Melbourne. These are under the control of the New South Wales Association and the Victorian League, respectively.

"Last season we introduced the game in South Australia and Tasmania, and efforts have been made to introduce it into Western Australia, and I have not a doubt that they will be as successful as other efforts have been to popularize the American sport.

"For the benefit of those in the United States who take an interest in what we do, I would like to say that we play the game here for the pure love of it. Professionalism is entirely absent, and would be stamped out as soon as it made its appearance. Those who take part are generally devotees of cricket, which is played in the summer months, and consequently we are compelled to play ball in the winter, which accounts for a good number of lame arms among our pitching brigade. We only play once a week and on holidays, and if we do get but little encouragement we know that we are progressing all the time.

"The standard of Base Ball in Australia is steadily improving each season, and the visit of the United States fleet to our shores gave our players a much-needed practical lesson in the finer points. Up to last season we had been self-taught—taught by studying the rules as they are laid down in *Spalding's Guide,* with the assistance of a casual visitor from the United States, who would be willing to impart any knowledge of which he was possessed. It was eagerly devoured by our players, who were only too glad to obtain it, and in turn they imparted it to their comrades.

"I am told that the quality of Base Ball which is played in Australia at present is quite up to the standard of amateur Base Ball in the United States.

"The pitchers of the ships of the United States fleet were too much for our batters, but I fancy that it would not have been very long before we would have been able to hit them all over the diamond. The speed with which they threw the ball was something new to us, and we are ready to admit that we know very little of the art of throwing. We are going to learn to attain pace, and I hope to be able to tell your American readers that in a few years we possess a 'Mathewson' among us.

"When the fleet landed its sailors for games with our clubs we were all delighted. It seemed like putting an American League of Base Ball clubs among us to instruct us in the game which we had played with so much enjoyment.

"The teams of the fleet played four contests in Sydney. Two were against New South Wales and two against All-Australia. In three of these contests the Americans won. They lost the second game to the All-Australia nine, but it was a well-played contest and the enthusiasm and applause which resulted while it was going on well repaid us for our efforts in behalf of Base Ball and certainly gave pleasure to the American visitors who took part in the games against our boys.

"The field work of the American players was slightly better than ours. They seemed to know better how to handle themselves to look after certain plays, and of course that was to be expected in view of the long training which they had as compared with the teaching that had been given our boys in the effort to bring up the game to a proper standard in Australia.

"We could not help but observe the work of their pitchers with admiration, because it gave us an inkling of what pitching was like in the United States and was totally different from our conception of delivering the ball to the batter. McCreary, Scott and other pitchers of the American fleet, who were put in the box against us, were batted very little because of the pace with which they delivered the ball. On the other hand, the batters from the fleet did not prove to be so wonderfully effective against our pitchers.

"I desire to inform the ball players of the United States of the excellent sportsmen whom we met in the fleet players. All the games were most enjoyable, and right through the series we found our opponents grand fellows, and just as splendid sportsmen as were Lieut. Weaver, U. S. S. 'Connecticut,' and Midshipman Cohen, U. S. S. 'Kansas,' who had charge of the teams representing the fleet. To both of these gentlemen we are greatly indebted for much information and for the assistance given to further the game of Base Ball in New South Wales."

Speaking of Base Ball in Natal, the *Natal Witness*, of Pietermaritzburg, Natal, says:

"The presence of a number of Strathcona's Horse in the city induced the Canadians in our midst to seize the opportunity of indulging in the American national game—the first played in the city. Accordingly teams were selected from the regiment and Canadian residents, and they met on the Polo Ground on Saturday to try conclusions. The result was eminently successful to all concerned, an excellent afternoon's sport being witnessed, and it is quite on the cards that future matches will be played. There were a number of spectators, who had not previously seen the game, but who became interested in it, and admired the dexterity of the players. The match throughout was well contested, the civilians coming off victorious by 13 runs to 9. Lieut. Stevenson captained the losers, and displayed considerable ability in the pitcher's box, while on the civilian side Hargraves and Ward creditably shared the same position, and the batting of Ferguson, Hargraves and Myles was a feature.

"Mr. Hugh V. Ferguson, formerly of the *Globe*, but now of the *Times,* of Natal, who was one of the civilian team, writes: 'If we have but the opportunity to play a few more games I fancy Base Ball will catch on here in Natal.'"

CHAPTER XXVIII.

BASE BALL MATCH AT KEIO, JAPAN BETWEEN U. S. SAILORS OF THE AMERICAN FLEET
AND THE STUDENTS OF KEIO UNIVERSITY

CHAPTER XXVIII.

1905–1910.

O F ALL countries into which Base Ball has been introduced in recent years, none has developed greater interest in the sport than has Japan. The fact is quite in keeping with what might have been expected from the little brown men of the Orient. In an early chapter of this work it was asserted of Base Ball that it is a combative game. That the Japanese have the spirit of combat recent history abundantly demonstrates. It is no wonder, then, that this progressive island nation, whose people have been so quick to adopt American civilization, customs, business systems, manufacturing methods, should also grasp with avidity a form of pastime so peculiarly adapted to their alert, intelligent natures.

It is not true of Japan, as it is of this country, that Base Ball is played everywhere in the Empire. But it is true that there, as in Australia, in all the larger cities and localities where there are important universities ball clubs are maintained. The government not only gives its countenance to the playing of the game but also aids it substantially in many ways. The rapid progress made by Base Ball in Japan during the past few years makes it certain that the next decade will see it spread generally throughout the Empire, wherever there are boys and men who can take time for such a sport. It must be remembered that conditions in Japan are not favorable to the enjoyment of field sports by the masses. Who may say that in years to come Base Ball may not have liberated multitudes of the youth of that land from their conventional thralldom?

Several years ago students of the leading universities of the Japanese Empire adopted Base Ball as their most popular form of outdoor pastime. The Keio University and the Waseda Imperial University both organized strong teams and have played frequent matches, attracting thousands of highly interested and enthusiastic witnesses.

Twice, at least, teams from Waseda University have visited America.

Writing for *Sporting Life*, R. S. Ransom describes an interesting game played at Los Angeles, in 1905, between the Waseda University team and a nine composed of American Indians from the Sherman Government Institute, California:

> The meeting of the little brown men from the realms of the Mikado and the red men from Sherman Institute at Fiesta Park in this city, May 20, under the management of Walter Hempel, marked an epoch in the history of our national game which is deserving of more than passing mention in the columns of America's greatest Base Ball paper. For the first time a Base Ball game was played by teams whose players were from two races that have adopted a sport heretofore distinctively that of the white man. And victory rested with the men from across the sea because of their all-around superiority in every department of the game, coupled with the steadiness and excellence of Kono's masterly work in the pitcher's box. This young man is a marvel, and his work a revelation to our twirlers, who consider themselves overworked if called on to pitch

two games during a single week. Already the Japs have played three games here—May 17, winning from the L. A. High School team by the score of 5 to 3; May 18, when Caucasian triumphed over Mongolian, Occidental winning by a score of 6 to 5, and May 20, when Red and Brown met, with disaster to the Native Sons by a score of 12 to 7. In all these contests Kono, a veritable iron man, did the twirling, showing marked improvement in each successive game.

"All these contests were witnessed by large crowds, the attendance at the Jap-Indian game being by far the largest of the series. During this game, which stands as an event unique in the annals of Base Ball, the Orientals from Japan had it over the Aborigines during all stages of the game, with the exception of the sixth inning, when the Sherman braves with a whoop broke from the reservation and went tearing madly about until six of them had scored before Field Marshal Hashido and his aides drove them back.

"The Japanese players represent the Waseda Imperial University and are being sent on a tour of the United States at the expense of the government. They have been coached by Fred Merrifield, an American, who is a professor in the university. When he first introduced the American game he was startled by the rapid manner in which the brown men picked it up. They were playing good amateur ball in no time. As they improved, a trip to the United States was talked of, and finally the government made the appropriation. The touring party includes: I. Abe, manager; Fred Merrifield, coach and trainer; K. Hashido, shortstop and captain; M. Obara, center field; A. Kono, pitcher; S. Suyama, third base; M. Yamawaki, catcher; U. Swzuki, left field; K. Shishiuchi, right field; K. Oshikawa, second base; S. Izumitani, first base; S. Morimoto and S. Tachihara, substitutes. After completing their engagements on this Coast the team will go to Chicago.

"When it comes to handling the ball these little brown men are all stars, but when it comes to a wise interpretation of the rules they get up against it. The other day the Japs were playing a tight game against Stanford. With a Jap on first base, no outs and the score tied, the Jap at bat hit the ball straight into the air back of first base. The runner on first crouched for the start and the minute the catch was made, zing! he was off for second. Of course he was thrown out by something like forty feet, and when their traveling Jap Base Ball coach was asked to unravel this play he responded something like this: 'Well, you see, sar, the rule he say the runner he shall not proceed until the ball he is catch. So he wait for the ball to be catch and then he go down to the number two base. Is it not correct to follow the rules of the game?'

"And the sport who asked the questions went away and batted his head against an oak tree. The Japs have the old Indian trick of 'sighting' with the ball before throwing it. Some of them have

BASE BALL IN THE ORIENT

1. Y. M. C. A. Team, Seoul, Korea   2. Christian College, Macao, China

3. American Protestant College, Assiout, Egypt

wonderful wings, their pitcher having the most marvelously developed arm ever seen in a pitcher's box.

"As indicative of the aptitude shown by the Japanese players in the development of the game, it can be said that when they arrived in this country the 'bunt' was entirely unknown to them. After their first game a class in instruction was held, with the result that this style of playing was at once assimilated, and the brown men 'worked the trick' successfully thereafter.

"Here is a description that fits perfectly the pitching wonder, 'Iron Man' Kono: 'This little, strong-winged brown man is the goods. He pitches every day, never seems to weaken, and is always the last man to complain of being tired. He has excellent control, and while his curves have not reached the development of the American professional, they are as good as those of the average amateur."

In the fall of 1909 a team from the University of Wisconsin visited Japan, playing nine games that had been scheduled by the Athletic Association of Keio University, whose guests the American college men were.

The Keio champions had some trouble defeating the Wisconsins, winning three games out of four by very close scores of 3-2, 2-1, 5-4, and losing the fourth game by 8-0 in favor of the Americans.

The Wisconsins won two out of three games with the Waseda team by 7-4 and 5-0, and losing the third in a shut-out, 3-0.

The Wisconsins easily defeated the Tokio team in two contests, 10-0 and 8-7.

In the spring of 1911 a team from Waseda University visited the United States, first playing in California, where they acquitted themselves with credit in games played by fine teams. In fielding the Japs are first-class. They are no match for the best American batsmen, and they have not yet developed pitchers equal to our stars.

Following is the story of a game played some time ago

at Tokio, between a visiting team from Honolulu and a nine from the Keio University. It serves to show what an excellent imitation can be given of America's national game on the opposite side of the globe. The story is told by Mr. E. S. Wight, in the Philadelphia *Evening Telegraph:*

"Base Ball is as popular in Japan as it is in the United States, and when the Honolulu team played Keio University the game was a great function, attended by representatives of the Imperial Court, the Diplomatic Corps, officers of the Army and Navy and some 10,000 others.

"The crowd lined the bleachers around the field. More than two-thirds wore European dress, though no more than a hundred Europeans and Americans were present. The crowd was typically Japanese, containing all classes, from rickshaw men to courtiers, but no women.

"The athletic field at Keio University is several miles from the center of Tokio, and is reached through miles of streets, with their bird-cage houses, temples and shrines, graveyards and parks. The entrance is guarded by a great arch of evergreen, across which in flaming colors is the English word, 'Welcome,' done in huge chrysanthemums.

"The field is as large as any big League park, with a bamboo fence surrounding it, over which the verdure of pine, palm and bamboo can be seen. Japan's weather is such that the game can be played the year round, which certainly is a fact calculated to make the big League magnates of the United States jealous.

"On this occasion the imperial band played 'Bedelia,' 'The Stars and Stripes Forever' and 'The Little Tonquine.' It was the one false note. The music sounded like a kennel of pups with the hydrophobia, kioodeling their death song.

"The ground was without grass, but rolled as smooth as a tennis court. The players used English terms, and it was positively weird to hear a Japanese crowd shout: 'Good eye!' 'You're the candy!' 'Line 'em out!' But they do it, and the Japanese umpire says, 'Stlike one,' 'Two bowl,' in a manner that would turn Silk O'Loughlin green.

"The college yell of Keio is 'Rah! Rah! Rah! Keio.' Not a banzai was heard, but there was as much handclapping and inarticulate yelling as at home. There was no rowdyism, dirty ball or disrespect to the umps. Base Ball in Japan is Base Ball with the rowdy part kept out.

"The game went thirteen innings, ending 5 to 3 in favor of Keio. It was refreshing to see such a game for from 10 sen (5 cents) to 60 sen (30 cents).

"A liberal translation, condensed, of the account of the game given in Tokio's great independent newspaper, *Jiji Shimpo,* is as follows:

"'The heaven-born Honolulu team, by grace of the gods, won the toss and the Keio Invincibles had first chance to swat the honorable ball—that emblem so beautiful of Uncle Sam. The honorable Kauki, of the first base, descendant of a hundred Samurai and beloved of all, grasped his bat as if it were the two-handed sword of his ancestors. Alas! his honorable legs were not winged and the ball beat him to the first rice bag.

"'No score was made by either of the honorable sides, though they hewed holes in the atmosphere like foresters. In the fifth inning the gods smiled on Honolulu and the team scored one honorable run, then the gods laughed while the honorable Keio boys piled up three tallies.

"'Keio's 4,000 rooters then drew in their honorable breaths with a pleased hiss, waved their royal purple flags and exploded like a bunch of firecrackers, with the weird war cry, "Skidoo, doo, doo, for Honolulu," "Razzoo, Razzoo, and 23 for you." At least an American present said this was what the boys meant.

"'Not till thirteen innings had been played was Honolulu vanquished, when the whole Keio team, with innate courtesy apologized for their breach of hospitality in beating a visiting team.'"

The spectacular side of Base Ball around the world is pretty well known by this time, but there is another side that would touch the heart of any ardent American. Take, for instance, the little group of men who represent a big oil company up in the wilderness of upper Burmah. There are just enough of them to form two nines, and when they have an afternoon off, or when their day's work is over, they get together and "batter up" in the good old way. They are far from home; practically exiles, but when they are in the midst of a smashing game under a tropical sun, with the natives staring at the audacious energy of the white men, they probably feel themselves much nearer home than at any other time.

AMERICAN BASE BALL TEAM AT YENAMGYAT, UPPER BURMAH

CHAPTER XXIX.

THOMAS J. LYNCH

CHAPTER XXIX.

1860–1910

UP TO this point consideration has not been given
to the Umpire. In this omission I have not
been unmindful of the importance of that functionary
to the game; nor have I forgotten how extremely difficult
it has ever been to secure for him the deference due to his
position from managers, players and the public. But, as
the umpire has been in evidence from the very inception
of the sport, and is to-day a more potent factor than ever,
I have deferred treating of him and what is due to him
until it might be done in a chapter devoted exclusively to
that subject.

To secure the presence of intelligent, honest, unprejudiced, quick-witted, courageous umpires at all contests
in scheduled games has been one of the most vexatious
problems confronting those in control of our national
sport. The combination of attributes required is very
difficult to find in any individual. It is not easy to put
one's hand upon a man who possesses any two of these
several qualifications; and yet the efficient umpire must
have them all.

The umpire must be intelligent. And by intelligence

405

I do not mean that he must have education or culture. The best umpire in the National League would not shine as a scholar in a gathering of college professors. But he could outclass the entire faculty of any university in America in promptly and quickly deciding the fine points of a game of Base Ball, and that because he has the peculiar quality of intelligence required for his duties. The rules in vogue for the government of our national pastime are not so numerous that one of ordinary acumen may not be able to acquire them. However, the acquisition of information and the ability to apply it are two very different things. One may have the capacity to commit the rules so thoroughly to memory that he can repeat them forward or backward, in the order of their setting or any other order, and such freakish accomplishments may only serve to unfit him for the duties of umpire, for they may overwhelm him with an "embarrassment of riches" along the line of multiplied rules which he has no talent to apply.

He must be honest. A crooked umpire at a ball game is as offensive as a scoundrelly jurist on the bench. His power to beget disgust for the sport is even greater than that of the judge to bring the law into reproach. The umpire does not deal with unfamiliar, abstruse, legal technicalities, whose veiled meaning needs to be explained by the citations of other judges in other cases in other courts. He must hand down his decision instanter before an audience composed of hundreds who know Base Ball law as well as he—or who think they do.

He must be absolutely without prejudice. Did you

ever think what that means? Consult your own feelings at the next contest you witness. Note how perfectly free you are from bias against the visitors. Put yourself in the umpire's place for a little while. Let a team bluster, and kick, and play horse, and dispute your decisions from the opening of the game. Let them play rowdy ball, seeking thereby to gain unfair advantage not only of the adversary, but of you. Let them encourage rooters in the grandstand to hoot, and howl, and insult and browbeat you in your earnest efforts to be just. Let them encroach upon the rules far enough to strain without breaking them. Let them invite the imposition of fines for petty offenses. All this let players do—you being the umpire—and remain without prejudice, *if you can.* Perhaps if you are endowed with superhuman graces you may put aside the desire to give them the worst of it—not otherwise. Is the picture overdrawn? I don't think you will say it is if you have been an attendant at many games.

The umpire must be quick-witted. He may not, like the wise old owl of the bench, look over his gold-rimmed eyeglasses, inform the assembled multitude that he will "take the matter under advisement," and then adjourn court for a week or two to satisfy himself how he ought to decide. No, indeed. He must be "Johnny-on-the Spot," with a decision hot off the griddle, and he must stick to it, right or wrong—or be lost.

The umpire must be courageous. With perfect composure and dignity he must render judgment, though he knows that in so doing he is likely to precipitate a riot, with himself as the object of a cowardly mob's unreasoning frenzy. He must stand in the midst of a team of recalcitrants like "Patience on a monument, smiling at grief," listening, until patience ceases to be a virtue, to the jibes and jeers and innuendoes of all before imposing the fine authorized by the rules.

Do you wonder that, during the evolution and development of our national game, the umpire problem has been so difficult of solution? Are you surprised, with such a requisition of heaven-born attributes, that now and then an umpire fails to measure quite up to the standard of perfection called for? Do you regard it as passing strange that, in the half-century of professional Base Ball, difficulty has been occasionally experienced in finding men equal to the requirements of this most exacting position?

But I have not mentioned nearly all the attributes demanded of every umpire. Until, in the course of the development of the game, the double-umpire system was introducd into certain leagues a few years ago, it was required of the umpire that he should be not only Omniscient, knowing everything about the game; Omnipotent, having power to control players, rooters, spectators; but he must be also Omnipresent, standing behind the batter, to judge of balls and strikes at close range; behind the pitcher, to watch for infield plays; at first base, to decide when base runners beat the ball; at second base, to determine the result of a slide or a double; at third base, to note if the runner touched that sack.

When I visited England in 1874, with competing teams of star ball players, the severest criticism I met from real English sportsmen on the American game, and that which I found most difficult to answer, was that the Base Ball umpire has too autocratic power. It seemed strange, didn't it, to have men living under even a limited monarchy censuring the great American Republic's game as too autocratic? And yet so it was. And the autocracy is there all right. The umpire *is* clothed with absolute power. It must be so from the very nature of the game. Base Ball is governed by inflexible rules, and it is the function of the umpire to enforce the laws to the letter. Just insofar as he can do this to the satisfaction of magnates, managers, players and spectators he is efficient. It is gratifying to note that marked improvement in this respect characterizes the game of to-day over that of even a few years ago.

There was a time when the umpire was simply tolerated as a necessary evil. He was known to be essential to the playing of the game; hence he was permitted to be there in an official capacity. But he was feared and hated alike by members of both teams engaged, and was the special object of derision and abuse on the part of occupants of both grandstand and bleachers, because his authority did not extend to them. He was always the scapegoat for the defeated nine and their apologists. There has been noticeable improvement in this regard. The slugging of umpires by players is no longer an essential part of the programme, and their mobbing by spectators, though occasionally indulged in, is not encouraged by public opinion.

Still later on, it became necessary to protect umpires against the outrageous machinations of club owners. The

THE UMPIRE—AS HE WAS

THE UMPIRE——AS HE IS

practices of certain managers at one time threatened the very life of the game itself; for always and everywhere the prosperity of Base Ball has depended upon public confidence in its integrity, and whenever and wherever that has been withdrawn serious injury has followed.

Some years ago unprincipled, narrow-minded men in control of league teams conceived the idea of working umpires for rulings uniformly favorable to their players by vicious methods. If the president of the league happened to be a weakling, they would manage it through him. Umpires who would not give their nines the best of every close decision would be protested and changed. The telegraph wires were kept hot with messages from such magnates demanding that this umpire be sent here, and that umpire be sent there, and the other umpire be sent elsewhere, to meet the whims and caprices of these persistent mischief-makers. The result was that upright umpires lost heart and withdrew from the game. Weak and dishonest umpires were handled at will, to the disgust of players and the public, and to the very great injury of the sport.

There was a time when the owner of the New York club practically dictated what umpires should and should not officiate at games upon the Polo Grounds of that city, and at that time this practice was general throughout leagues where weak-kneed presidents would permit it. The result of the pernicious action was shown in many ways. It caused the presence in the game of dishonest and incompetent umpires; it offered a premium on rowdy ball; it begot disgust and mistrust on the part of the public——

and when that began to affect the patronage of the sport, the evil had to be checked.

The establishment of the Supreme Court of Base Ball in the organization of the National Commission, or Board of Arbitration, has accomplished wonders in the way of eradicating this abuse. The rules have been greatly strengthened by requiring this enforcement. Managers who now interfere with umpires in any way are liable to severe punishment. Players who are guilty of offense against the presiding official at any game are subject to heavy penalties, and even spectators may not go too far in the way of personal abuse; for the presence of minions of the law is now required to preserve the peace.

In closing this chapter, I desire to speak a word for the umpire of the present and the future. As I have already said, he is essential to the game. There can be no Base Ball without his presence. His position at the best is not an enviable one. In every game there will need to be close decisions. He must give offense to somebody in each recurring contest. That every umpire will make mistakes is true. What, then, is to be done about it?

First, then, I answer, we must be fair to him. We, of America, pride ourselves upon love of fair play. Former President Roosevelt's claim for a " square deal " echoed throughout the land and found an answering echo in every true American heart. Each mother's son of us is ready to shout himself hoarse in approbation of a square deal for himself, his " sisters, his cousins and his aunts." But how about this square deal for the Base Ball umpire? Is he different? ' Is he outside the pale for those to whom fair dealing is to be extended? We all know the nature of his duties. We know that he must give his decision with lightning-like rapidity. Is it a square deal to dub him "rotten" if he doesn't give our team the close decision every time? Is it? I have stood in the pitcher's box and seen Ross Barnes, while covering second base, take a ball thrown by the catcher, whirl, and with a motion quick as flash apparently put the runner out. Later, I have asked in a low voice:

"Ross, did you put it on him?"

And the answer would come in a whisper, "Not by a yard."

That is one of the commonest tricks of the game. In this case Barnes fooled the umpire. He had fooled me. But down the line there were spectators who had not been fooled. They could see that the runner was safe, and they howled. But was that a square deal? Was it fair play? The umpire *believed* he was right. I *believed* him to be right. Those who were in a position to see from an angle impossible to him and to me *knew* that he was wrong. But he had made the decision according to his best judgment. He couldn't change it. He, and not the spectators, was judge. He was standing at the time back by the catcher's box, and if I, only a few feet away, and watching as closely as possible, could not see the play, it surely was not fair nor square to dub the umpire "rotten" because he couldn't.

And so, in behalf of the sport we love, and to the exploitation of which the umpire is absolutely essential; because the future success of the great American national game depends upon it; because as Americans we are committed by nature to stand for "fair play"; because as men we believe in a "square deal" for everybody, I bespeak for the Base Ball umpire always and everywhere the same consideration that we so freely accord to the wearer of the ermine on the bench, the difficult exactions of whose office in many respects are not to be compared to those of the man who holds the indicator in his hand at a Base Ball contest.

In recent years public sentiment has been rapidly crystallizing along the line of according to the umpire his proper position in the game. Time was, as I have said, when he was looked upon as a necessary evil—to be tolerated, but not respected. It is not so to-day.

As illustrative of progress that has been made in the direction of widening the scope of the umpire's jurisdiction, I recall an incident of which I was witness during the World's Championship series of 1910. It was on the grounds of the Philadelphia Athletics and upon the occasion of the first game of the series. The Chicago Cubs had captured the pennant of the National League, the Athletics being in possession of the same trophy of the American League.

The magnificent grandstand of the Philadelphia club was thronged by a mighty multitude of Base Ball enthusiasts. For several years the National League had held the World's Championship flag, and, although betting favored the Cubs, the knowing ones felt that the Athletics had more than a fighting chance to win. So the great crowd, although good natured, was highly wrought up.

Among the spectators that day, as might have been expected, were many magnates of both major and minor leagues. Chairman Herrmann, of the National Commission; President Lynch, of the Nationals, and President Johnson, of the Americans, together with other old-time and modern Base Ball lights, were present in the best places in the grandstand.

The gathering of such a galaxy of celebrities naturally attracted the camera fiend, and he was there, conspicuously, and in large force. The teams were engaged in preliminary field practice, while the batteries were warming up and onlookers were watching the play and singling out their favorites, when a very active photographer, with paraphernalia of his craft, appeared before the grandstand directly in front of the central and most crowded section. For some moments he plied his art, snapping groups here and there, when a murmur of protest began to be heard from those whose view he was obstructing. The umpire had taken his place and was about to make announcement of batteries, when the hubbub increased.

"Down in front," "Move on," "Cut it out," "Bounce him," "Throw him out," were some of the ejaculations hurled at the artist.

The picture-taker paid no attention for awhile, but finally the remonstrance became so widespread and general that he was forced to take notice. Removing his hat, the photographer said, politely but firmly, "Gentlemen, I am within my rights here. I have the permission of President Johnson to make these exposures."

"Oh, get out; we've got some rights, too," derisively shouted someone. "I paid $3 for this seat," yelled another, "and I want to see something." And then a refrain went up from the throats of thousands: "Too much Johnson," "Too much Johnson," "Too much Johnson."

Suddenly a hush fell upon the great assemblage. The umpire was approaching the stand. The camera man turned, saw hope in the man of the indicator, and shouted out to him a repetition of his claim that he had permission of President Johnson, of the American League, to make his snap-shots.

"Time is up," called the umpire. "I am about to call the game. You'll have to get out." *And he got.*

I was seated near President Johnson. I had seen him arise as if to corroborate the claim of the artist, but upon the appearance of the umpire, and hearing his fiat of authority, the great Ban Johnson, blushing like a schoolgirl, took his seat, while thousands upon thousands cheered the verdict of the man in temporary but absolute control of the game.

This chapter would be incomplete without reference to the honor that has recently come to a National League umpire in his selection to the presidency of the National League and, by virtue of that office, to membership on the National Commission, the Supreme Court of arbitration in Base Ball.

Thomas J. Lynch, of New Britain, Conn., is the man thus honored. He is 52 years of age and served as umpire for eleven years, part of the time for the Eastern League, and for the National League from 1896 to 1899, when he retired from the game until his election to the presidency. He has an excellent record as umpire, both for his ability to make accurate and prompt decisions, and for his unswerving integrity in his treatment of players, management and the public.

CHAPTER XXX.

JOHN T. BRUSH

CHAPTER XXX.

PLEA FOR THE BASE BALL MAGNATE—A SOMEWHAT ABUSED
INDIVIDUAL WHO CARRIES A BURDEN OF DUTIES AND
RESPONSIBILITIES OF WHICH THE PUBLIC KNOWS LITTLE
AND CARES LESS. 1860–1911

I F IN these chronicles it has not been made to appear
that our national game owes something of both prestige and perpetuity to the men who have directed its
business affairs, then have I failed in one important point
of my undertaking; for, during my connection with Base
Ball, as player, captain, manager, magnate and league
official, I came to know much about men who have managed its destinies. I know something about their duties,
their trials and their responsibilities, and I have sought
in these pages to accord to them their due meed of praise
for the success that has attended their patriotic and painstaking efforts to preserve Base Ball as a game worthy
the great American Nation.

The public is not always discriminating in its judg-
ments. It is prone to throw bouquets at those who tickle
their senses and forget the men who are to be credited
with the selection and employment of these favorites.
The men who, uncomplaining, have lost fortunes in vain
attempts to further the interests of clubs they have owned
and managed, and whose players have delighted countless
thousands, are lost to memory. Those who have played
the part of " angel " to teams that have been forced to

ARTHUR H. SODEN

disband for lack of patronage are, of course, unknown or lost to sight. But the magnates who have made good are known to everybody. They are exploited by the bright young men of the press; they are looked upon by the general public as beings to be envied; as men without a care in all the world, except to expend upon their persons and their pleasures the alleged countless coins that flow in an unending stream through the turnstiles of their clubs. That these men have any other vocation in life than to enjoy an uninterrupted good time, a succession of blissful holidays, with free ball games as a continual performance, seems never to enter the minds of many.

It is to correct this very serious error that this chapter is written. I shall not here refer to the unlucky financiers whose enthusiasm for the game has led them into the backing of forlorn hopes in hopeless territory; nor shall I dwell upon the misfortunes of those who have gone to the wall by reason of inability to meet competition on the business side of the game. I shall undertake, however, to show that the Base Ball magnate who achieves what the world denominates success is up against a serious enterprise; that he must go "the pace that kills," that ownership of a great ball club in a populous and prosperous city involves man-killing experiences; that the management of a major (and sometimes of a minor) league club often works havoc to the health and happiness of the man who undertakes it, and that the long list of physical and mental wrecks strewn along the shores of Base Ball history tells a story of sacrifice to our national game that is not generally appreciated or known.

FRANK DE HASS ROBISON

A few years ago I happened to be paying a business visit to a city of some importance in the Middle West. The owner of the local club, whom I had known in former years, learning of my presence, sent a complimentary invitation to attend a series of ball games then scheduled for that city. I went, and from the grandstand sent my card to the magnate who was on the bench below, pencil and card in hand, industriously keeping score and directing his players in the game. He responded at once by coming to my side.

I was not prepared for the change I noted in my friend's appearance. He had been a ball player in other days, a fellow of fine physique, active and strong. Now he was attenuated; his hand trembled as he marked the score card; deep furrows crossed his forehead; his once dark hair had turned to gray; he was prematurely an old man. The game progressed, and favorably for his team. When it was ended he said: "Thank God, we've won. We needed that game very badly." Then he added: "Spalding, do you know that I'm a miserable, mental and physical wreck? I can't stand the strain much longer. My wife, too, is disgusted with the whole business. I've made some money, and we're going to buy a farm and get out of Base Ball." It was a simple story, but it portrayed the experiences of many another.

The responsibilities of a Base Ball club owner are great and his trials are many. While those who are ignorant of the troubles that beset his path regard him with envy, he is an ever-present "buffer," receiving the oft-repeated blows of opposing interests. He must stand

A. J. REACH

between the public and its relentless demands for impossibilities. He must provide grounds easily accessible, and fit them up with elaborate grandstand, bleachers, club house and toilets, that shall meet all requirements of comfort, cleanliness and convenience. His grounds must be located as close by many avenues of rapid transit as possible. He must make sacrifice of much money to save time for patrons who want to come late to games in great throngs and depart early in a solid body. If the trolley lines provide inadequate facilities for handling the crowds, the magnate is to blame!

He must stand between the press and the interests of his club in many ways. At least twice a day must he receive representatives of evening and morning papers, and by "soft words" turn away the "wrath" of adverse criticism that is always seeking to discover something with which to find fault. He must be ready to answer diplomatically, satisfactorily and promptly any impudent question that may come from the lips of an irresponsible reporter. "Why don't you release Murphy?" "What do you play O'Brien on second for?" "Why don't you strengthen your pitching staff?" "Say, are you going to sell Corrigan?" These are a few samples of conundrums that come to the club owner, and which he must adroitly answer, skillfully parry, or invoke the ire of the interrogator, with its inevitable results.

He must stand by his team, good, bad or indifferent. He must receive the brunt of hostile comment directed against his players, whether merited or not, from both press and patrons, apologizing for shortcomings where

CHRIS VON DER AHE

they exist, excusing as accidental errors in play that cost him infinitely more than they could possibly cost anyone else on earth.

He must hear and patiently consider the never-ending stream of complaints growing out of jealousies and ambitions among his players, and must, for the sake of the game, and in his own personal interests, maintain the *esprit de corps* of all members of the team. He must listen to fault finding on the part of the men with the manager he has placed over them, and, acting as judge, must be patient, impartial and just, insisting upon proper deference being paid to the official and at the same time requiring the manager to be fair and reasonable in his treatment of players.

He must be present at as many games as possible, watching the individual work of the team, that he may be personally advised of the capacity of each in order to weed out the weaklings. Meanwhile it is important that he should have his eye on the players of other teams in the league, in the hopes of picking up here and there an artist unappreciated by the manager under whom he is playing. He must be on the grounds to see that order and decorum are preserved, and on occasion he must stand between the umpire and the mob.

Again, he must be big enough to rise above the petty annoyances that thrust themselves upon him. Put yourself in the magnate's place a moment for illustration of this point. All the afternoon you have sat watching the game. It has been characterized by many embarrassing incidents. It has been an " off day " for your team. The

PRESIDENTS OF NATIONAL LEAGUE CLUBS

boys have made too many errors, and the visitors have been on their mettle. Every close decision has seemed to be against you. The game has ended with a score showing your nine to have the small figures. Everything has gone wrong. The attendance has been light. The crowd is glowering in disgust. You turn from the grounds, thinking to escape to your home, where you may forget the Base Ball business and its discouragements for just a little while. But, alas! Every man you meet is loaded with the same question. "What was the score to-day?" You are perfectly aware that your interrogator knows the score as well as you do. You saw him in the grandstand, where he caught your eye half a dozen times just as errors had been scored against your team. But you must feign a cheerfulness you do not feel and make a civil answer. Then you must control the ire arising within you as he asks: "What in the d—l is the matter with *your* club, anyhow?" "Can't *your* boys play the game any more?" "Where on earth did *you* get the lobster *you* are playing on third?" Remarks similar to these come from every man you meet on the homeward path. And next day, when the game has been brilliantly won by your team, the bombardment of exclamations and interrogatories is hardly more satisfactory, for now the jubilant fan, in the exuberance of his joy, shouts to the ears of all the world, "How was that?" "What's the matter with *our* boys?" "Say, it looks as if *we'd* got the flag cinched for sure this year, don't it?" And so forth and so on. *Your* club in defeat, with anathemas on the side for *you*. *Our* team in victory, with the bouquets for *us*.

CHARLES COMISKEY
CHICAGO

BENJAMIN F. SHIBE
PHILADELPHIA

FRANK J. NAVIN
DETROIT

FRANK J. FARRELL
NEW YORK

BANCROFT B. JOHNSON
PRESIDENT
AMERICAN LEAGUE

CHARLES W. SOMERS
CLEVELAND

JOHN I TAYLOR
BOSTON

THOMAS C. NOYES
WASHINGTON

ROBERT L. HEDGES
ST. LOUIS

PRESIDENTS OF AMERICAN LEAGUE CLUBS

And at night when, harrassed and worried by the embarrassments and perplexities of the day, the magnate seeks needed rest, thoughts of other trials, troubles and tribulations force themselves upon his mind, driving sleep from his tired eyelids. And, if perchance sweet sleep shall come to restore in part his wasted energies, that ever-ready instrument of torture, the telephone, is used by the ubiquitous reporter to call him and ask for the line-up of to-morrow's game.

The magnate must be a strong man among strong men, else other club owners in the league will combine in their own interests against him and his interests, and by collusion force him out of the game.

Nor is the league official exempt from his woes. As a magnate of magnates, he comes in for his tribulations, too. He, also, is called upon to act as "buffer." Indeed, that seems to be his special calling. He must not only stand between the players and managers and magnates of his league, but, if a member of the Commission, he must at times receive the jolts of players and managers and magnates of all the leagues, major and minor, and what he does not learn of trouble in the politics, management and playing of the game, and in the administration of discipline, he may find in the hospital for the insane to which his trials are likely to drive him.

Are these pictures here presented of the vexations of magnates overdrawn? Are they mere phantasies of the imagination? Let us see. Only a short time ago Harry C. Pulliam, the bright young President of the National League, put the muzzle of a revolver to his head and ended

JAMES A. HART

his life. Unable to endure the strain of meeting the trying problems that confronted him in life, he gave up the battle.

That heroic figure in base ball history, William A. Hulbert, lived only a few years after taking upon his shoulders' the burdens of the National League. The brothers, DeHass and Stanley Robison, so long identified with Cleveland and St. Louis Base Ball interests, both died in managerial harness before their allotted span of life. The names of Harry Wright, Ford Evans, Chas. H. Byrne, John I. Rogers and others occur to me as those of men who have given up the fight right in the midst of battle.

And in addition to these are those who fill the ranks of magnates still living, but who have either been forced to leave active Base Ball management in order to escape nervous collapse, or who are yet in the field, carrying on the work, but all the time conscious that they must soon retire—or join the silent majority.

I met James A. Hart, late President of the Chicago Base Ball Club, of the National League, one day after he had sold his interest to its present owner. He had retired, broken in health and completely discouraged. He had greatly improved when I met him, and I said: "Well, James, you're looking fine. Don't you regret having got out of the game?" "Not a regret," answered he. "I'm getting all right again, and life is going to be worth living once more; but it wouldn't be with a ball club on my hands."

There are Base Ball magnates—a few—who seem to

be equal to the emergency; men of strong physical and mental fibre, and of temperament just suited to the work. August Herrmann, Chairman of the National Commission—the Supreme Court of Base Ball—is such a man. With a jovial, Teutonic temperament, nothing seems to disturb his equanimity. B. B. Johnson, President of the American League, is another of quality suited to the place he holds. He is not likely to wear out. Thomas J. Lynch, the new President of the National League, is a man of strong parts who will probably endure. John T. Brush, President of the New York National Club, is one of those thin, wiry men of steel whom nothing seems to wear out, and Mr. A. H. Soden, of the Boston Nationals, is strong; but such men are exceptional. Very few magnates continue as these men have, year after year, under the relentless strain of Base Ball management.

And so, concluding this plea for the Base Ball magnate, I ask, simply in the interests of fair play, that when one feels inclined to bear down too hard on the man behind the club some consideration be given to facts herein set forth; for, like that of Mr. Gilbert's policeman, the lot of a Base Ball magnate is not always "a happy one."

CHAPTER XXXI.

WILLIAM A. SUNDAY

CHAPTER XXXI.

IT CANNOT be claimed for Base Ball that it is essentially religious, either as to its features or its objects. During the history of the evolution and development of the pastime, magnates, managers, even players, have been known who were not conspicuous examples of personal piety. So far as the sport has developed any religious side whatever, it can be said of it that, thus far it has avoided sectarian bias or control—though it must be confessed that it escaped that once by only "the skin of its teeth."

While all this is true, it will not be denied that about every religious cult known has had representatives among its votaries. Perhaps the term " Pan-denominational " might properly be employed to describe its constituent elements. Moreover, that word seems to be useful as suggesting the Pandemonium which has sometimes characterized its councils and its exploitation. During my long connection with Base Ball I have known among its managers and players Agnostics, Baptists, Catholics, Dunkards, Episcopalians, Fanatics, Mormons, Gentiles, Israelites, Hebrews, Jews—but why go through the entire alphabet to show that the game has within its ranks

439

Lutherans, Methodists, Presbyterians, Quakers and all the rest? Everybody knows that.

However, it is of interest to know that churchmen, of high and low estate, have been as fanatical in their love for Base Ball as they have been zealous in their religious predilections. Billy Sunday, who seems to be about the most successful evangelist in the Presbyterian Church, was converted while playing ball professionally, and it is said that his contracts from that time on eliminated Sunday ball for Sunday.

The following special telegram, from the Hoosier capital, tells of Billy's work in the early days of his evangelistic career:

" INDIANAPOLIS, July 12, 1904.—'Billy' Sunday, who was known in Base Ball circles years ago as the renowned outfielder of the Chicago Club, is doing missionary work in the Indiana gas belt towns and is talking to crowds of laboring people every night. He has become as widely known as an evangelist as he once was as a Base Ball player, and though it is many years since he was associated with Anson, Pfeffer, Kelly, Burns and others who made up the Chicago aggregation, he often refers to his old chums and the kind words they gave him when he determined to reform.

" He is telling the story of his conversion and the happiness the new life has brought him to Indiana audiences every night and, incidentally, he has woven into his addresses the story of how prayer, as he verily believes, saved a game of Base Ball. As he tells the story, the fight for the pennant was between New York, Chicago and Detroit that year, but it finally narrowed down to the two last-named cities, and the final bout with Detroit came. The score was close. Everybody was excited and the players were nerved to the highest pitch by the great responsibility that rested upon them.

"'The last half of the ninth inning was being played,' says the ex-ball player. 'Two men were out and Detroit, with Charley Bennett at bat, had one man on second and another on third. He had two strikes on him and three balls called, when he fell on a ball with terrific force. It started for the clubhouse. Benches had been placed in the field for spectators and as I saw the ball sailing through my section of the air I realized that it was going over the crowd, and I called, " Get out of the way." The crowd opened and as I ran and leaped those benches I said one of the swiftest prayers that was ever offered. It was: " Lord, if you ever helped a mortal man, help me get that ball."

" ' I went over the benches as though wings were carrying me up. I threw out my hand while in the air and the ball struck and stuck. The game was ours. Though the deduction is hardly orthodox, I am sure the Lord helped me catch that ball, and it was my first great lesson in prayer.

" 'Al Johnson, brother of the present Mayor of Cleveland, ran up to me and handed me a ten-dollar bill. " Buy a new hat, Bill," said he. " That catch won me $1,500." ' "

The following news item, from the San Diego, Cal., *Sun*, 1911, seems to prove that Rev. " Billy " finds his evangelistic work garners financial returns as well as converts:

"BILLY SUNDAY IS SURE GETTING IT.

" ERIE, PA., July 20.—William A. Sunday, quondam professional Base Ball player, now professional revivalist, closed the evangelistic season of 1910-11 here the other day $70,507.77 to the good as a result of his year's work ' winning souls to Christ.'

" This return for about ten months' work, more than the President of the United States has drawn for the same time, is evidence that from a monetary standpoint, evangelistic work is more profitable than playing professional Base Ball. The Rev. Mr. Sunday recently refused an offer to go back to the ' majors ' once more. The inducement was but $500 a month.

" Seven thousand a month looks better to Billy. Besides he thinks he can do more good in the world preaching than playing ball!

" During the past season Billy Sunday broke all evangelistic records for money earned. It brings the cost of Sunday's services to about $2 a ' convert.' "

In point of dogma it is a far cry from the tenets of Evangelist Billy Sunday to those of Cardinal Gibbons, but since both are identified with Base Ball in their personal records, Billy as a player, and the Cardinal as a " fan," the placing of their names in juxtaposition here may not appear as an ecclesiastical inconsistency.

Some years ago the Baltimore team visited St. Charles College at Ellicott City, Md., where, in the presence of

Cardinal Gibbons, Bishop Curtis, of Wilmington, Del., the faculty of the college and a number of visiting Catholic priests from Washington and Baltimore, they gave an exhibition of professional ball playing. The feature of the occasion was the comments on the game made by the Cardinal at the dinner given to the players in the college refectory, of which the following paragraphs are worthy of special note as being a valuable endorsement of the merits of professional Base Ball as exhibited by the most expert exemplars of the game known to the National League in 1896. The Cardinal said:

"I am not what you might call a crank, but I am surrounded (referring to a number of clergy seated at the same table with him) by several excellent critics of the game, some of them even being well enough versed in the pastime to lay claim to the title of authorities. From them I have learned the merits of Baltimore's Base Ball players, and, without hesitation, say that these young men, who have obtained such prominence in their chosen profession, are worthy of the praise bestowed upon them, and both the State and city can well afford to be as proud of their achievements as they themselves no doubt are.

"Let me say," he continued, "that I favor Base Ball as an amusement for the greatest pleasure-loving people in the world. It is necessary that there should be popular amusements, and in consequence it is wise that the most generally patronized of these amusements should be innocent, since, were the opposite the case, the opportunity of committing sins of greater or less degree would be too openly set before the public. Base Ball is a clean sport. It is an innocent amusement. Never have I heard that the games were being used as vehicles for gambling, the most insidious of vices, and this one fact alone raises it above the level of the average sporting event. It is a healthy sport, and since the people of the country generally demand some sporting event for their amusement, I would single this out as the one best to be patronized, and heartily approve of it as a popular pastime."

The Cardinal's words were listened to with the closest attention by the players and the clergymen, who had remained in the room after the body of students had filed out. He finished in silence, but his words had made a deep impression on his hearers, and especially upon the players, not one of whom could find words sufficient to thank him for the glowing eulogy of the national game that he had delivered. The Cardinal displayed the greatest interest in the game, toward which he had been looking forward for some time, and which was arranged especially for him at his invitation. The curving of the pitched ball attracted his attention at the outset, and he spent some time in investigating the phenomenon from behind the wire screen. No detail of the game escaped his watchful eye.

The following reprint from the Chicago *Tribune*, in 1906, is presented as showing what a strong hold our national game has upon some very excellent and highly religious people, whose counterparts live in every village and city in America:

"Rev. Mr. Perkins (so-called because that isn't anything like his real name) is one of the shining lights of the Episcopalian Church in Chicago, a man noted for his high ideals and his good works.

"Rev. Mr. Perkins has a son who strayed into strange ways, and finally wound up as a Base Ball reporter—and a corking good one. Indeed, he is almost as well known in his line as his reverend father is in his.

"The son never laid any claim to being wise in his father's line, but Rev. Mr. Perkins always has had quite an idea that he would have made quite as good a Base Ball reporter as minister.

"Thereby hangs a tale. Last year the son was an ardent and faithful supporter of the Cubs. His heart was with Comiskey, but he couldn't see how Commy's bunch ever could beat Murphy's crew. His father, who attends Base Ball as often as there is no service, or meeting of the guild, was a wild and woolly admirer of the Sox, and one of the most ardent believers that they could beat anything on earth. And at home, instead of starting a discussion on higher criticism, the father and son debated strongly upon the relative merits of the South and West Side teams, and the debate waxed hotter and hotter as the post-season series came nearer.

"Comiskey heard of it, and was so tickled that he sent the minister seats for all the post-season games—and it is stated that the church ser.ices during that week were adjusted to fit the post-season schedule—up to Sunday.

"Rev. Mr. Perkins witnessed all the games, but on Sunday he was absent. It is stated that the afternoon services were cut short and that within a minute after pronouncing the benediction he was at a phone inquiring the score.

"And that night he wrote to Comiskey a letter of congratulation, and at the close he said:

"'It appears to me unfortunate both for myself and my church on this occasion that I was forbidden by my calling to wager upon the outcome. Otherwise I should have won enough to pay off the parish debt.'

"There was another fan who, on that memorable Sunday afternoon when the Sox clinched their claim for the world's pennant, suffered. He is one of the best Base Ball cranks in Chicago, a rooter for the Sox and an ardent supporter of Comiskey. He has the good fortune (although he didn't think so that day) to have a good and pious wife, who is one of the leaders in a little church up in Edgewater. This fan isn't particularly religious, but he respects and admires his wife's stand in the matter, and during fifteen or twenty years of married life has assimilated more or less of her belief and feelings.

"The post-season series, however, was too much for him. He attended five games and admits that he was planning to attend morning services with his wife and make a sneak to the ball park in the afternoon. Luck, however, was against him. A special afternoon service of great importance was announced, and his hope of seeing the deciding game evaporated. He knew he could not offer any excuse that would satisfy his wife, and that a plain explanation meant to hurt her feelings. So he decided to make a martyr of himself and attend the special service.

"It is not believed that the service did him much good. His mind was away down on the Base Ball field.

"He was sitting there, picturing the great throng on Commy's park, the excitement, the noise, the enthusiasm, and pulling hard for the Sox to win.

"He wasn't even giving a thought to what was going on in church, and twice his wife had to pull his coattails to get him to stand up.

"Suddenly he saw Deacon Morris arise and tiptoe into the vestry. He knew there was a telephone there, and for five minutes he had been wondering if he dared slip out and ask what the score was.

"About five minutes later Deacon Morris tiptoed back up the aisle, smiling, and sat down just across the aisle.

"The fan slipped along the pew, leaned out, and an instant later the worshipers in the surrounding pews heard him ask in a stage whisper:

"'What's the score?'

"And without a flicker of hesitation Deacon Morris whispered back, so he could be heard by half the church:

"'Sox got 'em beat in the sixth.'

"For just an instant everybody looked startled, and then the minister, whether by accident or design, no one knows, remarked:

"'Let us sing the long meter doxology.'

"But there is a minister out on the Northwest side who made himself one of the most popular men in the district on that same Sunday afternoon, when all Chicago and most of the world waited to hear the news.

"There was a meeting of the Bible class called for 4.30 in the afternoon. This class is the biggest thing in the church, and almost all the men and women, especially the young ones, are members.

"That Sunday afternoon the lecture room of the church was crowded—and the minister was late. He usually started things off, and then turned over the meeting to the class itself, explaining and helping only when needed or called upon. So the meeting was opened without him.

"Shortly thereafter he came in, red from rapid walking, and beaming with smiles. He sat down until the hymn was finished, and then, walking forward, remarked:

"'Ladies and Gentlemen: I have glorious news for you. The White Sox are champions of the world—I stopped to learn the score, feeling that we could study better if we knew.'

"And the class broke into cheers."

Some twenty odd years ago the local department of the *Brooklyn Eagle* happened to be rushed with work during the absence of the Base Ball editor, and it was found necessary to assign the religious editor to the task of writing up the Base Ball match of the day at the Capitoline grounds. The writer in question went to the game, watched the contest to its finish, and the next morning sent in the following report:

"A very refreshing season of Base Ball was experienced in the Capitoline Vineyard yesterday afternoon, affording exceeding unction to a congregation of fully two thousand souls. Brother Murphy, of the Brooklyn Class, first wielded the rod, even as did Moses at the rock of waters, and smiting the ball with prodigious smite was richly blessed with two bases. It then became the blessed privilege of Brother Fitzgerald to stand forth, but, despite his most fervent efforts, Divine Providence interfered with a foul tip, and the brother harvested naught. During this season Brother Murphy had experienced a change of bases, garnering unto himself the third thereof, whereat there was great rejoicing, mingled with lamentation and rending of garments among the disciples of the conflicting tribes. At this critical point in the salvation of the class Brother Maloney came among them as a physician of souls, but the sheaves of great rejoicing were not for him. Like Jacob he wrestled, and like Nathan he fell, for his adversaries were plenteous and their wisdom that of the serpent, forasmuch when he smote the ball so that it soared they that were as Philistines unto him did congregate around about that the ball might not escape them, and did hold forth each man his hands, until their fingers in number were like unto the lilies of the valley, and they seized the ball and bore it thence in triumph."

On reading the story before sending it out to be set up, the city editor called the writer to the desk, and asked him, as he handed him the report:

"What's all this got to do with the game I sent you to write up?"

"Anything the matter with it?" asked the writer.

"This is no way to write up a ball match."

"Why not?" queried the writer indignantly. "That's the way they did it," he continued, "and that's my way."

"But, man alive," resumed the editor, "this reads like a sermon."

"What if it does," was the reply. "Have you any objections to sermons? If you don't like my style of writing the game up you had better send some secular cuss to the next game when the old man is absent."

The report was sent in and it created quite a sensation for the time being.

CHAPTER XXXII.

ERNEST L. THAYER

G. G. Spalding Eg
Dear Sir   Point-Loma, Cal
        Casey at the Bat — was communicated first in the San Francisco Examiner
was forever copy furnished by me
The poem had no history. it was
written in the regular course
of business where I was a journalist on
the staff of the S.F. Examiner
                Yours truly Ernest L. Thayer
April 9, '05

CHAPTER XXXII.

LIKE every other cause worthy the best efforts of
writers of note, Base Ball has a literature peculiarly
its own. Love has its sonnets galore; War its epics in
heroic verse; Tragedy its sombre story in measured lines,
and Base Ball has "Casey at the Bat."

To this day men of splendid mental equipment are
burning midnight oil in labored efforts to solve the authorship of the immortal productions usually accredited to
the "Bard of Avon." It is not, therefore, passing strange
that more than one individual has taken to himself the
honor of having written the popular Base Ball classic.
At various times in the early history of this poem its
authorship was assumed by Joseph Quinlan Murphy, Will
Valentine and Ernest L. Thayer. That Mr. Thayer was
its author has long been established beyond the perad-
venture of a doubt, the false claimants fading away as
soon as the real author was brought to the front.

The poem, "Casey at the Bat," was first published in
the San Francisco *Examiner*, June 3, 1888, and won
instant favor among the Base Ball fraternity. But it
needed the impetus given it by DeWolf Hopper to bring
to it the widespread popularity that it has since attained,
and which not only calls for its repetition whenever

Hopper appears before the footlights, but which also demands its publication at frequent intervals in the daily press.

I shall not undertake to determine as to whether the poem made Hopper great, or Hopper made the poem great. As a friend of Hopper, and an admirer of the poem, I am inclined to the opinion that each owes a good deal of popularity to the other. The poem as usually published consists of eight stanzas, beginning with the words: "There was ease in Casey's manner as he stepped into his place." As originally printed, however, it embraced thirteen stanzas, and in its perfect form, as written, was as follows:

CASEY AT THE BAT.

(A Ballad of the Republic. Sung in the Year 1888.)

The outlook wasn't brilliant for the Mudville nine that day;
The score stood four to two with but one inning more to play;
And then, when Cooney died at first, and Barrows did the same,
A sickly silence fell upon the patrons of the game.

A straggling few got up to go, in deep despair. The rest
Clung to that hope which "springs eternal in the human breast;"
They thought, If only Casey could but get a whack at that,
We'd put up even money now, with Casey at the bat.

But Flynn preceded Casey, as did also Jimmy Blake,
And the former was a lulu and the latter was a cake;
So, upon that stricken multitude grim melancholy sat,
For there seemed but little chance of Casey's getting to the bat.

But Flynn let drive a single, to the wonderment of all,
And Blake, the much despised, tore the cover off the ball,
And when the dust had lifted and men saw what had occurred,
There was Jimmy safe at second, and Flynn a-huggin' third.

Then from five thousand throats and more there rose a lusty yell,
It rumbled through the valley; it rattled in the dell;
It knocked upon the mountain and recoiled upon the flat,
For Casey, mighty Casey, was advancing to the bat.

There was ease in Casey's manner as he stepped into his place;
There was pride in Casey's bearing and a smile on Casey's face,
And when, responding to the cheers, he lightly doffed his hat,
No stranger in the crowd could doubt 'twas Casey at the bat.

Ten thousand eyes were on him as he rubbed his hands with dirt;
Five thousand tongues applauded when he wiped them on his shirt.
Then, while the writhing pitcher ground the ball into his hip,
Defiance gleamed in Casey's eye, a sneer curled Casey's lip.

And now the leather-covered sphere came hurtling through the air,
And Casey stood a-watching it in haughty grandeur there,
Close by the sturdy batsman the ball unheeded sped—
"That ain't my style," said Casey. "Strike one," the umpire said.

From the benches, black with people, there went up a muffled roar,
Like the beating of the storm-waves on a stern and distant shore.
"Kill him; kill the umpire!" shouted someone from the stand;—
And it's likely they'd have killed him had not Casey raised his hand.

With a smile of Christian charity great Casey's visage shone;
He stilled the rising tumult; he bade the game go on;
He signalled to the pitcher, and once more the spheroid flew;
But Casey still ignored it, and the umpire said, "Strike two."

"Fraud," cried the maddened thousands, and echo answered "Fraud,"
But one scornful look from Casey, and the multitude was awed.
They saw his face grow stern and cold; they saw his muscles strain,
And they knew that Casey wouldn't let that ball go by again.

The sneer is gone from Casey's lip; his teeth are clinched in hate;
He pounds with cruel violence his bat upon the plate.
And now the pitcher holds the ball, and now he lets it go,
And now the air is shattered by the force of Casey's blow.

Oh! somewhere in this favored land the sun is shining bright;
The band is playing somewhere, and somewhere hearts are light.
And somewhere men are laughing, and somewhere children shout;
But there is no joy in Mudville—mighty Casey has Struck Out.

Mr. Thayer, the author of "Casey at the Bat," has his home at Worcester, Mass. His father being a wealthy manufacturer, young Thayer, after finishing his course at Harvard University, from which he graduated in the class of 1885, started out to "do" the world. He had been the editor of the *Lampoon* while at college, and was looked upon by his classmates as a particularly bright and witty fellow. Upon arriving at San Francisco, the youth—to show his independence of parental patronage— sought and received employment on the *Examiner*, in whose columns the poem appeared during his term of service.

The following letter, being the second in a series establishing his authorship of the poem, explains itself:

"ROME, Grand Hotel du Quirinal,

"To the Sporting Editor of the *News*:   "February 4, 1905.

"Since writing to you the other day, other facts about 'Casey' have occurred to me which, perhaps, will be of interest to you. Except as originally published in the *Examiner*, 'Casey' has never been correctly printed—barring one or two cases in which I have furnished the copy. When the poem was first copied into an Eastern paper—I think by the New York *Sun*—the clipping editor cut off the opening stanzas and began where Casey advances to the bat. Later on, Mr. Hopper began to recite the complete poem as it was given to him by Mr. Archibald Clavering Gunter, who saw it in the *Examiner*. Some one who heard Hopper's recitation wrote out the first five stanzas from memory—and a very bad memory he must have had—and tacked them to the mutilated version as it was printed in the *Sun* and many of its exchanges, and then published a combination which has been printed up and down the land as 'Casey at the Bat.' I think that if the matter were of any importance the easiest way to establish the authorship would be to let the different claimants furnish a copy which might be compared with the poem as it was first printed in the *Examiner*.

"I may say, in conclusion, that though some of the mutilated reprints of 'Casey' have my name on the title page, I have never authorized them. I have left the poem to its fate—except that once I had a few copies printed for circulation among my friends, and only recently, when I am charged with falsely claiming the poem, has it seemed to me my duty to say something of my connection with it. Finally, while a certain Will Valentine may have written a Base Ball poem in a Sioux City paper before 1888, it could not have been 'Casey at the Bat,' and if anyone is anxious enough to search the files of that paper this fact will become patent. With apologies for troubling you,   Very truly yours,

"ERNEST L. THAYER."

Among the mountain of clippings in the collection of the late Henry Chadwick I find the following, without newspaper credit or date. I am therefore compelled to print it in this form, or not at all:

" Casey is dead!

" There are many Caseys, dead and alive, but this particular Hibernian won fame because he was ' Casey at the Bat.'

" Not only fame for himself, but a reputation for DeWolf Hopper, who was a sort of foster father to him, did he win, and with his demise is learned for the first time the identity of his author.

" Wherever Hopper is known, Casey of bat fame is an acquaintance also. For seventeen years Hopper has recited the poem relating to Casey's wild blows at the ball in nearly every city in this country, and in London as well. At benefit performances, at Lambs' gambols, at regular performances—in fact, at nearly every gathering which Hopper has attended since he became known upon the stage— he has been called upon to recite ' Casey at the Bat,' and he always has responded.

" And until yesterday the original of the poem which has found such favor was not known.

" The Casey who just died was John Patrick Parnell Cahill, a former Base Ball player. On the Pacific Coast he was very popular as a player, and after his retirement from the diamond still held his head high, for he had been perpetuated in verse under the name of Casey. His demise occurred in Pleasanton, California, last Friday, of consumption.

" Exactly seventeen years ago, when Hopper appeared in ' Prince Methusaleh ' at Wallack's, he first used the poem. No less known a person than Archibald Clavering Gunter, novelist and dramatist, called his attention to it. By so doing, Hopper believes Gunter did as much to earn him a reputation as any role he ever played.

" Gunter approached him one evening and asked him if he would like to have a novel poem. Hopper replied in the affirmative, and Gunter handed him the ' Casey at the Bat ' verses. Hopper was highly pleased with them and used them at Wallack's Theater. They made an instantaneous success.

" Gunter did not know the authorship of the verses, and Hopper spent three years in an effort to find out. He had about despaired of ever learning the name of the man who penned the lines, when by chance the information was borne to him. The comedian was billed to appear at Worcester, Mass. From an old friend of his family residing in that city he received a note asking him if he would like to meet the man who wrote 'Casey at the Bat.' Hopper accepted the invitation gladly and the next day was presented to Ernest L. Thayer, of Worcester. Thayer admitted the authorship and told the circumstances which led up to the penning of the verses."

Another poem, of equal literary merit, a parody on Macaulay's "Lays of Ancient Rome," which appeared about the same time, and which is supposed to have first been printed in the St. Louis *Globe-Democrat*, seems to have been lost to literature, unless this reference to it shall result in its reproduction. I have been unable to secure a copy, but a friend recalls the opening stanza, in these words:

> " Ho, lictors, sound the war note;
> Triumvirs, clear the way;
> The great barbarian ball teams
> Will play in Rome to-day."

The reference, of course, is to the World's Tour of the Chicago and All-America teams, in 1888-9.

It will be manifestly impossible to reproduce here a tithe of the meritorious verse that has been written on our national game. From a collection of many poems the following are selected as representing the wide range over which the Base Ball Pegasus has roamed:

THE SPORTSMAN'S CODE.

From Harper's Round Table.

> Now these are the laws of the athlete,
>   That stretch the length of the field.
> They make the code of the runner fleet
>   Who has never yet learned to yield.
> They tell you how to lay your plan,
>   And how to carry it through.
> They help the man, who's done what he can,
>   To bear his Waterloo.

You shall give the foeman all his due,
    And let him win if he can;
But keep all rights that belong to you,
    For that is the law of man.
You shall hold the ground that is yours by right,
    And yield not a foot you have trod.
But grant his right in a stand-up fight,
    For that is the law of God.

If you row with the crew in the boat,
    It's a wretched thing to spy.
There's plenty of work when you leave the float,
    But little to do for the eye.
There's plenty to do to swing and slide,
    And steady the fragile shell;
But to gain your strength from the other side
    Is a method sent from hell.

No man shall yield on the foot ball field
    Till the final whistle sounds.
No man shall show by a single blow
    That he has no place on the grounds.
But when the foe is in racking pain
    And cannot move or fight,
You shall help him up to his feet again,
    And chafe his bruise and bind his strain,
To show the make of your own good grain,
    For that is fair and right.

The strength of the team, or nine, or crew
    Is not the strength of the " star."
'Tis what the body together can do
    That carries the victory far.
So you shall give your mite to the rest
    To bring the whole team through,
And then at the time of your single test
    They shall give their strength to you.

And these are the laws of the athlete,
    You can heed them or not, as you like,
But they make the code of the runner fleet,
    And they check a man when he'd strike.
They tell you how to lay your plan,
    And how to carry it through.
They help the man, who's done what he can,
    To bear his Waterloo.

"TEN THOUSAND EYES WERE ON HIM AS HE RUBBED HIS HANDS WITH DIRT"

"BUT THERE IS NO JOY IN MUDVILLE— MIGHTY CASEY HAS STRUCK OUT"

"WHENEVER HOPPER APPEARS BEFORE THE FOOTLIGHTS"

"CASEY AT THE BAT"

BASE BALL.

By S. D. Richardson.

'Tis a glorious game, with a well-earned fame,
　A diamond in royal setting;
And its beautiful rays light up our days
　From the field with an emerald fretting.
So day after day I am watching the play,
　Absorbed in the outings and innings;
Though I risk not a dime, I'm gainer each time,
　And the joy that it gives is my winnings.

But sometimes on a day my mind is away
　From the game with an idle perusing,
And I think of another so much like the other
　That I blend them together in musing:
'Tis the old game of life, with its conquest and strife,
　With its wonderful outings and innings;
Where the umpire of fate forever doth wait
　Giving gladness and sorrow for winnings.

There's the man at the bat, he's a king on that plat,
　And he watches the ball that is fleeting
'Till his blow meets the same, and it soars o'er the game
　And receives from the people a greeting.
'Tis the man who doth wait while fortune that's great,
　Changing hands like the shuttle in weaving.
Comes and touches his mace, and he runs every base,
　While the people shout, "Luck is retrieving!"

See the pitcher, whose aim is surely not tame,
　While his curvings are often perplexing;
And the poise of his fist, with the twist of his wrist,
　To those running the bases is vexing.
'Tis the man who in fame hits the mark all the same,
　Though he throws a curved ball there to do it;
And the one who would steal a base on his field,
　Will have cause to remember and rue it.

And the catcher with nerve that all good might deserve,
　And a visor drawn low for the danger;
With a smile by that base that's as cruel to face
　As the blow of a spiteful sky-ranger—
'Tis the man of strong nerve, whom no terror can swerve,
　And who laughs where the peril is thickest;
And he guards the home base 'gainst the strong in the race,
　And outs them with hand that is quickest.

There's the guard at each base who, alert in his place,
  Knows his work and performs it with pleasure;
And the fielders that stand with the game well in hand
  And consider high balls but a treasure.
'Tis the men of each age, who on history's page
  Have written their names with their actions;
Catching fame on the fly, though it comes from the sky,
  And ne'er bothered with foolish attractions.

So the old game of life, with its conquest and strife,
  Ever moves, with no pause or delaying.
The wise and the great and the foolish with fate
  On the field of the great world are playing.
And the games will ne'er close 'till the books shall disclose
  All the wonderful outings and innings,
With the sun 'neath the West and the players at rest,
  And the blest with their bountiful winnings.

THE SLIDE OF PAUL REVERE.
Grantland Rice, in Atlanta Journal.

Listen, fanatics, and you shall hear
Of the midnight slide of Paul Revere--
How he scored from first on an outfield drive
By a dashing sprint and headlong dive—
'Twas the greatest play pulled off that year.

Now the home of poets and potted beans,
Of Emersonian ways and means,
In Base Ball epic has oft been sung
Since the days of Criger and old Cy Young—
But not even fleet, deer-footed Bay
Could have pulled off any such fancy play
As the slide of P. Revere, which won
The famous battle of Lexington.

The Yanks and the British were booked that trip
In a scrap for the New World Championship—
But the British landed a bit too late,
So the game didn't open till half-past eight,
And Paul Revere was dreaming away
When the umpire issued his call for play.

On, on they fought 'neath the Boston moon,
As the British figured—"Not yet, but soon"—
For the odds were against the Yanks that night,
With Paul Revere blocked away from the fight—
And the grandstand gathering groaned in woe,
While a sad wail bubbled from Rooters' Row.

But wait—Hist!   Hearken! and likewise hark!
What means that galloping near the park?
What means that cry of a man dead sore?
" Am I too late?   Say, what's the score? "
And echo answered both far and near,
As the rooters shouted, " There's Paul Revere!"

Oh, how sweetly that moon did shine,
When P. Revere took the coaching line!
He woke up the grandstand from its trance,
And made the bleachers get up and dance—
He joshed the British with robust shout
Until they booted the ball about—
He whooped and he clamored all over the lot
Till the score was tied in a Gordian knot.

Now, in this part of the " Dope Recooked "
Are the facts which history overlooked—
How Paul Revere came to bat that night
And suddenly ended the long-drawn fight—
How he singled to center and then straightaway
Dashed on to second like Harry Bay—
Kept traveling on with the speed of a bird,
Till he whizzed like a meteor rounding third—
" Hold back, you lobster "—but all in vain—
The coachers shouted in tones of pain—
For Paul kept on with a swinging stride,
And he hit the ground when they hollered "**SLIDE!** "

Spectacular plays may come and go
In the hurry of Time's swift ebb and flow—
But never again will there be one
Like the first American " hit and run."
And as long as the old game lasts you'll hear
Of the midnight slide of P. Revere.

BALTIMORE'S LAMENT.

Baltimore American.

When the team from Podunk Centre comes to play in Baltimore
We will see the game presented as it was in days of yore.
When the score was in the hundreds as the coming shades of night
Called it at the seventh inning, and the players had a fight;
When 'twas " out " if any fielder caught the ball on its first bound,
And they " crossed the runner out " before he'd travelled half way
     round,

Oh, they'll give us old time Base Ball, with the old time sort of
  score,
When the team from Podunk Centre comes to play in Baltimore.

The Orioles will hustle for the annual championship
Of the Turnpike League; they'll try to beat the team from Hutner's
  Slip,
And the nine from Perkin's Crossing must play ball its very best,
While the Punkintown star pitcher's curves will be knocked " galley
  west."
The club from Sleepy Hollow will agree that Jerry Nops
Has a way of giving pitchers' fancy inshoots knockout drops.
"Oh, kill him! Kill the umpire!" will the bleachers loudly roar
If the team from Podunk Centre tries to win from Baltimore.

Our " Mugs " McGraw will do his best to play Base Ball and win,
And he'll wear some zephyr coaxers on his broad, determined chin;
And " Robby," too, will say " B'gosh " and chew a wisp of hay
To conceal his strong emotion when a liner gets away.
The Turnpike League will have a pennant made of green goods
  bright,
And each team will play to win it with all their strength and might,
So we'll see the game played this year as it was in years before
When the team from Podunk Centre comes to play in Baltimore.

CHAPTER XXXIII.

RALPH D. PAINE

HUGH S. FULLERTON   WILL S. IRWIN

CHAPTER XXXIII.

THE prose literature of Base Ball began with the game itself, and has kept pace with it in attractive form. If it is true, as has herein been said, that whenever the elements are favorable and wherever grounds are available the game is in progress, it is quite as true that wherever and whenever newspapers and periodicals are printed in America literature of the game is in process of making. Not only volumes but libraries have been written. Historical, statistical, descriptive, narrative, technical and humorous articles and books, in unlimited numbers, have flooded the country for years, and the cataclysm continues its supply of literary matter in an ever-increasing deluge. Recently the high-class magazines have taken up the subject, and the foremost publications of America are devoting much valuable space to the exploitation of features of the American game.

From out of this vast ocean of material one can only present, in a work like this, a few excerpts, touching divers phases of the general theme. In selecting these, I have only chosen such as here appear as representing types of Base Ball writing, each peculiar to its author or its class.

The following characteristic editorial is from the New York *Sun* of April 18, 1908:

"THE GREATEST LIVING WRITER.

"Our valued and vertiginous contemporary, the Chicago *Tribune*, has not given up to stockings and gloves what was meant for the permanent happiness of mankind. In spite of its ferocious war on Gloversville and Hosierdom it is still true to the felicities, rarities and preciosities of style. Ithuriel Ellery Sanborn was present with all his squadron of language at the 'christening' of the Chicago Base Ball season last week. We invite students of the living speech to the works of the 'master':

"'The Cardinals were outbatted by many parasangs.

"'Big Jeff Overall cut the cardiac region of the plate.

"'The turnout from Bugville was surprisingly large.

"'Zimmerman makes winning clout.

"'One on a pass, the other on a puncture.

"'Compiling a double.

"'There was a gay yelp when Steinfeldt smashed.

"'After Overall had whiffed.

"'Overall caught him off balance, accomplishing Roger's demise.

"'But for Brown's unfortunate decease he could have scored pulled up.

"'Moran poked a hot one.

"'The little fellow stabbed it.

"'There were two dead Cubs.

"'A couple of underground shoots.

"'Manager Frank had not touched the pan.

"'Arbiter Klem showed him a slewfoot print on the edge of the rubber.

"'Opposed to the Cubs' star was Left Handed Lush.'

"If Mr. Joseph Medill were here to exult in the glory of the 'master' and the Cubs he might need an interpreter at first, but he would instantly applaud the originality, the tang, the bite, the procession of home bagging parts of speech that belong to the Hon. Ithuriel Ellery Sanborn. May his vocabulary increase, if such a thing is possible. We take the liberty of nominating him as a member of the Hon. Henry Cabot Lodge's Academy. Is there another living writer who can produce in quantities to suit such muscular, meaty and animated English?"

The following appeared a few years ago in the editorial columns of the Memphis *Appeal*:

"THE GAME OF BALL.

"Ball playing is looked upon as the national sporting game of this country, just as poker is looked upon as the national gambling game, and never was ball playing so popular as it is at present. We have national leagues of all kinds. Every city of consequence has its Base Ball club, a member of some league or other. Semi-professional clubs are numerous. Big business houses maintain amateur clubs. Every vacant lot has its ball players organized and unorganized. The public streets are occupied by ball tossers who avail themselves of every opportunity to throw a ball across the street to some one else quite as eager as themselves. Base Ball is the topic of universal conversation, and keeping the percentage of the several clubs is making us a nation of mathematicians. On the streets, in the alleys, in business offices, in public resorts, in private houses, at morning, noon and night, young and old, rich and poor, are discussing Base Ball and arguing in favor of their particular favorites. The boy or girl of 15 who does not know the batting record of every member of the local league is looked on with pity. A game at Red Elm Park attracts 7,000 people who pay to get in. People go wild with excitement as they did long ago when they watched the contests in the arena in the Circus Maximus, in the stadium, or as they did who lined the road from Marathon to Athens to watch the footrunners. Bourke Cockran drew an audience of 6,000 people during a time of political excitement, but they paid no admission. Demosthenes, risen from the dust of ages, and advertised to deliver a new philippic, could not draw a paid audience of 7,000. The country is Base Ball crazy, and it is a pleasant form of dementia. The game is harmless and healthy, and those who witness it feel a relief in leaving dingy offices or dull workshops and going where they can fill their lungs with pure air and shout to their heart's content."

The professional ranks of actors, musicians and artists have always contained large numbers of lovers of Base Ball, and many of them have divided their time between devotion to their arts and to the game. DeWolf Hopper's reciting of " Casey at the Bat " into world-wide fame has been spoken of. The cartoons of Davenport and other famed artists have contributed great pleasure to enthusiasts. John Philip Sousa, the popular bandmaster, not only has an organized team among his instrumentalists but occasionally writes upon the subject. The *Base Ball Magazine* of February, 1909, contains a very interesting contribution from the pen of the great band-

JOHN PHILIP SOUSA'S BASE BALL TEAM

master, together with a halftone cut illustrating some of his members—himself among them—in full Base Ball uniform, with the word " Sousa " emblazoned on every breast.

The following was published in the Chicago *Inter-Ocean*, Tuesday, May 5, 1891. It is in a vein characteristic of its author, Leonard Dana Washburn, an *Inter-Ocean* writer, who lost his life in a railway accident, in Indiana, a few months after this Base Ball story appeared:

" You can write home that Grandpa won yesterday.

" And say in the postscript that Willie Hutchinson did it. The sweet child stood out in the middle of the big diamond of pompadour grass and slammed balls down the path that looked like the biscuits of a bride. The day was dark, and when Mr. Hutchinson shook out the coils of his right arm, rubbed his left toe meditatively in the soil he loves so well, and let go, there was a blinding streak through the air like the tail of a skyrocket against a black sky. There would follow the ball a hopeless shriek, the shrill, whistling noise of a bat grippling with the wind, and a dull, stifled squash like a portly gentleman sitting down on a ripe tomato.

" Then Umpire McQuaid would call the attention of a person in a gray uniform to the fact that circumstances rendered it almost imperative for him to go away and give somebody else a chance.

" There were ten of the visiting delegation who walked jauntily to the plate and argued with the cold, moist air. Mr. Field lacerated the ethereal microbes three times out of four opportunities to get solid with the ball, and Brer Lewis Robinson Browning walked away from the plate with a pained expression twice in succession. The Gastown folks found the ball six times. Two of their runs were earned.

" Mr. Staley, who pitches for the strangers, did not have speed enough to pass a street car going in the opposite direction. His balls wandered down toward the plate like a boy on his way to school. If our zealous and public-spirited townsmen did not baste them all over that voting precinct it was because they grew weary and faint waiting for them to arrive. Dahlen continued his star engagement with the bat, getting a single, a slashing double, and a triple that missed being a four-timer only by the skin of its teeth.

" Even with all this, it is probable that Pittsburg would have won the game had it not been for a party named Miller, who played short for the wanderers. He covered about as much ground as a woodshed, and threw to first like a drunkard with a cork leg. By close attention to details Mr. Miller rolled up four errors, and three of them cost three runs.

"The town boys won the game in the first and second innings. Ryan hit an easy one to Miller as soon as the procession started. Mr. Miller picked up the ball with great agility and hurled it with wonderful speed at an elderly gentleman on the top row of the bleachers. Then Reilly threw Cooney's effort so that Beckley could easily have landed it had he been eighteen feet tall. Carroll's two-bagger brought both Colts in.

"In the second Wilmot removed the ball to the left field fence. Mr. Browning threw to Miller, who at once fixed his eye on third base and threw the ball with unerring directness at President Hart, who was posing on the roof of the grandstand with a haughty smile. Wilmot scored. And in the seventh Willie-Forget-Me-Not Hutchinson hit the ball a lick that brought tears to its eyes. Kittridge, who was just due, got a strong reverse English on the leather and started an artesian well in far-away left. Willie came right home.

"Bierbauer's single and a measly throw by Kittridge gave a run to O'Neil's pets in the second. Beckley's beautiful triple, and a sacrifice by Carroll fetched another, and in the ninth Reilly hit the ball a welt that caused it to back out over the north wall. That was all.

"Grandpa Anson wasn't feeling real well, and said several saucy things to the umpire out loud. He was on first and Dahlen was on second when Carroll hit down to Bierbauer. That person choked the ball on the ground and thereby removed both the man Anson and the man Dahlen. The former claimed interference and tried to explain things to McQuaid in a voice that could have been heard at the stockyards. McQuaid pulled out his watch and began to study the figures, whereupon the big captain moved grandly to the bench, and the show went on."

Mr. Ralph D. Paine prefaced one of his able articles on our national game, published in the *Outing Magazine* a few years ago, with these words:

"After the allied armies had stormed the walls of Peking, seven years ago, the British officers hastened to lay out cricket and hockey fields in the spacious grounds of the Temple of Heaven. Before skirmish-firing had ceased to vex the city's suburbs 'The Peking Field-Sports Club' had been organized, with an 'honorary secretary' of the Bengal Lancers. We correspondents viewed these proceedings with much interest and began reluctantly to agree with the popular opinion that the English are the only genuine sporting race.

"Not long after this, however, a squad of British officers rode into the vast enclosure of the Temple of Earth, where were encamped the khaki-clad troopers, 'dough-boys,' and gunners of Uncle Sam. The visitors were amazed to hear from beyond the yellow-tiled roofs a mighty roar as if an army were shouting itself black in the face. The terrific commotion rose and fell in waves of wrath and jubilation, and the puzzled Englishmen pushed on until they came to rows of templed walls and marble terraces, swarming with hundreds of blue-shirted fighting men.

"Here in one of the most sacred and inviolable places of all China—a place for ages dedicated to an annual pilgrimage of solemn worship by the Emperor—a thousand lusty Americans were using the very altars for 'bleachers' while they 'rooted' for the rival nines of Riley's Battery and the Sixth Cavalry squadron. The American Army League was in full swing for the Peking championship, and the hoarse volleys of 'Rotten umpire!' 'Soak it to her, Kelly!' 'Wow-w, slide, you lobster!' re-echoed from gray parapets that had never before been profaned by a foreigner.

"It was all as typically American as it was a unique episode in history. Those athletic Englishmen from India had their eyes opened to an appreciation of the national pastime of eighty-odd million Americans, and before the occupation ended they were deserting their own fields to enjoy the thrill of a fiercely fought nine-inning battle on the diamond of Chaffee's Camp.

"These Yankee exiles fell to 'playing ball' as naturally as to foraging, and while they were engaged in driving the festive three-bagger through the startled air of North China, jackies in white duck were circling the bases in blazing Cuba and Honolulu, or landing from revenue-cutter patrols to stake out a home-plate on frozen Alaskan beaches; and soldier and sailor teams were swinging their bats from one end of the Philippines to the other. As the British drum-beat has encircled the globe, so has the slogan of 'Play ball!' followed the Stars and Stripes, proclaiming the reign of the finest outdoor game ever devised."

In the May number of the *American Magazine* for 1911, writing on "Hitting the Dirt," Mr. Hugh S. Fullerton, of Chicago, had a forceful paper from which the following is a reprint:

"Base stealing, the gentle art of sprinting and 'hitting the dirt,' is the finest drawn and most closely calculated play in Base Ball, and the one that, above all others, reveals the mathematical exactitude of the national game. A player who can run eighty-five feet in three and one-third seconds from a flatfooted start, ought to reach second base exactly tied with the ball, nine times out of ten starts, if the play is perfectly made by the runner, pitcher, catcher and baseman. The slightest inaccuracy or hesitation decides the play.

" It seems a simple matter to run ninety feet while a ball is being thrown sixty-eight feet and caught and thrown back, approximately one hundred and thirty-two feet, caught again and held in position to touch the runner. Yet there is art and science in the feat. All pennant winning teams are base running teams. Every manager urges base running, tries to train his men to it; and then, except in rare instances, refuses to permit them to run, and plays the hit-and-run and sacrifice game instead.

" The figures show that the sacrifice hits average about one-third more per season than the stolen bases, and that the hit-and-run is used sixty per cent. oftener (this in major leagues) than stealing bases. The figures also prove that base stealing succeeds in about sixty-three per cent. of the times tried, and the hit-and-run in less than sixty-six per cent., and further, that the hit-and-run results in almost seven per cent. of the times it is attempted. In the face of these figures and of the expressed desire to increase base running, few managers will order a base running attack except when a pitcher opposing his team is notoriously weak at ' holding up ' runners and watching the bases.

" In the average seasons of the two major leagues—the American and National—89,156 face the pitchers. Of these 27,058 reach first base—19,154 of them on safe hits, 1,303 on errors that permit them to achieve the first ninety feet—645 by being hit by pitched balls, and 5,950 on bases on balls. These figures are the averages of the two leagues for five seasons. Of the 27,058 who reach first base, 17,138 arrive at second, 12,822 at third, and 8,272 score.

" Yet the average number of stolen bases in the 1,232 games of the two seasons of the major leagues is only 2,744. That is, out of 55,988 opportunities to steal bases, only 2,744 are improved.

" The figures appear to prove that the pitchers and catchers have acquired a mastery over the runners. The truth is that the cause of the degeneracy of the art of base running is twofold; first, the hit-and-run play and the sacrifice, and, second, the tendency toward stereotyped playing. Of the 2,744 pilferings, 1,951 are of second base, 744 of third, and 19 from third to the final goal."

It would be of interest, did space permit, to present Mr. Fullerton's deductions to prove his proposition that it is easier now than ever before to steal bases.

In *Pearson's* for May, 1911, Christy Mathewson, the famous pitcher of the New York " Giants " of the National League, wrote under the caption, "Outguessing the Batter," and the following incident is from his article:

"Many things have been said and written about pitchers outguessing batters, and batters outguessing pitchers, and to tell the truth there has always been a question in my mind about the outguessing proposition. I have seen so many instances where guesses went wrong—so many hundreds of instances—that I am about the last human being in the world to pose as an oracle on the subject of pitching psychology. Nevertheless, there certainly is a lot of psychology about pitching a base ball, * * * Joe Tinker, the clever little shortstop of the Chicago club, is a man with whom I have fought many battles of wits, and I am glad to acknowledge that he has come out of the fuss with flying colors on many occasions. There was a time when Tinker was putty in my hands. For two years he was the least dangerous man on the Chicago team. His weakness was a low curve on the outside, and I fed him low curves on the outside so often that I had him looking like an invalid every time he came to the plate. Then Joseph went home one night and did a little deep thinking. He got a nice long bat and took his stand at least a foot farther from the plate, and then he had me. If I kept the ball on the inside edge of the plate, he was in a splendid position to meet it, and if I tried to keep my offerings on the outside, he had plenty of time to 'step into 'em.' From that day on Tinker became one of the most dangerous batters I ever faced, not because his natural hitting ability had increased, but because he didn't propose to let the pitcher do all the 'outguessing.' "

The following extract from some periodical was also found among Mr. Chadwick's effects without a credit or date attached:

"The rules of the game will continue to shift one way and the other in the eternal duel between pitcher and batter, between attack and defense. For thirty years this effort at adjustment has been like the struggle between big guns and armor-plate. The science of pitching developed much faster than ability to hit the ball. Therefore the pitcher was handicapped in various ways, and the batter permitted to smite the missile freely until the tide swung the other way again. In recent years the 'slab-artist' has been given the advantage, and the complaint grows that there is not batting enough. This feature of the game has by no means reached a final solution.

"The revision of the rules has always been entrusted to the professional experts, and their edicts are obeyed by at least a million of players, all the way down to the barefooted tots who whang a three-cent ball with a barrel stave and wrangle over 'the foul-strike rule.' The vast army of amateurs must, therefore, look to the leagues for every change or improvement in the game, and in this way the professional element dominates the Base Ball of eighty millions of Americans. Unlike the history of other sports, professional Base Ball has helped instead of hindered the game of the amateur. Where one State league plays its circuit of six or eight small cities, a hundred amateur nines are springing up to pattern after the organization of the professionals, and with uniforms, managers, and regular schedules, boom the game for the pure fun of it. In Greater New York alone more than two hundred clubs of amateurs and semi-professional players contest regular series of games in private grounds and in the public parks.

"As a 'national game,' Base Ball has no more than begun its conquest. One of the great, popular awakenings of this generation has been the 'outdoor movement,' in which the gospel of fresh air and wholesome exercise has been preached from every housetop. The public schools are teaching it, employers are promoting athletic clubs for their working people, and a million dollars is not considered an extravagant sum to invest in the equipment of a college athletic plant. The average American is so constructed that athletic endeavor bores him unless it is enlivened by the spirit of competition. He must be trying to 'lick the other fellow' or he will quit the game in disgust. Base Ball is the one sport open to all, without any barrier of expense, and with rivalry enough to rivet the interest of its players.

"The pallid student with bulging brow may croak that it is a wicked, economic waste for thousands of grown men to be paid large salaries for hitting a ball with a stick of wood. On the contrary, these clean-built, sunburned, vigorous athletes of the league diamonds are the faculty members of the National University of Base Ball Culture, and their pupils are to be found in every other American home.

"The greatest day of the sporting calendar is 'the opening of the league season.' Then it is worth the price of admission just to see twenty thousand cheering Americans banked half way round the velvet turf in the sparkling April weather; when the heroes in their spick-and-span uniforms parade grandly across the field behind the band; when the big flag soars to the top of the tall pole; when the Mayor or Governor tosses the dedicatory horsehide sphere from his box; when the first gladiator strides up to the home plate, and the umpire croaks 'Play ball!'"

CHAPTER XXXIV.

FRED W. THAYER   JAMES A. TYNG

CHAPTER XXXIV.

WHILE writing this book, I have purposely avoided touching upon the technique of the game of Base Ball in its several departments, for the reason that the opinions of up-to-date, scientific experts so widely and so honestly vary as to what really constitute important methods that there is no intelligent hope of bringing them together by opening in these pages a discussion of the many playing features of the game.

However, I may, with perfect consistency, touch upon certain beginnings of things within my own recollection, welcoming any amendments to them of fact that may be antedated by the memories of others.

The first glove I ever saw on the hand of a ball player in a game was worn by Charles C. Waite, in Boston, in 1875. He had come from New Haven and was playing at first base. The glove worn by him was of flesh color, with a large, round opening in the back. Now, I had for a good while felt the need of some sort of hand protection for myself. In those days clubs did not carry an extra carload of pitchers, as now. For several years I had pitched in every game played by the Boston team, and had developed severe bruises on the inside of my left hand. When it is recalled that every ball pitched had to be returned, and that every swift one coming my way, from infielders, outfielders or hot from the bat, must be caught or stopped, some idea may be gained of the punishment received.

Therefore, I asked Waite about his glove. He confessed that he was a bit ashamed to wear it, but had it on to save his hand. He also admitted that he had chosen a color as inconspicuous as possible, because he didn't care to attract attention. He added that the opening on the back was for purpose of ventilation.

Meanwhile my own hand continued to take its medicine with utmost regularity, occasionally being bored with a warm twister that hurt excruciatingly. Still, it was not until 1877 that I overcame my scruples against joining the "kid-glove aristocracy" by donning a glove. When I did at last decide to do so, I did not select a flesh-colored glove, but got a black one, and cut out as much of the back as possible to let the air in.

Happily, in my case, the presence of a glove did not call out the ridicule that had greeted Waite. I had been playing so long and had become so well known that the innovation seemed rather to evoke sympathy than hilarity. I found that the glove, thin as it was, helped considerably, and inserted one pad after another until a good deal of relief was afforded. If anyone wore a padded glove before this date I do not know it. The "pillow mitt" was a later innovation.

About this time, 1875-6, James Tyng, catcher for the Harvard Base Ball Club, appeared on the Boston grounds one day, and, stepping to his position, donned the first

wire mask I had ever seen. This mask had been invented
and patented by Mr. Fred W. Thayer, a Harvard player,
now a prominent lawyer of Boston. Like other protective
innovations at that stage of the game, it was not at
first well received by professionals. Our catcher, James
White, was urged to try it, and after some coaxing consented. I pitched him a few balls, some of which he missed,
and finally, becoming disgusted at being unable to see
the ball readily, he tore off the mask and, hurling it toward
the bench, went on without it.

This wire mask, with certain modifications, is the
same that has been used by catchers ever since.

In June, 1908, the New York *World* had the following
version of the introduction of the mask:

"Very few, even of the old-time Base Ball fans, could tell who
had the distinction of being the first player to don a Base Ball
mask. Dr. Harry Thatcher, of Dexter, Me., at that time a resident
of Bangor, is the man, and the mask was invented by a Boston
man and a captain of the Harvard Base Ball nine.

"It was way back in the '70s that the Base Ball mask was
first invented. The national game was a rather crude affair compared with what it is now, but the principles of the game were
about the same and the players of those, early days realized the
troubles of the man behind the bat. At that time catcher's and first
baseman's mitts were unheard-of things, and those players caught
the ball bare-handed.

"It was a few years prior to 1878 that Fred Thayer, of Boston,
at that time a player on the Harvard nine, realized the necessity
of a covering for the face of the catcher in a Base Ball game.
He set about to see what he could do in that way, and the result
was a Base Ball mask. It had its beginning then.

"When Mr. Thayer had a mask which he thought would answer
its purpose, he introduced it in the games which the Harvard nine
was playing at that time and of which he was captain and third
baseman. Harry Thatcher was 'the man behind the bat' on Captain Thayer's team, and it fell to him to don the mask for the first
time.

"It is said that Dr. Thatcher did not take to the idea very

well, for the players on the Harvard team guyed him not a little for wearing it, as they said that it was 'babyish' and cowardly to wear a protection to the face. So the doctor was not seen very often after that wearing Mr. Thayer's invention, but instead used a rubber mouthpiece to protect himself from foul tips and the in-shoots of the slab artist.

"Shortly after Mr. Thayer got out the first sample of his invention Mr. Spalding saw the possibilities of the Thayer invention and sought to get control of it. Finally the matter came to a head in a lawsuit over who had a right to the patent. Finally, February 12, 1878, Mr. Spalding was granted a patent.

"F. H. Davis, of Bangor, has the mask that was worn by Addison Hamlin, of that city, when the catcher on the Harvard nine during his college course, and it differs in appearance from the modern Base Ball mask very little.

"Of course, it is somewhat cruder in appearance than the finished product of the present day, but it has the same general features. The padding is of cotton batting with long leather strips wound around the wire to keep it in place. The wire shield to the face is different from the masks of to-day in that it comes to a sharp point in front, so that if a ball should hit it it would glance off."

That Dr. Thatcher was *not*, and that James Tyng *was*, the first catcher to wear the mask in a regular game it is quite possible to demonstrate by competent witnesses, but in doing this a slight discrepancy in time is introduced. In a letter quite recently received from Mr. Fred W. Thayer, the inventor of the mask, that gentleman writes:

"116 FEDERAL STREET,
"BOSTON, May 18, 1911.

"MY DEAR MR. SPALDING:

"I am in receipt of your favor of the 9th instant. You shall have the facts in regard to the catcher's mask, and I think you can feel assured that the data are all correct.

"In order to give you the whole story I shall have to ask you to go back to the year '76 that you may know what the conditions were in Harvard Base Ball matters.

"Thatcher was the catcher in the season of '76. He left college at the end of the year.

"You will recall the fact that college nines especially had rarely more than one, possibly two, substitutes, and these were 'general utility' men.

"Tyng was the best all around natural ball player of my time. He had played third base, center field, and helped out in other positions, including catcher, in the season of '76. In one or two games in which he caught behind the bat he had been hit by foul tips and had become more or less timid.

"He was, by all odds, the most available man as catcher for the season of '77, and it was up to me to find some way to bring back his confidence.

"The fencing mask naturally gave me the hint as to the protection for the face, and then it was up to me to devise some means of having the impact of the blow kept from driving the mask onto the face. The forehead and chin rest accomplished this and also made it possible for me to secure a patent, which I did in the winter of 1878.

"Tyng practiced catching with the mask, behind the bat, in the gymnasium during the winter of '77, and became so thoroughly proficient that foul tips had no further terrors for him.

"The first match game in which the mask was used was on Fast Day, in Lynn, against the Live Oaks, in April, 1877. Thereafter the Harvard catcher used it in all games.

"I hope this will give you the data which you wish. At all events it gives you the real facts in regard to the Base Ball mask.

"Yours faithfully,

(Signed) "Fred W. Thayer."

In a communication from Mr. George Wright, the famous old-time ball player, bearing date Boston, May 17. 1911, he says:

"The first time I saw the mask and it being used was by Tyng, when catching in a game on the Harvard nine in 1877. What game it was I cannot remember. But that fall Mr. Thayer, by appointment, brought the mask to my store on Eliot street. Harry Schafer, being there, put it on, when we threw several balls at it, which glanced off, he not feeling any jar or effect from them. We pronounced it a success and decided it would come into general use. I made arrangements at the time with Mr. Thayer to patent the mask, control the sale of it, and pay him a royalty, and, as you know, after the above date the mask gradually came into general use. Who the first professional player was to use it I cannot say. The mask was patented 1878."

To Roger Bresnahan, manager of the St. Louis Nationals, belongs the credit of the recent introduction of shinguards for the catcher.

When sliding, as an aid to the base runner, began, I

am not prepared to state with authority. I do know, however, that its introduction was not by "King" Kelly, as has sometimes been claimed. As early as 1866 (Kelly began to play as a lad in 1873), at a game at Rochelle, Illinois, Robert Addy startled the players of the Forest Citys by a diving slide for second base. None of us had ever witnessed the play before, though it may have been in vogue. Certainly we were quite nonplussed, and just as surely the slogan, "Slide, Kelly, slide," had not been heard at that time.

All the varied modifications of the slide have been well known for many years, and, but for the fact that different players adopt different methods of "getting there," not many changes have been introduced, some reaching the bases "head-on," others feet foremost, still others sliding sideways, and a few by a low dodge and grab of the sack with one hand.

The bunt sacrifice hit is a comparatively recent introduction to the game. Years before it was thought of much attention had been given to placing hits in exposed portions of the field, and some batsmen had gained considerable proficiency in the science. Others made a specialty of the long, high drive, in the hope of a muff or of aiding base runners to advance after the ball had been caught, with only one man out. But to stop the ball at close infield, with the expectation of giving advantage to base runners, and with the forlorn chance of beating the ball to first, was not adopted systematically as a feature of the game until much later. I regret that I am not able to give the name of the player who introduced this very important innovation or the time of its first presentation.

As a matter of fact, from the time of the adoption of regular playing rules by the old Knickerbockers, changes in the technique of Base Ball have been remarkably few in number as compared with the great advances in skill and science of play. The ball has been recently improved, but is still of practically the same size and weight. Bats are substantially of the same form and material as at the beginning of professional Base Ball. The masks and gloves and mitts have been somewhat bettered in material and workmanship, and uniforms and shoes are better; but the same general quality of fabric and fashion are yet employed in their making.

In one department of the game, however, the change has been very marked. Pitching has undergone a complete revolution. Indeed, the word "pitching," which was properly applied to the act of ball delivery at first, is to-day a misnomer. The ball as now presented to the batsman is not pitched, but thrown. Whereas, in the early days, it left the pitcher's hand with a peculiar snap of the wrist from an unbent elbow, and below the hip, now it may be hurled in any manner at the pitcher's option.

Perhaps at this point it may be of interest to consider briefly the causes that resulted in the change from the old-time straight arm pitch to the present unrestricted delivery of the ball. First, then, it must be conceded that the method employed at the beginning was never acquired by many men. It seemed to be a natural gift to a few players in the early seventies and before, but, in spite of the earnest efforts of hundreds to acquire the science of delivery as required by the published rules, less than a dozen pitchers were using it up to 1876, and only half a dozen gained eminence as pitchers at this time. These were Brainard, Cummins, Matthews, McBride, Spalding and Zettlein. All the above named, with the exception of Cummins, who began pitching in 1873, were in the game from 1870 to 1876, when the National League was formed, following which, in 1884, after numerous modifications, the straight arm delivery was finally abrogated.

The fact that so few ball players were ever able to acquire the "knack" of straight arm pitching led to many embarrassments at the beginning of professional Base Ball. The game was rapidly growing in favor, new clubs and new leagues were coming into existence all over the country, but the supply of pitchers did not correspondingly keep pace. Something had to be done. As the rules were unchanged, and as only a dozen legal pitchers were in the country, clubs were forced to put men in the box who attempted the straight arm delivery, but who only succeeded in presenting a very poor imitation. The effect of this course was to put the question up to the umpire, and if he ruled against the pitcher there was a disappointed crowd, no game, or an utterly uninteresting exhibition. If the umpire ruled in favor of the bogus pitcher, there was bitter controversy on the field and usually a protested game. Still, it was a fact that there were not enough legal pitchers to man all the teams, and the result of this condition was a growing tendency on the part of umpires to be lax in the enforcement of the rule. In most cases, where the demand of the captain of the club possessing a legitimate pitcher was not too strong, the umpire permitted the unlawful delivery of the ball rather than stop the game and disappoint the crowd.

It should not be understood that no modifications of the straight arm delivery had been made previous to 1884. There had been several changes, but each resulted in partial failure. The original Knickerbocker rules of 1845 required that

"The ball must be pitched and not thrown for the bat."

In 1860 the rule was revised by the original National Association of Base Ball Players, providing that

" The ball must be pitched, not jerked nor thrown to the bat."

In 1875 another change provided that

"The ball must be delivered to the bat with the arm swinging nearly perpendicular at the side of the body, and the hand in swinging forward must not be raised higher than the hip."

The National League, in the first year of its existence, in 1876, made a change providing that

"The ball must be delivered to the bat with the arm swinging nearly perpendicularly at the side of the body, and the hand in passing forward must pass below the hip."

In 1878 the National League again changed the rule, requiring the pitcher to deliver the ball

" Below his waist."

In 1883 the National League once more revised the rule, requiring that the ball should

" Be delivered below the pitcher's shoulder."

None of these changes were satisfactory. The requirement that the ball should be delivered with the arm swinging perpendicularly gave too much latitude to the umpires who did not agree in their interpretation of the term. The provision of 1878 induced pitchers to wear their belts abnormally high to elevate the " waist line " to the shoulder, and the rule of 1883, requiring delivery below the shoulder, was deceptive and differently construed by different umpires.

It was not, therefore, until the change of 1884, removing all bans and permitting the pitcher to use his own option as to his method of delivering the ball, that the need of further change was removed. I was present at the meeting of the League when this action was taken. I do not recall who presented the resolution removing all bans from the pitcher, but I remember that it followed much acrimonious discussion, and I was most heartily in favor of doing away with all restrictions.

The withdrawal of the old-time straight elbow restraint of course enabled pitchers to devote their talents to the development of new methods of delivery calculated to deceive the batsman, but long before this some efforts in that direction had been made.

Arthur Cummins, of Brooklyn, was the first pitcher of the old school that I ever saw pitch a curved ball. Bobby Matthews soon followed. This was in the early seventies. Both men were very light, spare fellows, with long, sinewy wrists, and having a peculiar wrist-joint motion with a certain way of holding the ball near the fingers' ends that enabled them to impart a rotary motion to the ball, followed by a noticeable outward curve.

In 1874 Tom Bond inaugurated the present style

of pitching or, rather, underhand throwing, with its in-curves and out-shoots. This style of delivery was then in violation of the straight-arm pitching rules, but umpires were disposed to let it go, and thus gradually, in spite of legislation, the old style gave way to the new.

In the first year of the existence of the National League several of its pitchers began the delivery of the curved ball, that is, a ball which, after leaving the pitcher's hand, would curve to the right or left, and could be made to deceive the batsman by appearing to come wide of the plate and then suddenly turn in and pass over it; or, appearing to come directly over the plate, to shoot out, missing it entirely.

The result of this work on the part of the pitcher was to make hitting much less frequent and small scores characterized all well-played games. In 1877, as a result of the curved ball, a hot controversy arose into which many scientists were drawn. Distinguished collegians openly declared that the " curved ball " was a myth; that any other deflection of a thrown ball than that caused by the wind or opposing air-currents was impos-sible. Men high up in the game clung strenuously to the same opinion. Col. J. B. Joyce, who had been a ruling spirit in the old Cincinnati Red Stockings, held to this view. It was absurd, he claimed, to say that any man could throw a ball other than in a straight line. A prac-tical test was made at Cincinnati in the presence of a great crowd to convert the Colonel. A surveyor was employed to set three posts in a row, with the left-hand surface of the two at the ends on a line with the right-hand surface of that in the middle. Then a tight board fence about six feet high was continued from each end post, also bearing on the straight line drawn. Will White, one of the most expert twirlers of the day, was selected to convert Col. Joyce. The test took place in the presence of a big crowd and was a success in everything but the conversion. White stood upon the left of the fence at one end, so that his hand could not possibly pass beyond the straight line, and pitched the ball so that it passed to the right of the middle post. This it did by three or four inches, but curved so much that it passed the third post a half foot to the left. Col. Joyce saw the test successfully performed, but he would not be convinced.

The following is from the Cincinnati *Enquirer* of October, 1877:

"During the entire summer of 1877 the question has been mooted whether or not there is or can be such a thing as curved pitching. Upon the subject a variety of opinions have been freely expressed. Some persons have stoutly maintained that the curve is a reality, while others have as decidedly affirmed that it was merely a hallucination of a willingly deceived imagination. At length the question was taken up by Prof. McFarland, of the Ohio Agricultural College, in the affirmative, and by Prof. Stoddard, of the Worcester University, in the negative.

"Prof. McFarland says: 'Of course, a curve throwing of a ball, causing it to deflect from a direct line, is possible, for if the ball be held in such a way that by a peculiar motion of the wrist and arm it is made to revolve on an axis other than its true one it must continue to revolve on such axis to the right or left as would necessitate from the pitcher using his right or left hand, and hold a positive motion in such deflected direction.'

"Per contra, Prof. Stoddard says: 'It is not only theoretically but practically impossible for any such impetus to be conveyed to a moving body as would be required to perform the action supposed, by inexperienced persons, to control the movement of what is termed a curved ball; for, as is well known, the motion of any body such as the ball is in the direction of the propelling force, and that being direct, and the ball itself having no volition or power to alter its own course, how can such a result occur? To cause the ball to curve would require the constant, attendant action of some controlling power along its entire pathway; but as no such accompanying agency exists there cannot possibly be such a thing as a curve to the right or left of the true line.'

"Professor Lewis Swift, of the Rochester University, thus set forth his ideas of the curved ball problem, correcting at the same time the erroneous report that he had predicted the feat as impossible.

"'In complying with the request to give a philosophical reason for the curvature of a ball by Base Ball experts, I do so the more cheerfully to correct an impression that I am a disbeliever in the performance of such a feat, which statement, unauthorized by me, was first promulgated in your paper. It is true that some time ago, when the subject was first broached to me, I denied that it was possible to do it, but when so many keen-eyed observers asserted that they had seen it repeatedly done, I began to investigate the matter, and soon saw, that instead of being impossible, it was in accordance with the plainest principles of philosophy. I will now as plainly and briefly as I can, consistent with clearness, proceed to give an explanation of what, at first thought, and without having seen it, one would suppose to be contrary to the laws of motion. In the first place, let it be borne in mind that when a ball is thrown with great velocity, and especially against the wind, the air in front is considerably condensed, but if the ball has no rotation, the only effect of the air's resistance is to impede the velocity, but not so when the ball rotates. 1. Suppose a ball to be fired from a rifled cannon—say to the east—the ball emerges with a rapid rotation at right angles to the direction of motion. One face of the ball is continuously in front, the upper, the lower, the north and the south sides of that face, pressing constantly and equally against the air, consequently it has by its rotation no tendency to deviate in any direction. It may be well here to state that the object in giving such a ball a rotation is (as no ball can be made equally dense in every part and perfectly round) to present every part of the forward face on every side of the line of motion, all inequalities, therefore, of density and symmetry are at every instant equally divided on all sides, and the ball will go undeviatingly in the direction desired.

"'2. Suppose a pitcher should throw a ball, say to the east, giving it a rotation whose axis should correspond with the northern and southern horizons. The air in front being more dense than in the rear, of course the friction of the rotating ball will be greatest on the front side, and will cause it to deviate, not to the right nor left, but slightly up or down, depending in which way the ball rotates.

"'3. Suppose the pitcher, at the instant the ball leaves his hand, should impart to it a rotation whose axis would lie in the zenith and nadir like a spinning top, such a ball, because the friction is greater against the compressed than the rarified air, will 'curve' either to the right or left, depending in which direction it rotates. If it rotates from the north, through the east to the south, which is the direction a right hand pitcher would most easily give it, it would curve to the left, and vice versa. If any one believes that the cause assigned is inadequate to produce the observed effect, let him imagine experiment No. 3 to be performed in a dense medium—water for example, and I think he will be convinced that a ball can be curved, but if he still doubts it, let him suppose the ball to be a croquet ball driven full of long, projecting spikes, and sent rapidly through the water, rotating as it goes. It would be the very essence of folly, and at variance with every principle of philosophy, to contend that it would move in a straight line.' "

The foregoing is only interesting from historical and scientific standpoints, since every careful observer in the grandstand, behind the batsman, is able clearly to note the very wide deflection given the ball by modern pitchers of every league.

Other deceptive deliveries than the "curved ball," with its in-curves, its out-shoots, its rise and drop, are later innovations. The "spit-ball," of which more was heard a few years ago than now, is one, and the "fade away," with a line of motion like that described by the undulations of a snake while crawling, is used by Christy Mathewson and a few others, I believe.

The removal of the straight-arm pitching restriction, by the amendment of the rules in 1884, was responsible for the evolution of the "Phenom." He came into the game from Keokuk, Kankakee, Kokomo and Kalamazoo. He was heralded always as a "discovery." His achievements were "*simply phenomenal.*" Once in a great while he "made good." Usually he proved to be a flat and unmitigated failure. The trying-out of these wonders became a very frequent occurrence, and the appearance of one for that purpose was sure to call out the ejaculation, "Hello, here's another phenom. Wonder how long he'll last?"

Ever since the introduction of the "curved ball," as has been already stated, very low scores have become the rule. The pitcher has come to be regarded as the most important man in the game, and, as a result of the strain to his wrist and arm, his numbers have had to be augmented, until now some league clubs employ half a score of twirlers.

Not until recently has there been any change in regard to the pre-eminent prestige of the pitcher in the game. Now, however, there are indications that a new order of things is about to be inaugurated which shall give the batsman great prominence; and this is due to the introduction of the cork-center ball, just adopted by both the major leagues as the Official League Ball.

For some years rule makers and close students of the science of Base Ball have been trying to devise some means by which the batting end of the game might be strengthened. A very low score, in the nature of things, makes a close score. But there is no reason why a larger score, involving sharper work on the part of every player on the team, under conditions equally favorable to both sides, should not still be a close score, with many more incidents to interest the spectator.

The ball that has been in use for so many years had a small core of solid rubber in the center. While it was about right as to size and weight, its resilience was not all that could be desired. It did not leave the bat with that live, crackling sound which betokens the force of the concussion and suggests a long hit. The new ball has a small core of cork, encased by a shell of rubber, which gives to it greater resilience and accuracy of flight.

Although at this writing the season is not over, the games thus far played have been characterized by many more base hits than have been recorded up to this time in recent years. It is possible that pitchers may not be altogether pleased with the innovation, but it is certain to delight the public, and it will incidentally give all other players on the team a chance to strengthen their averages.

CHAPTER XXXV.

OLD GRANDSTAND AT THE POLO GROUNDS, NEW YORK

CHAPTER XXXV.

FOR more than ten recent years each Base Ball season has seemed to be a climax of prosperity, only to find the succeeding season further advanced in every way than its predecessors.

I do not limit or attempt to define the qualification of prosperity and success by any material advantage which may have happened to each individual club of the major league circuits. Superficial observers of Base Ball conditions are too prone to believe that the general conditions affecting the national game are contingent upon the attendance in the greater cities.

It is true that prosperity in the cities means a certain amount of Base Ball interest in all the territory which is within the metropolitan influence, but it is also true that there has been a very wonderful and general growth of interest in sections which are remote from the major league circuits, and which are dependent for their professional Base Ball upon the so-called minor league organizations.

If we look for a specific date from which to measure the revival of conditions from the chaotic period which followed the organization and death of the Brotherhood

493

of Base Ball Players, in 1890, and the elimination of "Freedmanism," in 1902, we may accept the reorganization of the New York National League Base Ball Club as the beginning of the professional rehabilitation of the national sport.

Following closely upon that was the settlement of all disputes between Base Ball organizations and the signing of a new National Agreement, which provided for the sanest court of executive administration in the history of the sport—the National Commission—all of which tended to place Base Ball on a basis which commanded the admiration of the patrons and gave permanent assurance to promoters of the stability of their occupation.

As the seasons followed in natural sequence, that of 1910, through the cumulative effect of all the good which had been accomplished, surpassed all others in the broader interest which was taken in the pastime, the superiority of attractions from the purely professional standpoint, and the wider-reaching and firmer hold which Base Ball had attained upon the masses by reason of competent and able management at its fountain-head—that being carefully adjusted and well balanced organization with a fair deal for all.

The major leagues succeeded so handsomely throughout the year that at the finish of the season all of their clubs, with perhaps two exceptions, had balances to their credit ranging from small amounts to handsome sums. The exceptions, if they were losers, lost so little that they were not distressed financially, and in view of embarrassments under which they had been compelled to labor,

THE GRANDSTAND AT FORBES FIELD, PITTSBURGH, ONE OF THE LARGEST AND MOST COMPLETELY APPOINTED BASE BALL STRUCTURES IN AMERICA

THE MAGNIFICENT NEW STEEL AND CONCRETE STRUCTURE OF THE NATIONAL LEAGUE BASE BALL CLUB, POLO GROUNDS, NEW YORK CITY owing to the vicissitudes of the sport from a professional standpoint, were cheerful and optimistic as to the future.

Forty-nine organized leagues completed their season and were awarded championships in 1910. Probably about sixty leagues, working under direct rules and following the system which governs the parent major leagues, endeavored to make progress through the year, but some of them weakened through causes which experience teaches to avoid and were unable to last to the final games scheduled for their circuits.

In addition to these leagues, we must not omit in summing up general Base Ball conditions the great number of municipal and what are known as semi-professional leagues which were in existence from one ocean to the other.

How many of these are to be found in the States of the Union is without the pale of known data. In some cities there are as many as fifty such leagues. In others there are half a score. In general, it would not be far amiss to say that there probably are not less than 5,000 scattered throughout the cities. This may appear to be a high estimate, but when the radius of the national game is taken into consideration, and when the actual number of contests played on a certain day amount to more than 200, as was indicated in one Eastern newspaper alone, it would seem that the local leagues are a far greater factor in the national sport than many imagined.

Add to these the college and school games, which are also sufficiently well organized to become fixtures, and one can begin to conceive of the expansion of the national game, although still be far from anything like actual possession of the facts. There are 10,000 games played every day of which the public hears nothing; perhaps double that number.

So much for the activity of players on the diamond.

Principal causes for the growth in interest of the pastime have previously been stated. There is a great contributory cause which must not be neglected when undertaking to make a review of the progressive strides of the sport.

I refer to the erection in the larger major and minor league cities of permanent and substantial structures to house our national pastime.

When Base Ball first became established as a public sport, which requested public attention for its share, the conditions were so precarious that most of the Base Ball promoters felt that wooden stands, arranged with tiers of seats for the accommodation of patrons, were all that they could afford.

The earliest stands were small affairs compared with those which were erected along in the nineties. At various times the structures that were in use at Base Ball parks burned to the ground by reason of fires which started through accident.

As the stability of Base Ball became more assured, owners decided to branch out and erect fireproof buildings on their grounds. First of these stands was the concrete and steel affair which was built at Cincinnati by John T. Brush. In the course of time Mr. Brush became owner of the New York Base Ball Club.

When the huge, wooden stadium burned at the Polo Grounds, in the spring of 1911, Base Ball men sat aghast, because it meant much to the national pastime to lose the home of the most important National League club in the largest city of the United States.

There was some doubt as to whether Base Ball would be continued on the historic field, because of the possibility of a short lease, but Mrs. Harriet G. Coogan, owner of the Polo Grounds, through her husband, Col. J. J. Coogan, assured Mr. Brush that the lease would be extended as long as the life of the National League.

In effect, this means a permanent home for Base Ball in the city of New York. The moment that the lease was effected Mr. Brush announced that he would rebuild on the Polo Grounds and would erect a concrete and steel stadium, modeled after the style of the stand which was burned, but which would accommodate 50,000 spectators and would not have a stick of timber in it.

The estimated cost of this structure will be $100,000, but it is quite well assured that before the new stadium is completed it will cost more than that sum. However, it will be a lasting monument to Base Ball in the City of New York and something of which the city will be proud.

Shaped like a horseshoe, supplied with hundreds of comfortable boxes and seats, with no stairways, but easy ascents from all parts of the structure to another, it will be more like the fitting of an outdoor opera house than a ball park, showing that Base Ball promoters have progressed as well as the game.

Philadelphia has two fine plants, one of them fireproof

and the other nearly so. Chicago has one of the most magnificent outdoor grounds in the United States, equipped by Charles Comiskey, of the Chicago American League Club. Pittsburg has erected a stand which is a model, and Cleveland is the fortunate possessor of an up-to-date outdoor park which probably will stand as long as there is Base Ball. Every foot of the structure on this modern edifice is concrete or steel.

Washington has a new concrete and steel stand and the Boston American League club shortly is to have one. St. Louis owners contemplate building and will put in concrete and steel whenever they improve their parks. The Chicago National League club contemplates a new structure that may eclipse them all. So, everywhere, there is a tendency to add to the solidity and the permanency of the sport, which assures more comfort for patrons.

Nor is the lavish expenditure for better accommodations for Base Ball patrons confined to the larger cities of the major league circuits. Indianapolis and Toledo, of the American Association, have new and expensive plants.

Newark and Baltimore, in the Eastern League, have recently rebuilt their grounds, while Toronto, in the same circuit, possesses a new, fireproof stand.

Atlanta, in the Southern League, has an equipment far better than most major league clubs could boast ten years ago, and at Birmingham, Ala., the owners of the Base Ball club have a new concrete and steel structure which is a gem. It well belongs to the "Gem City of the South."

In connection with the subject of new stands for the convenience of patrons, it may also be added that most Base Ball concerns are finding it advantageous to purchase the property on which their parks are located. As in most cases this necessitates buying real estate of much value, the fact that such holdings become permanent for the purposes of outdoor recreation is confirmatory of the stability of the national game after its years of evolution.

In the major leagues both of the St. Louis grounds, both of the Chicago parks, that at Detroit, the one at Cincinnati, the field at Cleveland, Pittsburg's new park, the Washington ground, both of the Philadelphia grounds, the Boston National League ground, a new field to be provided for the accommodation of the New York American League club, and the Polo Grounds in New York, since the recent agreement between its owner and the owner of the New York National League Base Ball Club, are permanent.

The field in Brooklyn is leased, as is that of the Boston American League club, but it is said that the Boston American League club has purchased a plot of real estate in that city on which a structure will be built for the national game corresponding in all its details to the best that have been built elsewhere.

The value of this real estate is rather hard to conjecture, for it is located in varying sections of different cities. Presumably it would be out of the question to estimate the property which is used by the New York club at less than $300,000. It comprises two city blocks and might bring that amount at forced sale. As this is probably the most valuable plot in the major league circuits, the other fifteen clubs may be accepted as playing on real estate which is worth anywhere from $50,000 to $100,000. Some of it may be less valuable than $50,000, but, as population increases and the cities expand, it is noticeable that Base Ball values enhance as well as everything else.

The estimated attendance at the National League games in 1910 was 3,705,574. That at the American League games was 3,550,951. The total for both leagues was 7,256,665. Very likely there was not so large a paid attendance as the above figures would indicate, because where the attendance is made public by the authority of some of the club owners they are accustomed to give the paid attendance and the free attendance conjointly.

More spectators attend Base Ball games on passes than many imagine. It is a rather sad commentary on our municipal politics that history is filled with incidents where those in temporary authority have seemed to be impressed with the idea that Base Ball promoters were operating clubs for their benefit and for that of their friends. Were the names of those on the free lists in some of the large cities to be published, perhaps even the hardened conscience of the American voter might be shocked.

If we go on the basis of 6,000,000 paid admissions to major league games, which is a liberal estimate, and figure that the average admission was thirty-three and one-third cents per spectator, which is also fair, we find that the gate receipts of the major leagues in 1910 were about $2,000,000.

Of that sum, less than a quarter of a million was returned directly to the promoters for their interest in their investment. True, some of them made large profit, which was offset by very small profit on the part of others, and perhaps a trifling loss on the part of one or two.

So that in the same breath in which we can point to the great strides which the game has made, to its popularity, to its signs of assured permanency, we can also say that it is not a pastime which robs the public in any way, for the bulk of its income is turned directly back into circulation through salaries to players, expenses for travel, and the hundred and one incidentals which are a part of any great amusement enterprise.

It is by no means a selfish game, operated for purely mercenary motives. If that were the case, there is more than one man who has been prominent in Base Ball and who is still prominent in Base Ball councils who would have given up his share of the burden of maintenance long ago.

Indeed, we may go further and state that it is only within recent years that there has been anything like reasonable financial return to the investors. There are many men who have expended thousands of dollars on the national pastime who never realized a penny of income from it in their lives.

Until there was a new National Agreement, which gave the sport stability, the life of the minor league club owner was one of annoyance and hazard.

The coming of the new National Agreement was the dawn of an era of prosperity in the minor league circuits which has enabled owners to venture upon $50,000 and $100,000 plants for their patrons.

Without the National Agreement, there was no minor league owner who was sanguine that he would hold his players over night. Confident now in the stability of his organization, and able to realize something for his team by development of his resources, the minor league owner is willing to risk.

Becoming thus enterprising, he provides better Base Ball for his patrons, and the result is that the attendance has steadily increased in every minor league circuit in the United States, with perhaps a half dozen exceptions, for the last five years.

Roughly estimating, probably 10,000,000 spectators see the games in the ten largest minor league circuits of the country. That is a very conservative estimate and is established more on the paid spectators than on the actual total attendance.

At other minor league games there may be another 10,000,000 during the season. Suppose that we credit the minor organizations in general with 20,000,000 for the year. Even if a little too large it will not be too large in another year or two, and the figures are conservative enough for immediate data.

The minor and the major leagues together, therefore, would have an estimated attendance of 26,000,000 for the season. Until one realizes that 26,000,000 are six times the population of New York City, one scarcely begins to comprehend what Base Ball attendance amounts to in the course of a season.

GRANDSTAND OF SHIBE PARK, PHILADELP

A CROWD AT THE WORLD SERIES, PHILADELPHIA

HOME OF THE ATHLETICS

NEW GRANDSTAND OF THE CHICAGO "WHITE SOX," AMERICAN LEAGUE

This is not all. No consideration has been given the college games as yet or the various public school games, the games of the amateur leagues and the games of the semi-professionals.

Yale and Princeton and Yale and Harvard draw crowds of 10,000 to 20,000 when they play. One public school boy game in New York attracted 20,000 spectators. Frequently these school boy games, given under the auspices of the Public Schools Athletic League, are attended by 10,000 spectators.

More than all else, who in the world is to be able to make any reasonable kind of estimate of the attendance at games when Smithtown plays Rockville and Rockville plays Jones' Falls?

At some of those contests there are from 2,000 to 3,000 spectators, and when it is probable that on Saturday, which is a sort of half holiday everywhere, there are at least 20,000 of those contests being played in the States of the Union, we begin to feel like holding up our hands in dismay and affirming that it is almost out of the question to express the growth of Base Ball and its present status except by the million mark. And millions denote it more accurately than thousands.

The future of Base Ball, to be judged by its immediate present, is practically limitless, for, in spite of the fact that its development is broader, sounder and better at present than it ever has been, there are manifold indications that it will thrive and not starve so long as the present admirable system of organization is maintained.

Without organization it loses at once its foundation,

and experience has proved that so repeatedly that the man who trifles with the present system of adjusting grievances and operating on a basis of mutuality will be a Benedict Arnold to his fellow associates.

Thirty years ago the greatest drawback to Base Ball, then coming into its own, was the lack of communication between the smaller cities. Many a time I have known a team of young ball players to take a tramp of four or five miles to play with the team in a neighboring town and walk all the way home after the game was over.

The interest in the sport was there. That same honest, high-spirited interest which exists at the present time, but the facilities were lacking in those days.

While we are speaking about the development of Base Ball, it might not be out of place to say that what the boys lacked thirty years ago the boys of to-day have at their doors.

Reference is made to the electric railroads which traverse the country from one ocean to the other. Nowadays it is almost invariably the case that the county seat is connected with all of the important towns of the county by electric railroad, and very frequently a chain of these railroads connects the smaller cities, so that it is only a matter of an hour's ride before a visiting team can be transported from its own town to that in which it is to play.

These " short hauls," as I believe the railroad men call them, have done a tremendous good for pure amateur Base Ball, and for Base Ball between the smaller city leagues which are not quite large enough to enter regularly into professional Base Ball.

One hears a great deal about the "Trolley Leagues" in these days and that is exactly what these organizations are—leagues dependent upon the trolley railroad for transportation. These organizations are composed of the sterling young ball players of the United States, and if the satiated enthusiast of the city becomes a little too well satisfied with the well doing of his favorite professional club, he need only to visit one of these "trolley league" games to find Base Ball in all of the glory by which he remembers it when he sat on the grass and cheered for the home team.

By contrast with other countries, the United States within five years has taken long strides ahead of England and France in the matter of stable and safe structures for an outdoor sport.

It is true that in London, and perhaps in Paris and Berlin, greater generosity has been shown to the citizens in leaving untouched certain fields for those who are fond of games which are popular in those cities, but in the matter of stands to accommodate patrons there is nothing which can equal such Base Ball palaces as have been built in Philadelphia, Chicago, Cleveland, Pittsburg and other cities, to say nothing of the improvement contemplated for New York, where both the American and the National Leagues will build on a grander scale than is in existence throughout the world of sport.

When conditions are sane and settled among the organizers of Base Ball there is no trouble to locate prosperity. It appears at the door and begs to enter.

Nothing can better illustrate this than to compare the

finish of the season of 1910, the best in the history of the national pastime, with that of the finish of 1890, the worst.

Base Ball values are to-day quoted at one hundred cents on the dollar, to use a phrase which is popular with the men in financial circles.

At the end of 1890, a season of war and strife between players and owners, Base Ball values had been whittled down to less than ten cents on the dollar.

There were some who had lost their all and who had been forced out of the game. Strife did it. Strife will invariably mar the success of any sport and, unless it is possessed of the vitality and intrinsic merit of Base Ball, ultimately will kill it.

Estimating the growth of Base Ball upon the basis which has been in evidence for the last five years, it is within reason to predict that the year 1920 will see 10,000,000 paid admissions at the contests of the major leagues.

The million mark expands the further one analyzes the steady growth of the sport, and looks forward to a future which may be blessed with safe conduct under a sane National Agreement and with level-headed men to conduct the administration.

CHAPTER XXXVI.

THE AUTHOR'S INTRODUCTION TO BASE BALL

CHAPTER XXXVI.

MOST everybody remembers the story of Horace Greeley's mountain ride with Hank Monk, the celebrated California stage driver of early days, and how that story was told and retold until it became the stock in trade of everybody on the Pacific Coast. Something akin to this is the widespread publicity given to a tale that I encounter frequently in all kinds of publications, relating to my introduction to the game of Base Ball.

This narrative declares that the first time I ever heard of Base Ball was when a veteran of the Civil War came to Rockford in 1863 and explained it to me. The story goes on to state that I immediately organized two teams; that three years later I was clerking in a Chicago grocery and went out to watch a game between two clubs of the Windy City; that the pitcher of one of the nines got his leg twisted, so that the game was likely to go by default, when I volunteered my services and pulled the unfortunate club out of its deplorable situation, etc.

Now, I dislike to shatter this beautiful fairy tale. Especially distasteful is it to me to wreck the bright halo placed upon my brow by some good natured, highly imaginative, but ill-advised historian; but the fact is that, with the exception of the opening statement that a returning soldier told me about playing the game in the army, there is hardly enough truth in the balance of the story on which to hang a feather. It was emphatically not true that I, at thirteen years of age, organized two Base Ball teams. On the contrary, I was at that time an overgrown, unbaked, country boy, as green as the verdant prairies of my native State, and so bashful that I was almost afraid to go out of doors, lest I should meet and be spoken to by someone not a member of my family.

I was boarding at the home of a relative at Rockford. It was my first prolonged absence from home, and memories of the homesickness of that period haunt me like a nightmare to this hour. The only solace I had, the only bright skies for me in those dark days of utter loneliness, were when I could go out to the commons to watch the other fellows play Base Ball. And then my diffidence was so great that I would go way down the outfield, take a seat on the turf and watch the boys have fun. I think no mother, parted from her young, ever had a stronger yearning to see her beloved offspring than had I to break in to those crude games of ball on the commons at Rockford. Oh, if I only *could* get in! But I'd rather have died than suggest such a thing, and the players were too busy to think of me. So I would sit, and watch, and yearn, and covet a place among the happy lads who were having such happy times.

One day the unexpected happened. The balls used in those days were composed of melted rubber, around which yarn was wound and a leather cover sewed on—sometimes. These balls would bound as high as a house and, if a fellow got a fair lick at one, it would certainly go some. On this particular day I was occupying my usual place, far out beyond center field, when one of the boys hit the ball square on the nose and it came soaring in my direction. Talk about special Providence! That ball came for me straight as an arrow. Impulsively I sprang to my feet, reached out for it with my right hand, held it a moment, and then threw it home on an air-line to the catcher.

When the game was over, one of the boys came to me and said:

"Say, that was a great catch you made. Wouldn't you like to play to-morrow?"

Blushing, I managed to stammer that I would; and I did, and from that day, when sides were chosen, I was usually among the first to have a place. And this was my real introduction to the game.

As to the Chicago incident, so graphically recorded in the story referred to, the facts are set forth elsewhere in this narrative. I was clerking at Chicago because I had already made good as a pitcher on the Forest City team and was wanted by the Chicago Excelsiors. But I went to Chicago after the close of one season and returned to Rockford before the opening of another. Hence, it is too bad for an imaginative writer to twist the poor pitcher's leg in a supposititious game played in midwinter, even though I appreciate his good-will in making me the hero of an impossible romance.

My early experiences in a business way were not

encouraging. The first salaried position I ever held was in a grocery store at Rockford. About the time I left that establishment it "busted." The failure was not due to the size of my salary; I received only three dollars a week!

My second engagement was with a Chicago wholesale grocery, where I was to receive $40 a week as bill clerk, with the understanding that I was to pitch for the Excelsiors during the Base Ball season. I was told by the proprietor not to mention the amount of my salary to fellow clerks. I hadn't been at work but a few days when a son of Frank Parmalee—of Chicago Transfer fame—who had his desk near mine, asked the leading question, "How much do you get?" I answered, "I don't know; my first pay day hasn't arrived." He told me that he got $10 a week, and I suppose he ranked me as about a "fiver." I only received one salary check at Chicago, when the sheriff came along and closed up the wholesale grocery store. I was not so sure of my innocence of the cause of this failure as I had been in the Rockford case. Forty dollars a week for such service as I was at that time capable of rendering seemed to me enough to "bust" almost any concern.

I was now without employment in a big city in midwinter. Happily, I had an uncle in the insurance business at that time, and he gave me work, soliciting insurance. Among other policies that I wrote up was one on a blacksmith shop on Lake Street. I had become acquainted with the proprietor as I passed back and forth between my boarding place and office, and, upon my eloquent presentation of the desirability of protection against loss by fire, he allowed me to write his risk in one of my uncle's companies. One night a big fire broke out on Lake Street, and the losses were so heavy that every company for which my uncle had an agency went broke. I heard that a large, two-fisted blacksmith, whose place of business before the conflagration had been on Lake Street, was looking for a tall, young insurance solicitor. During the brief remainder of my sojourn in Chicago I went daily a few blocks out of my way to avoid apologizing for a defunct insurance company, and incidentally to escape a "licking."

After the insurance failures at Chicago, I returned to Rockford and obtained employment as bookkeeeper in the Rockford *Register* office, also doing similar work for Mr. A. N. Nicholds, agent for the Charter Oak Life Insurance Co., with the understanding that I was to pitch for the Forest Citys. The newspaper soon got into financial troubles and the insurance company failed.

Having now been present as mourner at the obsequies of one retail and one wholesale grocery establishment, several insurance companies and a newspaper, I lost confidence in the ordinary channels of business enterprise and determined in the future to devote my energies professionally to the great American national game.

Therefore, when Harry Wright appeared at Rockford one day in the fall of 1870, with an offer of $2,500 per annum, one-fifth to be paid spot cash, I signed a contract to pitch for the original Boston professional club. The Base Ball history of the five following years is familiar to the public. It is not so well known, however, that, while playing with the Bostons, the great fire of 1872 occurred, paralyzing the business interests of that city and nearly wrecking the Boston Base Ball Club.

Following that fire, I found myself short $800 in salary, and was forced to accept the offer of an old friend to take a place on the New York *Graphic*, an illustrated weekly paper that had recently been established there. The *Graphic* soon failed, of course, and, my back salary having been made up and future payment of salary secured, I returned to Boston and devoted my time strictly to playing ball professionally, until I embarked in business for myself, since which time I have not been connected with any more commercial failures.

————

The first time I had to do with the selling of players was in 1887. I had withdrawn from active participation in the game as a player, but was President of the Chicago White Stockings, at that time the finest team of ball players in the world. Although the traffic in players, under the National Agreement, had been in vogue for some time, I had never looked with much favor upon it, rather from sentiment than any other reason, I suppose, for I knew that such changes usually benefited club and player alike. The newspapers had made much ado about the arbitrary authority given to managers along this line. It had been quite generally denounced by the press; and the public, influenced, no doubt, by the changes rung on such headlines as "Slave Traffic," "Another Ball Player Sold," etc., had come to regard the practice as awful.

The facts leading to my personal introduction to the system are as follows: The White Stockings were repeating in Chicago the history of Boston's first professional club. The players were so capable that they were expected to win every game. It did seem almost impossible for them to lose. Twice in succession they had captured the championship pennant; the prowess of the team was known throughout the land, and praises of the individual performances of Anson, Kelly, Flint, Williamson, Dalrymple, Gore, Clarkson, Pfeffer, McCormick and Sunday were on everybody's lips.

Now, experience had shown that the keeping of the same players together for too long a time is prejudicial to the interests of the game. I had learned that lesson in my notice of the effect of the four years of successive championship victories gained by the Boston team, and felt that the time had come for a change in the personnel of the Chicago nine. I was well aware that patrons, while appreciating good players, do tire of seeing the same faces year after year, and do enjoy the introduction of new blood into the team. And so I decided to let some players go. But what ones? That was a question not easy to decide.

I deliberated upon the matter for some days, and finally persuaded myself that King Kelly was the man to sell. In arriving at this conclusion, I was not led to the determination entirely by the certainty that Kelly would bring the most money. I knew, of course, that he was as popular abroad as he was at home, and would sell for a lot of cash. I also was aware that there would be a sad, sad wail when it was made public that the "King" was to go.   But there were imperative reasons prompting his disposal.   It was an open secret—else I would not exploit it here—that Kelly's habits were not conducive to the best interests of the club or his team-mates.   He was of a highly convivial nature, extremely fascinating and witty, and his example was demoralizing to discipline. Particularly was his influence objectionable upon the younger members of the nine.   Everybody in Chicago liked Kelly; all the players desired to be where he was— and to follow him was "to go the limit."

So one day I broached the subject of the proposed change to Captain Anson, asking him if he could spare Kelly.

"Spare him?   Sure.   Spare anybody," was the reply.

I then cautioned Anson to say nothing, as I felt that this matter was one which would have to be handled with gloves.   So I sent for Kelly and asked him:

"Kelly, how would you like to go to Boston to play?"

"I don't want any Boston in mine; Chicago's good enough for me."

"Well, you're good enough for Chicago, too," I said. "But if there should be something nice in it for you, would you object?   Wouldn't you like more salary?"

"Wouldn't Kelly like more salary?   Well, I guess."

"What salary would you go to Boston for?" I continued.

He thought a moment, then said, almost as if ashamed to ask it, "Four thousand dollars."   He was receiving $3,000 at Chicago, which was the limit in those days.

"I think I can get you $5,000!" said I.

He beamed all over at the prospect.

"Now, Mike," I said, "you don't care how much we get for your release."

"If you get me $5,000 I don't care a —— if you sell me for a hundred thousand."

"All right. Now keep mum, and let me conduct negotiations; and remember, if you get a letter from Boston, asking your terms, it's $5,000—not $4,000."

I took the matter up with the manager of the Boston club, telling him that King Kelly might possibly be secured. He bit. In a few days I received a letter, asking the price. I replied that $10,000 would purchase the King. He couldn't wait to write. He wired me, "Terms for Kelly accepted," and the sale was made.

Meanwhile Kelly had also been receiving telegrams, and got his contract for three years at $5,000. It was understood between us that he was at liberty to play the "poor Base Ball slave" act to the limit. He did his part with such splendid effect that I soon had the whole press of Chicago applying to me names that, to say the least, were far from complimentary. To these attacks I replied by having the check received from Boston published in fac-simile in the Chicago papers. I had learned to know the value of good newspaper advertising, and it came good and plenty as long as Kelly remained to weep and wail over his sad fate in being sold away from the city he loved so well.

But other members of the team soon caught on, and I found myself besieged by players begging to be sold into a slavery that would help them to redoubled salaries. After awhile the reporters got the right of it, with the result that a system which helped player and club alike was shown to be not so one-sided as had been sometimes supposed.

Subsequently Clarkson, the White Stockings' superb pitcher, was also sold to Boston, and later Gore went to New York, but we overdid the matter a trifle and lost the pennant that year. _____

In speaking of the events which led to my separation from the Boston Club, in 1875, it will be recalled that I accompanied Mr. Hulbert to Philadelphia, where it was stated that Anson and Sutton had already "been secured." It was not quite true that both these players had been *secured*. They had agreed to go with me to Chicago, but Sutton never went, and Anson found it very difficult to do so.

In what has here been written concerning the game and its producers I fear I may sometimes have done injustice to the players. If so, I wish right now to make amends. I certainly desire to be just to all, and I know a good deal about the temptations that assailed players during the evolution of Base Ball in those early days. I have known tricky players, dishonest players, drunken players, but I have also met and dealt with shiftless managers, double-faced managers and managers as corrupt as Satan himself.

As soon as it became known that Barnes, McVey, White and I had determined to go to Chicago, in 1876, every conceivable influence to induce us to break our con-

tracts and cause a change in our program was brought
to bear upon all alike. If there was any difference, perhaps I suffered less than any others from these attempts.
I was generally looked upon as the ringleader of the seces-
sionists, and it was not supposed that my plans could be
altered. But the other boys got it " good and plenty."
They were cajoled, coaxed, offered all kinds of money,
and finally browbeaten and insulted, but all to no avail.
The " big four " had given their words, and all bribes,
entreaties and threats were ignored.

At Philadelphia, of course, conditions were similar,
and the same scenes were enacted. Sutton and Anson
were besieged and besought; corruptive influences were
brought to bear upon them right and left. Most alluring
offers were made to both of them—and Sutton surren-
dered! Although his sacred promise had been given and
contract signed, he was not strong enough to resist the
temptation of a higher salary and advancement. He
capitulated, broke his contract, and remained with the
Philadelphia Athletics.

With Anson it was different. There would have been
some excuse for him. He had recently met and was
betrothed to the good woman who was to become his wife.
Her home was at Philadelphia, and she naturally wanted
her husband at her home. A most tempting increase of
salary, if he would remain, added its allurements to the
situation. Anson decided that he must not go to Chicago
and wrote to President Hulbert for his release. Mr.
Hulbert showed me the letter. I told him to pay no
attention to it—and not to release the player.

"Oh, what's the use?" said Hulbert. "He'll break his contract. We've lost Sutton; we'll lose Anson."

"It is true," I replied, "that we have lost Sutton; but we haven't lost Anson."

Time passed with Anson still insisting that he wouldn't come to Chicago. Mr. Hulbert was quite inclined to let him go. I persisted in refusing to give my consent. Anson continued to "bluff;" said that he wouldn't come West; that he'd break his contract before he'd come.

In the following spring, in advance of the opening of the season, the big first baseman came out to Chicago, determined to secure his release. He offered to pay $1,000 to be relieved from his contract, but Hulbert was now immovable. Anson then came to me. He went over the whole situation. The claims of his fiancee were urged. I told him she would be happier in Chicago. He referred to the offer of $2,500 a year—far more than he had ever received—and said:

"I can't afford to lose the money."

"You can't afford to break your contract," I replied.

"That's about so, too," he acknowledged; but still he held out. Meanwhile, in his determination to remain at Philadelphia, Anson had subjected himself to daily interviews in the Chicago papers, in which he stubbornly declared his intention of remaining and playing in the East. Mr. Hulbert was convinced that Anson was lost. I told him not to fear.

"Sutton has broken his contract, hasn't he?" he repeated.

"Yes," I answered; "but I never told you that you

could hold Sutton. I know Anson. You have his contract; he has promised me. He'll play with Chicago."

Next day the Chicago team went out to the grounds for its first field practice. Anson was there. He wore a high hat and was immaculately clothed with up-to-date trousers, vest and a Prince Albert coat. So far as personal appearance went he might have been President of the National League, or of the Nation itself. He was, however, apparently still obdurate in his determination not to play at Chicago. He stood around, watching the practice for a little while, and then he said to me:

" Toss me one, Al."

"What? With those togs on? Not any. Take off your hat and coat and get into the game."

He stood around for a few minutes longer, his face alight with the spirit of the sport, and then he peeled off his statesman's wardrobe and took his place. I fired him a few and said:

"Now, Anse, come to-morrow in uniform." And he did, and remained with the Chicago Club for twenty-one years thereafter as manager, captain and player. Such was Adrian C. Anson, one of the greatest ball players that ever lived—and a man whose word was always as good as his bond. How we won the pennant for Chicago that year, the first of the National League, is part of the recorded history of the game.

The disciplining of a Base Ball team presents problems not to be met elsewhere, I think. The manufacturer, the merchant, the farmer—every employer of labor—

has some experience with men who will not always "be good." But the alternative in such cases is usually the same, and always at hand. The refractory employe in the ordinary avenues of business can be summarily dismissed and his place soon filled. Not so in the case of the recalcitrant ball player. He may be the most capable man on the team; his presence may be absolutely essential to the success of the nine; his absence may mean the loss of confidence on the part of every other player. To dismiss such a player summarily may be followed by the withdrawal of public favor and patronage. It may cause much hostile newspaper criticism. It may result in all kinds of demoralization, discouragement and loss.

What, then, is to be done with a team whose members persist in a course which the management knows to be prejudicial to the interests of the game and which is extremely vexatious and annoying? I cannot better answer this question, or illustrate the case at point, than by recounting here an incident in my experience as President of the Chicago White Stockings about thirty years ago. The team was composed of fine ball players—there can be no doubt of that. It was playing winning ball right along, which made the administration of discipline all the more difficult. I knew that some of the men were drinking to excess; I was aware that these were keeping late hours; it was a notorious fact that their habits were altogether improper; but what reply could I make to their questions, "What's the matter with our game?" "Do you want us to win everything?" "Where's the team that can down us ?"

One day I was remonstrating with Kelly, who was the liveliest of the bunch, when he turned on me with:

"What are you running here? A Sunday School or a Base Ball club?"

I told him that while we were not exactly in the Sunday School business we would still like to have the boys reasonably clean in their habits. The subject was dropped for a while and then I began to get letters from the public. Some were from prominent citizens and patrons of the game; others were from personal enemies of some of the players; still others were anonymous; but all told stories of drunkenness and debauchery, in which members of the White Stockings were implicated. These recounted scenes of revelry and carousing that were altogether reprehensible and disgusting. Finally the newspapers took it up and began to berate the management for the actions of the players.

Forbearance ceasing to be a virtue, I determined that something must be done; but what? As to myself, I could not charge the men with offenses I had not seen them commit. And yet I was reasonably certain of the existence of fire where there was so much smoke. I again interviewed Kelly and some of the others, telling them of rumors I had heard; but all denied the charges *in toto*—there was nothing to it, they insisted.

Meeting Billy Pinkerton one day, I mentioned my troubles and asked him to put a man on the job, with instructions to ascertain the facts and make a full report. In a few weeks the report was ready, and when I got it I did not know what to do with it. It was on foolscap sheets and bulked about an inch in thickness. It began with Anson, and dropped him after two or three days as all right. So with Sunday and several others. But the records of seven out of the fifteen players on the team were too awful for patient consideration. The detective had followed them up and down Clark Street, all over the tenderloin districts, through the whole roster of saloons and "speak-easy" resorts, and kept track of their movements, in minutest detail, for days at a time—and the evidence was now in my hands!

But what to do with it? That was a question not easy to answer. If the full disciplinary powers of the League were applied, that meant the disruption of the team at the height of the season—the practical elimination of the White Stockings from the League. I gave the subject long and careful consideration, and at length decided upon a course to pursue.

One day I told Anson to have all the boys on the grounds next morning, as I had something I wanted to say to them. He asked me, "What's up?" and I told him to be there and learn for himself.

Next morning I met the team by appointment. I told them what had been done; how I had heard the stories of their dissipation; how I had received scores of letters of complaint; how newspapers had finally taken up the subject; how I had then employed a detective to learn the facts, and that I had his report with me. I then asked:

"Now, boys, what shall I do with it?"

"Read it," said one, and

"Read it," echoed the others.

I didn't propose to read that long grist again, and so one of the players was deputized to perform the task. He commenced with the report on Anson, and I heard one of the players ejaculate, "Here's where the old man gets off." A minute later someone whispered, "Here's where Billy (Sunday) slides out," and so on until the real business of the report began.

Unfeigned interest kept everyone silent until the reading had ended. Then Kelly broke the silence with one of his characteristic drolleries, saying: "I have to offer only one amendment. In that place where the detective reports me as taking a lemonade at 3 a. m. he's off. It was a straight whiskey; I never drank a lemonade at that hour in my life."

"Now, boys," I said, "what's to be done about it? I understand that you plead guilty to the indictment. What's to be the penalty?"

"That's up to you, sir."

"Anson, what's to be the punishment? Do you want to fine these men?"

"No," said Anson, "we don't want their money."

"I'll tell you what we will do," said I. "I appoint you seven men a committee to report the punishment to be inflicted upon yourselves."

"How much did you pay the detective?" asked one of the guilty.

"One hundred and seventy-five dollars," I replied.

"Well," said he, "there's just seven of us. Suppose we stand $25 apiece?"

"All right, I'm agreed," said one after the other, and thus ended the administration of discipline in that case.

As a sequel to this incident, another occurred a few days later. The White Stockings were about to leave for a series of games at Detroit. The train was ready to start. Standing on the platform was a great, green gawk of a fellow, staring with wide-mouthed interest at the departing players. Kelly caught sight of him and whispered something to McCormick. Then the "King" stepped up to the countryman and, after denouncing him in most violent terms as a Pinkerton detective, hauled off and smote him with all his might, while McCormick, coming up behind the bewildered "Rube," kicked the poor fellow's pants clear up on his shoulders. Then the bell rang and the belligerent ball players sprang to the platform of the rear car and went whirling Eastward.

As showing the importance of taking advantage of opportunities presented for the gratuitous advertising of the game, I recall an incident following the sale of Kelly to Boston. The newspapers of Chicago did not take kindly to this transaction. One paper—the Chicago *News*—then owned by Melville E. Stone and Victor F. Lawson, was particularly severe in its criticism. The *News* strenuously urged, among other things, a reduction in the price of admission to games, claiming that if Chicago was to have cheap players it ought to have cheap admission.

Frequent caricatures were printed, some of them occupying a half page, illustrating the slave pen of ante-bellum days, with the auction block, upon which, instead of the familiar forms of the unhappy slaves, abject ball players were displayed for sale to the highest bidder. Being at that time President of the Chicago Club, and having been instrumental in promoting the sale of Kelly, I came in for much notoriety. While these daily " roasts " were being served out to me I noticed that the attendance kept increasing. Many friends, outraged at what they deemed unfair criticism, wrote me, urging me to take some action that would stop the abuse, even if I had to kill the editor.

A prominent Base Ball writer of that day was "Harmony" White, who had obtained his sobriquet from an article published in one of the Chicago papers to the effect that the only way to gain a winning team was to collect a nine whose members were so mad with one another that they would not speak. I happened to meet White on the street one day, early in the summer, and asked him:

"What's the matter with the *News?* You haven't been giving me the usual amount of space of late."

He replied that he was absolutely *out of ammunition.* I offered to furnish him fresh ammunition if he would only keep up the onslaught. His incredulous look indicated that he was not impressed with my sincerity. I then explained to him that simply as a business proposition I could not afford to be neglected in his paper, for since he had let up in his attacks our attendance was dropping off.

"Well," said he, "if you feel that way about it, and

will supply the ammunition, I will open up again, for I certainly have instructions from the managing editor to go to the limit in roasting the management of the Chicago Base Ball Club."

As a result of this casual conversation it was then and there agreed that he would send a trusted messenger to my office on two certain days of each week to secure the necessary ammunition. This plan was carried out to the end of that season, and, as a result, the Chicago Club made more money that year than it had ever made during its history up to that time.

From this experience I became convinced that—so far as Base Ball is concerned—good, liberal roasts in newspapers of wide circulation are much more effective than fulsome praise, for the latter carries with it the idea that it is paid advertising, and is therefore only read as such, whereas under the roast program the matter is relieved from that suspicion and read by everybody with more or less of sympathy for the poor fellow who has no newspaper in which to defend himself, and this even though the "poor fellow" is supplying ammunition to his traducer.

CHAPTER XXXVII.

EDWARD MARSHALL

CHAPTER XXXVII.

CONCLUSION—THE PSYCHOLOGY OF BASE BALL—MR. ED-
WARD MARSHALL'S INTERVIEW ON THE EFFECT OF THE
GAME ON THE MIND AND OF THE MIND ON THE GAME.

I HAVE thought best to conclude this book with an article written by Edward Marshall on "The Psychology of Base Ball," and which appeared in the Sunday issue of the New York *Times*, November 13th, 1910.

My reasons for giving space to this article are:

First—Because it deals with a side of the subject (the psychological) which had been heretofore overlooked, and

Second—Because it contained many thoughts that had existed in my mind for years, but had never before been expressed in words.

Mr. Marshall has the happy faculty of interviewing one in such a searching manner that, without apparent effort, he enters the recesses of his subject's mind and brings to light the inmost thoughts of the one interviewed.

The circumstances leading up to the interview came about in this way: Mr. Homer Davenport, the celebrated cartoonist, and a great admirer of the American national game, said to me one day that Mr. Edward Marshall, the well-known author, had expressed a desire to "interview" me on the "Psychology of Base Ball," and asked if he might bring Mr. Marshall to call at my New York hotel for that purpose. I consented, and a meeting was arranged for the next evening.

Mr. Marshall explained the object of his visit and the general lines of the information he was seeking, incidentally remarking that he had never seen a game of Base Ball.

In answer to my surprised inquiry, "Where have you lived all these years?" he replied that he had been a war correspondent and had spent most of his time in Europe, and more recently in Cuba.

Here was I, facing a man who had never seen a game of Base Ball; yet this man wanted to write an article on the "Psychology of Base Ball," which, so far as I knew, although I had been connected with the sport almost from its inception, was a phase of the subject that had never before been brought out.

While he was arranging his shorthand notes, seated in an easy chair, with a pad carelessly resting on his knee, I confess that I had some misgivings as to his forthcoming article, and as a precautionary measure requested him to show me proof of the same before it appeared in print. To this he assented.

Shortly after this first and only interview with Mr. Marshall I was suddenly called to my home at Point Loma, California, and never saw the article until some days after it had appeared in the New York *Times* of November 13, 1910. Had I seen the proof I would certainly have blue-penciled some of the personal references. I do not claim to have the face of a "Greek Hero"; I do not assume to resemble a Bishop of any church, and I could not be the father of a game whose birth antedated mine by ten years.

Following is the article in full:

THE PSYCHOLOGY OF BASE BALL DISCUSSED BY
A. G. SPALDING.

THE GAME ELEVATES AND FITS THE AMERICAN CHARACTER—IT BRINGS INTO PLAY THE EMOTIONAL AND MORAL AS WELL AS THE PHYSICAL SIDE OF MAN'S NATURE.

By Edward Marshall.

His face is that of a Greek hero, his manner that of a Church of England Bishop, when I talked with him he was a candidate for United States Senator from California, and he is the father of the greatest sport the world has ever known.

You don't know him? You are unfortunate. There are in the United States at least a million men who do and who will yell at sight of him. I am writing now of A. G. Spalding, and he talked to me, the other evening, of the game's psychology.

"The psychology of Base Ball?" he said, thoughtfully. " I confess that the 'psychology of Base Ball' is a new one on me.

THE MIND AND THE GAME.

" I take it that you are trying to find out what effect the game has on the mind, and what effect the mind has on the game. The general impression among those who do not know, and, although there are several million people in this country who do know, still there remain a few who don't, is that Base Ball is simply a form of physical exercise which is interesting to watch and to take part in. Those who have played the game know well that it is more— much more. They know that it is quite as much a mental as it is a physical exercise.

" As a matter of plain fact, it is much more a mental exercise than a mere physical sport. There is really no other form of outdoor sport which constantly demands such accurate co-ordination between the mind and body as this national game of ours. And that is rather fine, when you come to think about it.

" Base Ball elevates, and it fits the American character. The emotional and moral as well as the physical side of a man's nature are brought into play by Base Ball. I know of no other medium which, as completely as Base Ball, joins the physical, mental, emotional, and moral sides of a man's composite being into a complete and homogeneous whole. And there is nothing better calculated than Base Ball to give a growing boy self-poise and self-reliance, confidence, inoffensive and entirely proper aggressiveness, general manliness. Base Ball is a man maker.

" Of course the professional Base Ball player is the one known to the non-playing public; he attracts attention through his superior talent, just as a great actor or a great singer does; but a great actor or great singer may start late, while a Base Ball player cannot. I do not believe there is a single player in the major leagues who had not demonstrated a peculiar fitness for the game, and made a reputation as a skillful player among boy associates, before he was fourteen.

"Yes; certainly the game has its psychology—a part of the fine, healthy, undegenerate psychology of the whole Nation. The professional Base Ball player is no thug trained to brutality like the prize-fighter, no half-developed little creature like the jockey, no cruel coward like the bull fighter. He is the natural development of the American boy's inborn love of manly, skillful, outdoor sport—sport busying brain and body and not harming any one or anything. The average boy who loves Base Ball is not the sort of boy who loves to go off with a gun intent on killing some poor bird. Base Ball has done a lot to keep the Yankee lad from being brutal.

"And he revels in Base Ball, does this American boy—good luck to him! No one ever has to urge the normal Yankee lad to participate in this clean game. He takes to it as a duck to water. He knows its rudiments before he learns to read and write. His father played Base Ball before him, and, of this generation, most of his forefathers. And it is a sport which parents may encourage, for it is neither dangerous nor demoralizing.

"The professional Base Ball player is doing more for his native country than any one engaged in any form of sport has ever done for any country in the past. They say horse racing has resulted in improvement in horse breeding; well, Base Ball has done something better, it has resulted in improvement in man breeding. Aside from giving outdoor recreation to the public, the professional Base Ball player is, by his example, encouraging the boy to healthy sport with which not one unpleasant feature is connected. Little gambling is associated with Base Ball. When the game first started as a professional sport there was an effort made to saddle it with all the gambling features which beset the race tracks—pool-selling and all—and from 1870 to, say, 1875, the gamblers practically had control of our professional Base Ball. Every Base Ball park had its betting ring. This made decent people stay away, and interest in the game fell to a low ebb. Every error made was charged to crookedness upon the player's part, and not always, probably, unjustly. William A. Hulbert, of Chicago, had become interested in the game, and I explained this all to him. I was actually afraid the game would have to go. He wanted me to take my winning club on from Boston to Chicago, and I told him that I would if he'd clean out the gamblers, and not otherwise. He said he'd try, and he did try, to mighty good effect. That saved the game, undoubtedly, and in the winter of the following year the National League was organized, and has been getting more and more important to the life of all America with the passage of each day since then.

GAMBLING DRIVEN OUT.

"The elimination of the betting evil was the cornerstone of the success of Base Ball as an exhibition game. The fight against it was a fierce one, lasting four or five years. Then we triumphed, and the cleanest game on earth had been established. No betting, no Sunday playing, no liquor sold upon the grounds! It was a revolution in the world of professional sport. Base Ball is the only game which suits the mighty populace and yet is wholly free from ties to bind it to the gambling and the liquor-selling element, whose aim it is to victimize that populace.

"That's part of its psychology—it is clean-souled. Another and important part of it is that it is a leveler. That makes it, in the truest sense, American. It is almost, if not exactly, the same game in all parts of the United States, and nowhere is it cursed by caste. Caste may not wreck a sport in countries where caste dominates the social life, but it would surely wreck Base Ball in this country. That's the finest thing about Base Ball. Its spectators, once they settle in their seats and glue their eyes upon the diamond, are absolutely equalized by their delight in what they see. The hod carrier, if his seat so placed him as to make it possible, would be pretty apt, in case of a good play, to beat the President upon the back in his enthusiasm with a cushion or his hat, and the President would almost surely turn and grin at him. I don't know that that has ever actually happened, but I have known a workingman in jumpers to so lose his memory of social and financial and political rank as to biff thus a grave Senator. It was a fine and significant spectacle, because—note this—the Senator was not offended. He couldn't clear his mind of frantic joy in time to be offended, and, better yet, he would not have been offended if he could have cleared it."

Right here I ought to explain something. This interview was quite a family affair. Across the room from me sat Mr. Spalding's nephew—a young scientist—and at my right, upon a couch, was Mrs. Spalding. She is a fit mate for her classically featured husband. She is really very handsome, has a notably delightful voice—soft, cultured, vibrant—and she does what the "advice to wives" departments in the women's magazines always urge young wives to do; she takes an interest in her husband's soul-enthusiasms. Interest? Well, some.

TWO CRANKS IN A FAMILY.

"Men at Base Ball games, all men at Base Ball games, are brethren, equal sharers in whatever joy or woe or protest the great game may bring," said she. "And utterly irreverent. Ban Johnson, the president of the league, was sitting near us in the stand, and a man wanted to make a photograph of him. Did the crowd sit awed and reverent? Not notably. That crowd admired Ban John-

son and, in a way, revered him, but the camera man was an obstruc-
tion. What a cry went up! 'Too much Johnson! Too much Johnson!' roared instantly unto the vaulted heavens."

Mr. Spalding smiled at her. "Two cranks in a family means
domestic bliss, if they are both Base Ball cranks," he commented,
thereby adding to his exposition of the game's psychology.

"Any one who blocked a crank's view of the game would meet
with instant criticism," he said proudly. "And if Teddy himself
were playing and made an error he'd be roasted by the best friends
he possessed upon the bleachers.

"But, in spite of this, Base Ball is the most good-natured pastime in the world. Partisans will rave and tear their hair, but how
often do you hear that one of them has torn another's hair on Base
Ball grounds? In the history of the world no such great crowds
have gathered to watch anything the world has ever known—sport
or anything else—with so few fights. Base Ball, you see, arouses
no brutal instincts. It is a turmoil rather than a battle. It is
more a war of skill than a war of strength. Foot ball often breeds
fierce fights. That game calls for heavy muscles, don't you see? as
well as skill, and I shall dare some critics when I say that foot ball
science is less delicate than Base Ball science. Brute strength in
one foot ball player can, and often does, overmaster the pure science
of another. In Base Ball this could not possibly occur.

The One Game in the Open.

"The game is in the open, too. Twenty thousand people can
cluster round a diamond and see every move the Base Ball players
on it make. There is no chance for secret cheating, therefore there
is no tendency in that direction. It is not alone the umpire who
can see what happens on the field, but every newsboy, every millionaire, among the spectators. In foot ball there is often chance for
hidden fouls.

"Professionalism has not wrecked Base Ball—it has merely
brought about a higher degree of skill in players by offering them
an income which permits them to keep up, after they have become
men, the sport in which they have excelled as boys. The professional is merely a grown boy, and, in the minds of a large number
of his fellows, a very lucky boy at that. His profession is his sport a
little glorified. He is the natural outcome of the boy's love for the
game—ah, how that same boy loves it!

"And it is the only professional sport I know of which it does
not hurt a boy to revel in. He worships the professional who wins,
and, doing this, he never worships a plug-ugly or a thug. Drunkards and all other moral undesirables are barred from real success
upon the Base Ball field by the very nature of the sport. The men
whom the boy 'roots' for are a very decent lot of fellows—such a

decent lot of fellows as no other professional sport the world has ever known could show. The professional Base Ball player, by his example, does not encourage his young devotees to anything unworthy. That's a fine detail of our national sport. Parents need not be alarmed if their young sons announce at breakfast some fine morning that they plan to be professional ball players when they reach maturity. In the first place, out of 500 boys who may express that firm determination, only one, upon an average, will ever make good in a major league, or minor league for that matter, and, in the second place, that one of the 500 will not, by making good, prove himself to be anything at all unworthy. Success as a Base Ball player does not plunge a youth into a vicious or a dissipated life, but, on the other hand, insures him from that sort of a career.

PROFESSIONALS LUCKY CHAPS.

"Indeed, lucky is the boy who can develop sufficient skill to get a place on a league team. That means a mighty good salary and a pleasant, clean and healthful life. The professional Base Ball player is no mollycoddle—there are no mollycoddles in the game; but neither is there any room for thugs in it. No training could be more severe than that of the league player. Under the present system of organized Base Ball, he must conform to the strictest mental, moral and physical discipline, and must develop wonderfully in patience, self-reliance and fair-mindedness. He must keep at the top notch in all these details of fine character if he would keep position in the game. Ability to take criticism cheerfully is one of the great requisites of real success in any line. I know of no profession which requires of those who win in it the disposition and ability to do this which Base Ball requires.

BASE BALL AND THE MIND.

"Now, as to the effect of Base Ball on the mind of the boy player. If a boy is naturally selfish, peevish or crab-minded the members of the team he plays with will soon knock that out of him, or drive him from the team. He won't want to leave the team, for Base Ball, you must remember, is ingrained in his blood. If he is inclined to be hot-tempered, the loss of a few games and the respect of his associates as the result will help mightily toward correcting it. If he is prone to be a cad, to put on airs, to assume a superiority over his fellow-players as a result of the social or financial standing of his family, a little joshing from his fellows on the errors he made upon the field will soon bring him down to earth again. If he is unduly timid and shows cowardice in a pinch, his mates will quickly cure him or eject him. If he is apprehensive, pessimistic—and no trait is more entirely un-American—he will soon lose his place upon the team. The lad who is continually predicting

a defeat will not last long in Base Ball. And the beauty of the
thing is, that rarely will he let his faults go far enough to bar him
from the game—his love of it is too instinctive and too real. Rather
will he let the game correct the faults. And there you are. It's a
man as well as a soul builder.

"The psychology of Base Ball? It is the psychology of success."

"I know of nothing which more fitly trains the body, mind and
soul. The game plays havoc with a boy's or man's emotions. In a
day the player may well rise to the fine heights of victory and sink
to the dark depths of black despair in a defeat. And it must be
the one or the other. There is no midway station. The score is
5 to 3. You win or lose, and quickly learn that nothing is accomplished by trying to lay the blame, if defeat comes, upon the umpire
or upon your fellow-players. Pleading a sore finger or strained
muscle or tendon wins nothing for the vanquished player in his own
mind or the minds of his associates. That is a good thing. After
many victories, and the defeats which are quite certain to go with
them, a player must, of sheer necessity, achieve self-poise, learn to
take winning calmly, and lose philosophically. He may well reach
that super-point where he looks grave in victory and smiles with
hope when he is vanquished.

IMPORTANT IN EDUCATION.

"Base Ball has for a long time been important in the education
of our youth—far more important than most people think—and it is
destined to become still more important. The day will come, I
think, when all American school authorities will supply the necessary
grounds to play the game on as an essential adjunct to every public
school. The game means countless benefits, and not a single danger
to the boy who plays it. You may have gathered from what I have
already said that I consider it the greatest game on earth. I do,
and, doing so, am proud of my good judgment. There should be
Base Ball grounds adjacent to or very near each public school
building in the United States.

"Base Ball is the only sport which is severe enough to benefit
and not severe enough to overstrain. Base Ball players live to good
old ages, almost always. I wish I had the list at hand. The lon-
gevity of ex-professionals would surprise you. I myself began to
play on the advice of my physician, and I made a business of it in
the end.

"Prizefighters, jockeys, foot ball players, oarsmen, even college
athletes, are not long-lived."

I had not asked so very many questions. They had not been
needed. Mr. Spalding puts his words across the plate as accurately
and as logically as, in the old days, he pitched his balls. But now
I asked one.

"Even if the game had not resulted in wealth and fame for you, would you still be glad you took it up?"

He laughed. The Greek countenance, framed with white hair, broke into a particularly winning set of wrinkles; the Bishop's face became that of the jolly monk in the world famous picture.

"I'm a candidate for Senator," he said, "and ought not to use slang, but—I—sure—would. Glad? Why, I tell you it meant health to me—the biggest thing of all. It has taken me around the world again, and yet again; it has thrown me into contact with the finest set of men this country ever has produced. It has taught me that humanity is, at the bottom, clean of mind and soul. It has made me a rank optimist—and it has kept me one. It is the only sport on earth. The prizefighter is brutalized and his heart bothers him; the rowing man is almost certain to be most unequally developed physically, and his heart, also, generally goes wrong; foot ball maims and brutalizes; horse racing sends its devotees to pieces morally and gives them little of the compensation coming from good exercise and honest rivalry. It is and always has been founded upon gambling.

Old Players Now Important.

"Find fifty men from all these sports who have outgrown them and reached real importance in the world! You can't. I could name a hundred Base Ball players—yes, two hundred, and then more—who have become important, worthy, and respected men in later years. There's John M. Ward, for instance. Senator Gorman was a Base Ball player once. John K. Tener, who, as we talk, is a candidate for Governor of Pennsylvania, was a professional and went around the world with us in 1888. Senator Bulkeley, of Connecticut, was a player first and then first President of the National League. Base Ball for a few years is one of the best character builders I can think of. An able boy's blood always runs high and the first thing he must learn, if he is to win success, is to control it. Base Ball teaches that, first, last and all the time.

"The game was fortunate from the beginning. It was spread throughout the country by the soldiers returning to their homes after the Civil War. Now it is in its third generation. I hesitate to guess what it will be when it has reached its fourth. The crowds to-day are big; the crowds of future days will be much bigger. Every boy, you see, plays Base Ball, and the players of to-day are the spectators of to-morrow. The human being who has ever got the germ of Base Ball in his blood, whether the infection comes when he is young or after he has reached maturity, never gets it out."

"What effect has your Base Ball record and enthusiasm had upon your candidacy for the United States Senate?" I inquired, really wondering.

HOMER C. DAVENPORT

"How do I know, yet?" he asked. But then he added: "Give me the Base Ball votes of California and my opponents may have the rest."

Across the room from me sat Homer Davenport, most famous of the world's cartoonists, and himself a Base Ball crank of advanced mania.

"Any man," said Davenport, not looking up from his sketch pad (which Mrs. Spalding, also, was intent upon), "who can pitch every game, every season, for the Boston team, for five long years, and win the pennant every time, and then go to Chicago and take the pennant with him in his trunk, as Mr. Spalding did, can capture a seat in the United States Senate on wet grounds, with a glass arm in the box and the rooters all against him. The political game is easy when you stack it up against Base Ball. You're talking to a Senator-to-be, all right."

He went back to absorption in his work and Mrs. Spalding flushed with pleasure.

Base Ball and Business.

"Has your Base Ball training helped you in your business?" I inquired.

"I never struck anything in business that did not seem a simple matter when compared to complications I have faced on the Base Ball field," said Mr. Spalding. "A young man playing Base Ball gets into the habit of quick thinking in most adverse circumstances and under the most merciless criticism in the world—the criticism from the bleachers. If that doesn't train him, nothing can. Base Ball in youth has the effect, in later years, of making him think and act a little quicker than the other fellow.

"They have now, in colleges, a course in which they call experimental psychology. The relation between thought and action is recorded by delicate instruments. These instruments, in the psychological laboratories of the colleges, show that the mental reactions of the athletes are quicker than those of any other students. And that of the Base Ball player is quicker than that of any other of the athletes. The sprinter, don't you see, has but to go from place to place. His thought is intent on the one thing—on getting there. The thought of the Base Ball player must take many other things— a thousand things—into consideration. He must think while he is going.

"Folks marvel at the great throngs which attend important Base Ball matches. They really need not be wondered at. The public likes the game, and, more than that, it knows that this one game, of all sports, is certain to be absolutely on the square. The spectators have been players, most of them, and understand not only the first principles but the fine points of the sport.

"Here, again, is the effect of the evolution of the game up

through the boy into the man. The boys of the past generation are the spectators of this; the boys of this one will be the spectators of the next. So, like an endless chain, Base Ball will last and grow as long as these United States shall last and grow. Each generation will produce a little higher type of citizenship than that which went before it, and Base Ball and the principles which underlie it will help to bring this about."

The old Base Ball player, the successful business man, the candidate for Senator, stopped talking. I looked at him inquiringly.

He said:

"PLAY BALL."

INDEX